CAPITAL
FOR
OUR TIME

CAPITAL
FOR
OUR TIME

THE ECONOMIC, LEGAL, AND

MANAGEMENT CHALLENGES

OF INTELLECTUAL CAPITAL

Edited by

Nicholas Imparato

HOOVER INSTITUTION PRESS

STANFORD UNIVERSITY   STANFORD, CALIFORNIA

URL: http://www-hoover.stanford.edu

Hoover Institution Press Publication No. 448
Copyright © 1999 by the Board of Trustees of the
    Leland Stanford Junior University
Chapter 5 © 1998 by Margaret Jane Radin and Erin Sawyer
Chapter 11 © 1998 by Steven M. H. Wallman
Chapter 12 © 1998 by Leif Edvinsson and Åke Freij
Chapter 20 © 1998 by Pamela Samuelson

First printing, 1999
05   04   03   02   01   00   99   9   8   7   6   5   4   3   2   1

Manufactured in the United States of America
The paper used in this publication meets the minimum requirements
of American National Standard for Information Sciences—Permanence
of Paper for Printed Library Materials, ANSI Z39.48–1984. ∞

Library of Congress Cataloging-in-Publication Data
Capital for our time : the economic, legal, and management challenges
of intellectual capital / edited by Nicholas Imparato.
        p.   cm.
    Includes index.
    ISBN 0-8179-9582-5
    1. Intellectual capital.   2. Intellectual property.   I. Imparato,
Nicholas, 1944–   .
HD53.C367   1999
658.4′038—DC21   98-27302
                                                          CIP

Contents

Part Three   Measuring and Extracting Value

Foreword

This volume reflects the Hoover Institution's interest in addressing issues of intellectual capital and associated property rights. Situated in the heart of Silicon Valley, we believe the Hoover Institution is an ideal location to launch a study of how we treat intellectual capital from legal, commercial, and ethical perspectives.

As an initial display of this interest, on June 19–20, 1997, we convened a conference on intellectual capital: business strategy, legal protections, and global competitiveness. At the conference, my Hoover colleagues Nicholas Imparato and Richard Sousa convened jurists, business professionals, journalists, and researchers— all scholars and practitioners in the field of intellectual capital—to discuss property rights, regulation and legal systems, technology, and their implications for intellectual capital.

That conference was the genesis of this volume; it contains a selection of presentations made at the conference (some of which were significantly revised by the authors on the basis of other presentations at the conference). This volume, we believe, captures the essence of the conference and the breadth of the discussion. The conference agenda is included as an appendix.

The Hoover Institution Program on American Institutions and Economic Performance addresses two overarching questions: (1) How can the U.S. economy provide an ever-higher quality of life, increased economic opportunity, and greater economic freedom for all? and (2) Why do U.S. government institutions, despite enormous expenditures of financial and human resources, seem incapable of, or at least have great difficulty in, solving persistent economic and social problems?

The content of this volume makes it clear that, although there are many international implications surrounding intellectual capital, the impact of decisions made in this arena affects the performance of the U.S. economy and the competitiveness of American business. Hoover's Program on American Institutions and Economic Performance is generously supported by prominent donors to the program, including Tad Taube, the Taube Family Foundation, the Koret Foundation, Joanne and Johan Blokker, and the Sarah Scaife Foundation, to whom we owe a great debt of gratitude. In addition, we would like to thank Cadence Design Systems, Informix Software, Pfizer Inc., Roche Holding Ltd., and the staff members at those corporations for their financial and intellectual support of the conference and this book.

John Raisian
Director, Hoover Institution

Acknowledgments

Any project of this sort is a collaborative effort. Authors had to present their views without repeating arguments made by others. The effort to avoid redundancy, as opposed to the useful reexamination of an issue, demanded rewrites and edits of original work that might have been more than what any participant had bargained for at the outset. Indeed, it was originally anticipated that this volume would constitute the proceedings of our June 1997 conference. Instead, the interaction and discussion at the conference were so lively and thought provoking that many authors felt compelled to integrate new ideas into their papers or, in several cases, to take their essays in different and unexpected directions. These efforts, too, exceeded original expectations about the time and work the project would require. Such cooperation and enthusiasm reflects many aspects of professional discipline, not the least of which is a willingness to bear the cost of intellectual honesty.

By the same token, neither the conference nor this book would have been possible without the professional assistance provided by colleagues at the Hoover Institution. Gerald Dorfman, Joann Fraser-Thompson, Teresa Terry Judd, Michele Horaney, and Mandy MacCalla gave generously of their time and effort. All the contributors and myself owe a special debt of gratitude to Patrica Baker, executive editor; Marshall Blanchard, production manager; Lyn Larson, administrative assistant; and Ann Wood, editor of the Hoover Institution Press.

Richard Sousa, associate director of the Hoover Institution, and Lea Limgenco were always prepared to offer the assistance I needed to get the project to the next stage. Their counsel, regarding everything from selection of papers to how to manage the paper flow, was invaluable. Director John Raisian supported both the conference and the book from an administrative role and, more important, helped shape the intellectual framework that was needed to proceed. The discussions with John and Richard about property, political economy, and the interaction between business strategy and public policy were among the most rewarding moments in the entire endeavor.

Colleagues at other institutions also were valuable sources of encouragement, most particularly at the University of San Francisco: Jay Folger, dean of the Law School; Gary Williams, dean of the McLaren School of Business; and faculty members Tom McCarthy and David Raphael. My assistants Joann Stradley and Crystal Roseberry, McLaren research fellow, not only attended to necessary details but also kept us mindful of our priorities.

Finally, on behalf of all those involved in the project, there is a special gratitude owing to family, friends, coworkers, and loved ones who endured the tribulations of proximity to those working on deadlines. In one sense the best of our work is theirs.

Nicholas Imparato

Introduction

Intellectual capital, as well as the related topics of intangible assets and intellectual property, has been getting increased attention from policy makers and business leaders over the past decade. Legal experts, in both academia and the world of commerce, contend that the fastest-growing portion of their profession revolves around matters pertaining to intellectual assets.

Other examples abound. Accounting and management consulting firms have established practices in knowledge management. Thoughtful journals and magazines have published major articles on the knowledge economy and the implication for employment trends, economic productivity, and social policy. The profit impact of brand, customer relationships, proprietary databases, design methodologies, and procurement procedures is getting more scrutiny. Some congressional leaders have cited the need to protect the nation's intellectual capital as a reason for thwarting "fast-track" legislation. A new organization, the agreement on Trade Related Aspects of Intellectual Property Rights (TRIPS) Council, has been created in the course of the treaty that established the World Trade Organization (WTO) and has been asked to oversee the development of new intellectual property norms for the international community. It is hard to find a CEO or government official who doesn't make reference to "human capital" when commenting about corporate or national competitiveness.

By one way of thinking, nonetheless, all the attention regarding intellectual capital is about a future we have already experienced. The issue has been with us for a long time, goes the argument, as long as the process of innovation itself. Indeed, inventiveness and associated property rights have been the engine of capitalism's success. There might be a number of arresting anecdotes about intellectual capital, and it might be a concept that spurs curiosity; but there isn't any real "news" to warrant all the commotion.

The contrary opinion, and the one that is generally represented here, is that the scope and depth of intellectual capital as a force in society are substantially different from what has existed before. This attitude, detailed in different ways in the subsequent essays, reflects an array of opinions about life in our times, including, as examples, recognition of intelligence as a basis of competition, concern for enforcing property rights in an emerging economic order, respect for the unwieldiness of the Internet, optimism about the promise of genetic engineering, and the general sense that knowledge-based services, not industrial production, hold the future for economic security.

To say that intellectual capital deserves attention now, however, is not the same as indicating which part of its story has first claim on our energy and resources. The broad economic and social structure questions, the property and legal issues, the business and financial strategy concerns, and the implications for advantage in a globalized marketplace all compete. Meanwhile, there is relatively little effort to bring together the different strands of the issue. That is, economists might debate hypotheses regarding the knowledge economy but have little awareness of what trade principles are at stake in discussions between the TRIPS Council and the World Intellectual Property Organization (WIPO). Corporate counsel might gain from knowing more about the goals of those constituencies who want to list intellectual assets on the balance sheet, and some executives could benefit from a more comprehensive understanding of the relationships among intellectual property, intellectual capital, and innovation. Still, there is no one place where the full scope of the issues that affect organizational or societal performance is examined or even outlined. In short, no integrative approach to the challenge of intellectual capital exists. This volume is among the first steps in that direction.

The Faces of Intellectual Capital

What I have done here is to bring together scholars and practitioners who are experts in the various aspects of what is broadly referred to as intellectual capital. Management writers, technology experts, law professors and attorneys, researchers, corporate executives, and economists, as well as representatives of government-related agencies and trade organizations, offer their perspectives. In the course of doing so, they lay out different ways to assess the importance and effect of intellectual capital for the individual, for the firm, and for the global economy. Additionally, they suggest, sometimes explicitly and sometimes indirectly, different ways we could define intellectual capital. In so doing they distinguish it from other ideas that have proved terminally ambiguous (remember human resource accounting?). Their contributions are organized into five sets of essays.

The first section, Intellectual Capital and the New Economy, looks at the larger picture of intellectual capital and the emergence of a new economy, including a fundamental change in business dynamics. The initial chapter, by Peter G. W. Keen, makes a distinction between intellectual capital and intellectual property and then proceeds to lay out the argument that an economy built on trust, defined less as a value and more as a skill, is essential when ideas trump land and labor. Michael S. Malone presents the broad thesis regarding the ascendancy of intellectual capital as a major strategy issue for business and hints at arguments made in later chapters about how intangible assets might be included on the balance sheet. Robert J. Barro tempers the enthusiasm for notions of intellectual capital by commenting on the underlying variables and assumptions on which new economic models might be built.

Part Two, Intellectual Capital and Intellectual Property: Issues of Protection, develops several themes headlined in the opening chapters and focuses on intellectual property (IP) and corresponding legal issues. Joseph Costello sets out the dilemma faced by the leader of a high-technology company, specifically, how the firm goes about balancing the need for collaboration while protecting its own IP within a legal system that is often ineffective. Margaret Jane Radin and Erin Sawyer examine the proprietary spectrum, evaluating Microsoft, Java and Linux, and explain how nonproprietary technologies challenge the standard economics of intellectual property. Richard A. Epstein provides an insightful discussion of intellectual property in the context of property rights more generally. Edward P. Lazear offers a broad analysis of the problems and potential solutions that are part of the intellectual property debate, combining reflections about law, economics, and business strategy. The interaction between the current IP system and innovation gets its most detailed treatment in a subsequent chapter by John H. Barton, which includes a discussion of administrative costs, follow-on innovation, and industry structure. Issues pertinent to information technology generally and the Internet specifically are discussed in two chapters. David Henry Dolkas presents a case regarding the collision of rights that can occur, and Barbara Simons reviews what the Internet means for traditional views of publishing, property, and related concepts. Her chapter concludes with an outline of legislative initiatives, giving a rich overview of the matters under scrutiny by lawmakers at this time. Finally, Abraham Sofaer, drawing from his roles as academic, mediator, and arbitrator, comments on the role of the litigation system in providing genuine protections and rewarding innovation.

Part Three, Measuring and Extracting Value, is primarily the work of executives concerned with how to measure and financially value intellectual capital, as well as how to deal with knowledge management, and expands the discussion presented earlier by Michael Malone. Steven M. H. Wallman, at the time of the conference a commissioner of the Securities and Exchange Commission, opens the discussion with a careful evaluation of the necessity to make information about intangible assets more widely available. The point of view and experience of two companies noted for their engagement with intellectual capital strategies are included next: Leif Edvinsson and Åke Freij review the Skandia experience in working toward a model of intellectual capital in the corporate setting. Gordon P. Petrash spells out the importance of intangible assets for market capitalization and then describes how Dow Chemical includes an intellectual capital (IC) perspective in internal measures of performance. Finally, Patrick H. Sullivan integrates several issues relating to definitions of intellectual capital (versus intellectual assets and human capital), the distinction between intellectual property management and intellectual capital management, and the role of intellectual capital in the firm. Tim Draper, a venture capitalist, offers a cautionary note for IC advocates and warns of the dangers of regulating the assessment and report of intangible assets.

Two chapters regarding biotechnology are collected in Part Four, The Burgeoning Challenge in Genomics. These are given a spotlight, as it were, to overcome the frequent tendency to focus inordinately on information and computer technology to the detriment of a wider understanding. Those laboring in biotechnology have a rich source of experience that is valuable to decision makers in other disciplines. In this spirit Clarisa Long examines the relationships among patent issues and the innovation process, with specific reference to the challenge presented by research in genomics. Thomas J. White and John J. Sninsky expand our understanding of the Human Genome Project and provide a detailed context in which to evaluate the conflicts and decisions driven by patent issues, regulatory hurdles, and ethical concerns.

The fifth and final section, Emerging International Regimes, looks at the international environment. Here the concern is not only with an author's or inventor's rights but also with matters of international trade and national economic welfare. Clarisa Long reports her research on investment, technology transfer, and the standards of property protection in Latin America. Crawford Beveridge shares elements of Scotland's strategy for competing in the knowledge economy and summarizes his vision for an environment that is more friendly to the exchange of intellectual capital. Pamela Samuelson surveys the issues in international coordination, examining how WIPO and the TRIPS Council operate, their need to broaden their perspectives and their attention to competition policy in formulating intellectual property rules. As the author of the final chapter, she concludes with another view of the issue introduced by Peter Keen in the opening chapter, namely, the relationship between intellectual capital and intellectual property and the relevance of the distinction, particularly for a global economy capable of sustainable innovation.

A brief epilogue is included to underline the point, as a final word, regarding the importance intellectual capital issues have for shaping the future.

Taken together the chapters and commentary present an overarching view of what constitutes the challenges of intellectual capital and illuminate not only problems but also potential solutions. The issue's relevance for policy makers and executives is apparent in every chapter, which in itself is a valuable observation. The promotion of intellectual capital begins with an appreciation of the interdependencies among processes and ideas that cut across professional disciplines as well as geographic boundaries. The payoff is both a vibrant, innovative firm and a vigorous global economy.

Part One

Intellectual Capital
and the
New Economy

Peter G. W. Keen

Transforming
Intellectual Property into
Intellectual Capital:
Competing in the
Trust Economy

The question this chapter aims at answering is how to turn intellectual property into intellectual capital. The two are not equivalent. *Intellectual capital* (IC) is a long-term economic asset. *Intellectual property* (IP) is a financial expense, which may or may not have value as capital. My college term papers are part of my own IP, but are hardly part of my capital. A design for a workable antigravity machine that is locked away in the inventor's drawer, unseen by others, represents *potential* IC but is at present just lost property.

Many of the ideas expressed in this chapter are the fruits of collaboration with my friends and colleagues Fernando Flores and Chaunchy Bell. I wish to thank them and acknowledge this product of joint trust in action.

Intellectual Capital and Intellectual Property:
The Collaborative Difference

By definition, *capital* means value; otherwise it's an expense to be written off, not an asset at all. Capital is built in the past, owned in the present, and deployed to create future value. Intellectual capital is intellectual property in action. Turning IP into IC means creating value from it. Value rests on innovation, which rests on collaboration and entrepreneurship. Collaboration demands sharing of IP and IC—a collaboration that may help turn today's property into new capital, make effective use of existing capital, or build new capital. Collaboration rests on trust. Trust is the central topic of my chapter.

The massive dilemma for firms whose future rests on innovating through IC is that they need to protect their intellectual property, which is often their largest investment, but that collaboration and sharing of information puts their IC at risk. High-tech and pharmaceutical firms are the most obvious examples. Those firms are as dependent on star talent as the National Basketball Association; the loss of a top software designer can be equivalent to a top guard's leaving the Chicago Bulls. An even more severe impact can be felt when the designer or researcher turns a competitor's team into stars. Stealing intellectual property can be one of the cheapest ways of gaining intellectual capital. As a result, IC and litigation are today almost synonymous. In Silicon Valley, a competitor's hiring key employees is a transfer of IC, and almost any innovation in hardware or software raises questions about patent rights and use of licenses.

Protection demands secrecy, but innovation requires some degree of openness in a world marked by complexity, interdependency, and scarcity of resources—especially people who create and embody firms' knowledge, skills, education, and experience and hence the foundation for their IC. The result is a growing tension between protection and sharing, between security and communication, and between doing it yourself and collaborating with others. And it means a heavy reliance on lawyers. Tim Jackson's detailed history of Intel, *Inside Intel: Andy Grove and the Rise of the World's Most Powerful Corporation*, provides a convincing and disturbing picture of both the semiconductor industry and Intel, one of the most innovative companies in the world. Innovation, litigation, and security seem to move in parallel for Intel. The book illustrates Grove's philosophy, which was the title of his best-selling book on management: *Only the Paranoid Survive.*

Perhaps. But paranoia is the extreme of distrust, and the evidence indicates that trust is becoming the new currency of our economy and the essential vehicle for exploiting intellectual property. I don't mean trust in what I call the *squishy* sense of the term, which sees trust as fundamentally a matter of values built on sincerity, getting to know each other, shared goals, and face-to-face communication. That's certainly a base for trust, although a limited one. The challenge is to build trust where you don't know each other, are competitors, and have entirely different interests. If everyone were sincere and honorable, we wouldn't need the term.

My view of trust is that it is a choice of and skill in *the design of relationships* and that it is the foundation for innovation and coordination of the supply chain, customer interaction, and market, product and service development. Some firms still choose to minimize or manipulate collaborative and trust-based relationships, but that is increasingly impractical. The Intel position is in opposition to what just about every segment of business and society is doing: searching for trust. The search is not easy, obviously, and it would be foolish to dismiss concerns about theft, misuse and maintaining secrecy that anyone with valuable property has. But, that said, we are now in a trust economy.

The Three Eras of the Trust Economy:
Product, Service, and Relationship

The trust economy, which has been evolving for more than thirty years, has moved through three distinct stages. The first was the era of trust in the product, launched by the intrusion of Japanese car manufacturers and makers of consumer electronics on the previously well-protected and oligopolistic U.S. market in the early 1970s. That era saw the effective invention of the customer; before that period, the customer was just a consumer. It's remarkable that the most influential management theorists of the time, including Chester Barnard, James March, and Herbert Simon, ignored the customer entirely; their focus was the internal dynamics of the firm. (Even today, economists view the customer primarily in terms of the purchase transaction, one consequence of which is a dismissal of trust as a relevant variable.)

The first era of the trust economy was sparked by consumers' having new choices and thus becoming true customers. Their opportunity to choose from a wide range of offers instead of from the narrow range of options provided by such oligopolies as the Big Three U.S. car makers generated a crisis precipitated in part by their growing distrust in the American product. *Lemon* and *made in America* became synonymous. Firms such as Sony, Panasonic, and Toyota displaced RCA and General Motors. Customers were ready to pay a premium for Japanese products because their quality, which is an element of trust, was better. The belated adoption of total quality management and related methods was targeted at rebuilding lost trust. Detroit was thrown into a rearguard struggle that took decades. Most U.S. consumer electronics firms disappeared, including RCA and Sylvania, which had been leaders in sales of television sets. There aren't *any* U.S. TV manufacturers now.

Quality—the trust-building agenda of the 1970s through the

mid-1980s—only peripherally affected banks, airlines, and other industries that did not depend on manufacturing. The second era, that of service—also an invention—took those industries by surprise but affected their oligopolies as much as quality affected Detroit. When customers had choices, they selected the best provider of service. McDonald's is an example of how a provider of a commodity good—hamburger—could come to dominate the world. Fast food is thus prototypical of the service era and of trust as a brand—you could count on McDonald's to keep its promise.

Again, service is a topic marked by its absence in the management theory of the early 1980s and in most business practices. Banks, airlines, and insurance firms were notoriously sluggish, bureaucratic, and indifferent to customer needs. They continued to see product as the premium offer to customers. As John Fisher, the retired chairman of Bank One, a pioneer in service, comments, banks did no real marketing or selling. Bank branches were sterile places, where customers had to stand in line to get access to their own property, and fill in a form for just about every transaction.

That is no longer the picture. There may be a gap between the claims of service and actual delivery, but *customer service* is now equivalent to *basic business*. The main drivers for change were the new generation of U.S. retailers, most obviously Wal-Mart, and deregulation in more and more industries, including telecommunications, airlines, and financial services. Combined with growing overcapacity, fueled by a combination of technology and globalization, service became as much a mantra as quality had been.

The focus on service has led, first, to an emphasis on convenience and availability and, second, to trust in the transaction as the explicit basis for the customer relationship: money-back guarantees, no-questions-asked return policies, twenty-four-hour service seven days a week, automatic teller machines (ATMs), push-button credit card account information, 1-800 ordering, pizza delivery, and many others. Ours is a convenience era; if the ATM is

philosophy and related social sciences tend to emphasize the multiplicity of identities, hyperflexibility of society, and loss of loyalties. The Internet is an illustration: you can take on any identity on the Net that you wish: age, sex, person, and personality.

I am not a philosopher, just an observer of business. But I see many counters to postmodernism: people looking for a base of personal identity, wishing for loyalties, and valuing trust. Yes, there has been a huge loss of identity, sense of future, and value from the naive and brutal downsizing, reengineering, outsourcing, and offshoring that have cut several million jobs from the United States and, now, European economies and badly damaged workers' trust in companies. But that does not end the search for and wish for new bonds. It will demand new styles of worker-employer relationships. It will be hard to rebuild trust, but trust is the foundation of relationships. It is relationships that now drive the customer business and business supplier innovations, rather than just product quality and service. It is relationships that drive innovations that rest on the use of intellectual capital—that is, that rely on turning property into capital. And it is relationships that seem to be the agenda for responding to the postmodernist world.

The Nature of Trust

So, what do we really know about trust? It's a word that appears more and more in discussions of customer service, organizational innovation, partnerships, intellectual capital, alliances, teams, brand equity, the virtual organization, employee-manager relationships, and leadership. It's recognized as fundamental to all relationships: commercial, interpersonal, and organizational. Trust is seen as a good thing and distrust as a correspondingly bad thing, but very much on the rise in the social and political sphere and inside many organizations in the era of downsizing and reengineering. Innumerable appeals for more trust appear in books, articles, CEO speeches, and mission statements.

Thus trust is widely talked about but rarely defined in an operational way; rather, it is left as an emotive summary for a wide range of personal characteristics, behaviors, and cultural norms. Other than raising hopes, those concepts don't help much in enabling management action. One of my aims in my ongoing research, writing, and consulting, of which this chapter is an early output, is to "desquish" trust: to get away from emotional appeals and value judgments that make many people in business wary of discussing it and at times suspicious of the intents of the speaker. (As one manager told me, "If someone talks about needing to trust each other, I check my wallet.")

If trust is so vital, how can it be systematically built and maintained? My thesis is that trust is a business resource that can be *designed*. Designing trust demands going beyond the view of it as integrity, honesty, and sincerity. It's much more complex, it's a discipline and a skill without which you cannot build trust-centered relationships, the main source of the trust advantage.

Conceptions of Trust

Some conceptions of trust as a good thing are either too vague to be useful or downright misleading. For example, many writers see trust as fundamentally a matter of shared values, a view shared by many business executives and the core of an influential book by Francis Fuyukama, which argues that trust is the social capital that explains the success of entire economies and the nature of business practices in individual societies. He terms it a form of *spontaneous sociability*. His conception of trust emphasizes that we trust people in the community who have the same values and norms as ourselves. That, however, is a formula for cronyism and for treating outsiders as people to be distrusted, hardly a way to handle the diversity of modern society and its increasing globalization of relationships.

Trust may then *limit* the building of social capital and *block* collaboration with others outside the community. As one scholar comments: "Culture sustains shared values and beliefs and thereby engineers mutual trust within a group. Trust economizes on information costs . . . it is sufficient to know whether someone belongs to the same group to know whether the information they supply is likely to be true or not." He adds that these may also lead to conformity, reduce variety, dull innovation, and stifle entrepreneurship.[1] If trust is based on shared values and encouraged on that basis in organizations, the losers are likely to be women, Hispanics, Asians, blacks, and gays. It would be ironic were trust as social capital to become the enemy of diversity.

Others see trust as cooperation but cooperation may be just compliance. Many management experts talk up Japanese companies as exemplars of trust; as one book on the experiences of a midlevel Japanese "salaryman" suggests, much of that apparent behavior is forced cooperation. This is a society of "insiders" and "outsiders" in just about every relationship, and the case could be made that Japan is both the extreme of a high-trust and the extreme of a low-trust nation at the same time. "Harmony prevails, but trust is rare . . . harmony is a process of social control . . . trust is a by-product of social controls."[2] No one can compel trust, but managers can manipulate compliance and force cooperation.

Cooperation may also be simple mutual self-interest and not trust: "I might be said to 'trust' the milkman to deliver my milk, and he may 'trust' me to pay him, but if either of us breaches the

1. Mark Casson, *Entrepreneurship and Business Culture*, Studies in the Economics of Trust (United Kingdom: Edward Elgar, 1995), page xii.

2. Noboru Yoshimura and Philip Anderson, *Inside the Kaisha: The Enigma of Japanese Business Behavior* (Cambridge, Mass.: Harvard Business School, 1997), page 80.

bargain, we can forget about future benefits from future exchanges. In such cases, adhering to the agreement can hardly be said to differ in any meaningful respect from simple self-interest. If this is all that trust is, it may influence tactics, but it really represents just an extension of conventional notions of self-interest."[3]

The many ways of defining trust and the many normative recommendations they lead to mean that the overall picture is largely one of confusion, ambiguity, conflicting interpretations, and absence of reliable principles. For many business practitioners, trust is mainly equated with reliability and predictability; this view, which is grounded in their own organizational experiences, indicates that they are interested in results, not motives. For others, trust is more equated with attitude, confidence, and interpersonal skills, the emphasis being on individual intentions. Again, that's often grounded in managers' specific personal experiences. Equally well-grounded in theory and in the experiences of the therapeutic and mental health fields is the notion that trust is a core element of individual identity and living in the world, with self-trust as the essential core for trusting in others; here, the focus is on individual perceptions and confidence. For many others, trust is a cognitive and rational assessment of risk, and thus a form of probabilistic reasoning.

Trust is thus variously defined in both theory and practice in terms of interpersonal skills, self-trust, rationality, faith, psychological states, self-confidence, competence, expectations, goodwill, and even gender differences.[4] So at one extreme are the views

3. Neil McKay, "The Economics of Trust," *International Journal of the Economics of Business*, July 1996.

4. Survey after survey shows that women are more trusted than men, but, as some scholars have commented, many advocates of trust in business and social life adopt a male-dominated view of it as competence—rational, abstract, and distanced from life—leaving out caring and what is associated with unequal power relationships.

of trust as a personal and interior response—"that trust has more to do with our own perception than with another's behavior," for instance.[5] If so, then there's minimal scope for viewing trust as a formal element in a relationship design in that there's nothing you as a firm can do: either your customer or your employee perceives you as trustworthy or he or she doesn't. At the other extreme of the concept, trust is merely about rational assessments of reliability, in which case it's a redundant concept. If it were either of these extremes, however, it wouldn't be as central as it is to the language of everyday life or be moving so rapidly to the center of business life.

When trust *is* seen as central, it's generally viewed as a fairly simple commodity and a positive virtue. Yes but . . . squish! The very notion of trust as good and distrust as bad are open to challenge. It can obviously be as foolish or even dangerous to over-trust—"ripped off," "sucker," and "patsy" are everyday words for this—as to undertrust. Distrust may also reflect a personal competence and a caring about standards; the widely reported increase in distrust of politicians may thus be more a matter of citizens' being aware of the standards they expect in performance, being knowledgeable about what's going on, and being more concerned about trust breakdowns than an indication of some radical decline in the standards of public life.

As one academic comments: "Political scientists have perhaps best documented that distrust in any set of political incumbents is functional for the continuance of democratic institutions. Distrust, in other words, also reduces complexity by dictating a course of action based on suspicion, monitoring, and activation of institutional safeguards."[6] Another expert mentions that James Madison,

5. Lee Jampolsky, *The Art of Trust* (Berkeley, Calif.: Celestial Arts, 1995), p. xi.

6. Daryl Kuehn, "Should We Trust in Trust?" *American Business Law Journal* 34, no. 183 (1996).

the designer of our most fundamental political institutions, designed them so that they would not be vulnerable to misuse of power; demagogues rely on misplaced trust. The principle underlying the Founding Fathers' decision was that trust in government was never supposed to be high. Thus, distrust can be either a pathology or a rational, self-aware prudence and careful evaluation that prevents foolish acceptance of information and approval of others' actions.

Trust is thus a responsibility that demands that the trustor take responsibility for trusting: "My niece fails to bring back all the groceries on the list. I trusted her to buy these groceries; she promised to do so. But I forgot that she does not know what kumquats are. Yes, the child broke her promise but I erred in inappropriately reposing too much trust in her."[7] Active distrust is not always a bad thing, either. Too much trust opens up opportunities for opportunism, as Baring's Bank and General Electric's Peabody attest to; both these companies lost billions of dollars from trusted employees' violations of procedures.

Madison did not believe in trust but built political mechanisms and institutions that have by and large worked well. Most economists don't believe in trust, either. Here's Oliver Williamson, the leader in transaction cost economics, one of the major modern influences on organizational theory: "Trust is for families, lovers, and friends. . . . It has no place in commercial relationships." For Williamson, trust is a murky surrogate for risk, and risk can be hedged through contracts and surveillance and other mechanisms. That strong position is rejected by many other scholars, but the economists do tackle a topic easily skirted: how to deal with "opportunism" and how to handle transactions in a relationship where

7. Robert Behn and Alan A. Altshuler, eds., *Innovation in American Government: Challenges, Opportunities, and Dilemmas* (Washington, D.C.: Brookings Institution, 1995), p. 317.

there is no established basis for trust. As two researchers on trust in organizations comment in offering an alternate view: "In transaction cost economics, actors lie in negotiations, cheat on any deals if it is profitable to do so, and exploit opportunities for renegotiating to their utmost. . . . Our [own] definition of trust rests on a view of organizational action based largely on good-faith effort, honesty in exchange, and limited opportunism."[8] The economists can counter that *largely* is hardly a sensible metric in a world that includes shoplifters, hackers, con men, lazy employees, suppliers looking for an edge, and people who may be honest in their own areas of self-interest but can't be guaranteed to look after yours.

All in all, trust is a contradictory topic: widely acknowledged as central to just about every aspect of our lives and at the same time only vaguely defined and understood. My conclusions from my review of research and practice and my own business experience are that trust is most meaningfully viewed in terms of future relationships and relationship design. Two apt comments that capture my perspective are that "we see that the primary function of trust as sociological rather than psychological, since individuals would have no reason to trust apart from social relationships. It has distinct cognitive, emotional, and behavioral dimensions which are merged into a unitary social experience"[9] and that "the practical significance of trust is the social action it underwrites."[10] Substitute the phrase *business relationship* for *social relationship* and the sentences become "the primary business function of trust is . . ." and "the practical business significance of trust is the social action it under-

8. Roderick Kramer and Thomas Tyler, eds., *Trust in Organizations: Frontiers of Theory and Research* (Thousand Oaks, Calif.: Sage Publications, 1996), page 10.

9. J. D. Lewis and A. Weight, "Trust as Social Reality," *Social Forces* 63, no. 4 (June 1985).

10. Ibid.

writes." Focusing on relationships forces attention to the intertwining roles of *both* parties—trustor and trustee—rather than on just the person doing the trusting, thus reducing the emphasis in much of the commonsense conception of trust on psychological and moral traits and instead shifting the focus on how to make the relationship work, rather than on how to build correct motivations and attitudes. That makes the management agenda the design of effective relationships, which in turn raises the issue of which relationships matter most and demand most attention and investment. The relationships that I have chosen to focus on in my work are those that seem to me to be central to business positioning today. Customer relationships obviously lead the list, followed by business partner relationships, collaborative work, employee-manager relationships, and electronic commerce relationships, for it is these that will establish competitive and organizational advantage in the coming decade. If my reasoning is valid, it will be the design of relationships that makes intellectual *capital* out of intellectual *property*.

Trust as Business Advantage

There are many reasons to believe that such trust-centered relationships will increasingly become a business differentiator. The first of these reasons is discussed in the next section, which reviews the environmental forces pushing trust from the background to the foreground of business. The second is culture specific: the forces of individualism in the United States that push in the other direction. There is ample evidence that trust is highly culture-specific, making it even harder to pin down. The following neatly captures an American trait: "Given our individualistic assumptions and practices, trust is not a given. Trust is a hard-won competitive advantage."[11] Hard-earned and well-managed may be more accurate phrases for the purposes of this chapter.

As indicated earlier, *trust is* basically *about future relationships*; it unbinds or binds the space of possibilities for the concerned parties: companies and their customers, suppliers, employees, and investors. The greater the trust space, the greater the possibilities—and the risks and vulnerabilities. Distrust closes down the relationship space. The concept of trust that sees it as a shared value illustrates this (and shows the limitations of that concept); the trust space is confined to the immediate community of shared values and norms. Others are excluded; the relationship space for interacting with them is close to empty. (An interesting research finding in this regard is that, in societies with low trust in authority and government, high trust-demanding organizations emerge that are explicitly restricted in their relationships: the Sicilian Mafia, Chinese triads, and Los Angeles street gangs, for instance. Is trust here *really* social capital?) To do business in a world of alliances, intellectual capital, globalization, and diversity, trust has to be built with people who differ from us in many ways: values, interests, cultural norms and assumptions, location, professional background, race, religion, to name a few.

The calculus of trust in such relationships, where the trustor can't easily validate the trustee and vice versa, places a heavy weight on recurrence and predictability. The implicit question is, Can we work together for the unknown future? For me to trust you is to take a risk and be vulnerable. A trust relationship has built into it the idea of ongoingness; this is not a one-off transaction, where cash or a certified check and contract substitute for trust (these are in themselves trust mechanisms, of course, that

11. Marietta L. Baba, Donald R. Falkenburg, and David Hill, "Technology Management and American Culture: Implications for Business Process Redesign," *Research Technology Management* 39, no. 6 (November/December 1996): 46.

meet the economist's concerns for safeguards; failures in the transaction here are not failures in trust but breaches of law: fraud, forgery, theft and breach of contract). Where there is no risk, it's hardly meaningful to talk about trust as anything more than a habit or sense of confidence.

One of my main arguments is that business and its customers are being pushed to *having* to trust by complexity, interdependence, and telecommunications networks, which are the basis for new and ever-tighter business links. Those forces raise the trust stakes: risks and vulnerabilities on the one hand and payoffs on the other. In many instances, the payoffs arise more out of competitive necessity than of opportunity; this is especially true in supply chain management, where customers and suppliers must abandon many practices of secrecy, of looking for an edge, and of aggressively focusing on individual self-interest or in business process integration, where departments have to abandon their functional area perspective, autonomy, identity, sense of expertise, and "we-they" mentality. That's not easy, as most companies have found. But it has to be done.

It's my sense of trust in business as a necessity, a skill, a design issue, and an organizational resource that has pushed me away from most of the research on and advocacy of trust as a value, a moral stand, or a personal trait. It's not that I discount these, but if everyone were honest and integrity were universal, we wouldn't need to build trust; we'd take it for granted. When our business success or our job depends on trusting others, although we obviously take their moral credibility into account, we look for evidence that they can be relied on or for protective mechanisms in place that will reduce risk and vulnerability. Such mechanisms include state licensing and professional self-regulation ("office-based" trust), and impeccable operations. Sincerity here is no substitute for technique, which builds reputation and includes contracting, use of trusted third-party agencies, and many other factors that can explicitly be *designed* and made a formal part of business planning and implementation.

Trust mechanisms expand the relationship space, as in the following examples:

- Consider buying Christmas presents: the standard U.S. policy of accepting returns without the receipt allows you to take more risks—maybe Uncle Ted really will like a Sega game machine. The policy provides you with trust in the transaction and in the buyer-seller relationship.

- Until the mid-1980s, using a credit card involved substantial personal risk, in that if the card were stolen, the account holder was responsible for all fraudulent transactions made before the loss was reported. Now the onus is on the merchant and card issuer; the card holder's losses are limited to $50. Consider the relationships that have become routine in our everyday lives: ordering flower deliveries and computer hardware and software by phone, faxing a form authorizing a credit card transaction, and leaving your credit card on file with your travel agent. (As I discuss later, the central block to a mass market for Internet electronic commerce is that a majority of consumers do not trust the Net and thus refuse to give their credit card numbers or put personal information on their computer screens. In doing so, they obviously explicitly decide not to enter a relationship space with sellers and forgo many relationship opportunities. When they feel sure that effective trust mechanisms are in place, they will develop the same frequency and continuity of relationships that they have with, say, Dell and 1-800-FLOWERS. Until then, the space is empty.)

- In retailing and auto manufacturing, the long-established relationship between customer and supplier has historically been marked by aggressive jostling for advantage, with the power retailers and car makers playing suppliers off against one another to improve prices and terms. Information on sales and margins was tightly controlled, and contracts were written to address all possible issues of liability. Relationships were a matter of negotiation, much in the mode of institutionalized mistrust economists such as Oliver Williamson view as the rational norm. All that is rapidly moving toward trust-centered contracting, open sharing of information, and long-term coordination and collaboration with a small number of suppliers, mostly because the parties have no choice. As firms are forced by the pace of change, competition, and time pressures into interdependencies with their suppliers, they must move toward entirely new levels of trust.

- Queried as to why Boeing was so slow to adopt cooperative work methods from Japan, a senior company executive commented: "Trust. We monitored them, supervised them, told them when to go to the bathroom. We didn't trust our own people."[12] He goes on to praise the increase in innovation, collaboration, teamwork, and productivity opened up by management's shifting from control to trust. Thus Boeing's widely documented success in cutting the time and cost to develop a new airliner, the 777, is attributed to the firm's establishing a new—and difficult to obtain—degree of collaborative trust among the firm's many internal communities, suppliers, and customers.

That trust is an advantage is seen in any situation where the firm depends on the scope, longevity, and collaborative nature of

12. Anthony Sampson, *Company Man. The Rise and Fall of Corporate Life* (New York: Random House, 1995).

a relationship. Given that more and more aspects of business now depend on such relationships, it's no surprise that trust has moved to the foreground of management thinking and language. Some key relationships are the cooperative links between customer and supplier that mark the rapidly emerging integration of the supply chain through efficient consumer response, quick response, and business-to-business electronic commerce; business process integration;[13] industry partnerships, alliances, and joint ventures; long-term outsourcing contracts; true employee empowerment; customer retention versus one-time customer transactions; professional collaboration and sharing of intellectual capital and intellectual property; and many others. Whereas for decades a business was defined variously by its brands, products, manufacturing facilities, stores, and balance sheet, it's now enabled or constrained by its relationship spaces. In other words, trust is part of its identity.

The Environmental Forces Driving Business Trust

Trust has become central to business for three reasons that have nothing directly to do with morality and ethics: (1) *complexity*, (2) *interdependence*, and (3) *telecommunications networks* in general and the Internet in particular. Each of these forces in itself raises the salience of trust, but their interaction is making trust the new currency of business. The following thumbnail sketch applies to just about every firm that has more than fifty or so employees and to many that are smaller.

---

13. "Process integration demands trust—sharing information, especially. Trust is a scarce resource in the USA: individualism, with its short-term horizons, heterogeneity. Variability of value systems. Not knowing the other's values, we cannot trust them, setting up a vicious cycle." Baba, Falkenburg, and Hill, "Technology Management and American Culture: Implications for Business Process Redesign."

Complexity

The company's business environment is more and more uncertain. Prediction, even in the short term, is difficult, and the firm must be ready to respond to business changes quickly. Cycle times have become shorter and shorter. Customers' expectations are growing ever higher, and they demand ever-increasing levels of service. Organizational structures must be kept flexible, with an emphasis on cross-functional processes and teamwork. It is difficult in many areas for the company to locate skilled staff; intellectual capital is the prime asset in an environment of change and complexity, with the "learning" organization a new priority. The firm has moved through a sometimes almost continuous flow of downsizing and outsourcing, with all the disruptions, policy issues, human resource concerns, and impacts on both victims and survivors. Regulation, environmental issues, and health care management increasingly consume time and resources. The nature of competition is changing, with many new and nontraditional players from outside the industry and many global entrants. Channels of distribution are more becoming more complex and varied, including phone service, the Internet, and electronic procurement. Customer and market segmentation pose new challenges, with no more "average" customers. Information technology, previously delegated to the firm's information services function, is now a central element in almost all operations, with many business executives feeling that they don't completely grasp all the issues and risks.

Interdependency

The firm is involved in a number of partnerships and alliances to handle shared sourcing, joint development, or distribution. It is a member of industry associations, consortia for regional development, and other shared interest groups. Suppliers work together on many issues, to the extent that they cooperate in the morning and compete in the afternoon.[14] They jointly share information and plan functions that were previously the domain of each individual party; those shared functions include inventory management, quality control, and forward planning for materials and distribution. The company has a number of long-term outsourcing projects under way that require continuing review and adjustment. In high-tech and engineering-dependent firms, there is a constant movement of staff within the industry, with both frequent sharing of intellectual property through licensing agreements and frequent legal skirmishes about protection of patent rights and of proprietary information. In many instances, competitors have to work together because customers demand it in such areas as telecommunications and information systems integration.

Telecommunications networks

Between 40 and 80 percent of the firm's cash flow is now on-line, through electronic data interchange for procurement, customer-supplier supply chain logistics, distribution, customer information and service, electronic payments systems and cash management, production planning, reservation systems, engineering design, inventory management, and a wide range of other functions. When the telecommunications network is down, so is much of the business. The firm has 1-800 number customer service links and it is investing in Internet operations that may be small scale or experimental but in the case of firms like Cisco and General Electric handle billions of dollars in transactions. It has intranets and extranets and uses global data communications networks, "value-added" industry networks, and many others. Many of its operations are remote from the firm's main locations. Customer service may

14. This phrase is Walter Wriston's description of banking in the information era.

be handled out of Ireland or Omaha, the telemarketing centers of the world. Back-office processing of, say, insurance and health care claims are routed via Mauritius. Programming teams in India link to the firm's computer complexes in New Jersey. Reservation service operators work in centers in Europe and Texas, with calls routed to them as customer time zones demand. Many employees work as much from their home as in the company building, with their laptops and modems key tools of business. The firm increasingly talks about the "virtual organization" to describe the use of telecommunications to make operations time- and location-independent.

None of this is "gee whiz" stuff. It's not the something of the future. It's the present. And it rests heavily on trust mechanisms. In the lists I've presented above, the items depend on the quality of the relationship and hence on trust.

Complexity and Trust

Complexity means that we have to draw on the skills and services of others; we can't do everything ourselves. In simple societies, tribes trust only their families and immediate community; in our society, we have to trust many people we do not know. Writers on trust in such fields as sociology, politics, and law highlight the function of trust in making complexity manageable, as follows:

- "Trust reduces complexity far more quickly, economically, and thoroughly than does prediction. Trust allows social interaction to proceed on a simple and confident basis where, in the absence of trust, the monstrous complexity posed by contingent futures would again return to paralyze action."[15]

- "Trust is rational in regard to the function of increasing the potential of a system for complexity. Without trust only very simple forms of human cooperation which can be transacted on the spot are possible. . . . Through trust a system gains time, and time is the critical variable in the construction of complex system structures. The satisfying of needs can be delayed, and nevertheless guaranteed."[16]

The most insightful and practical research on trust highlights its role in making complexity tractable. For me, this may be the single most important *managerial* aspect of trust.

Interdependence and Trust

Interdependence, the second of the three factors, forces trust; collaboration, supply chain management, teams, alliances, and the like are all trust-dependent ventures. Without trust, the space closes. The firm of the 1950s, run as a monolith, controlling all the resources it needed, set clear boundaries to outside relationships. Now, companies have to find ways to work together in industry consortia for research and development, joint customer-manufacturer product development (per Boeing's launch of the 777 airliner), and multicompany joint ventures. Interdependence demands an expanded space of relationship opportunities; without

15. J. D. Lewis and A. Weight, "Trust as Social Reality," *Social Forces* 63, no. 4 (June 1985): p. 969.

16. Nicklas Luhmann, *Trust and Power* (New York: Wiley, 1979), pp. 88–89. Lewis and Weight, "Trust as Social Reality"; Casson, *Entrepreneurship and Business Culture*, p. ix.

skills in and mechanisms for trust, the space stays closed, whatever the stated goals of the parties.

Interdependence lies behind making the team rather than functional department the building block of the organization. Michael Schrage, an insightful commentator on the dynamics of collaboration, makes the point that although businesses routinely talk about teamwork, it's not natural to Americans; at school, it's called cheating. We join teams to win. A new college graduate at a job interview was asked if he were a team player. His answer was, "Oh, yes! I'm very much a team player." "And what position do you usually play in a team?" "Oh, captain, of course."

Trust is obviously at the core of both teams and collaboration, but because the two are not the same thing, the type of trust demanded by them is very different. Teams generally succeed when they have a common purpose and set of values; the more similar they are, the easier it is for them to build mutual trust. Here trust and values go closely together. The danger comes from relying too heavily on smoothing and consensus. Collaboration—literally, to *work* together—aims at innovation; expert collaborators don't need to like each other, seek agreement, or feel abashed about standing out as different. Famous teams of collaborators were notoriously critical of each other, especially in the arts and sciences. They did, though, trust each other's ability, commitment, openness to ideas, and expressiveness.

Innovation, everyday entrepreneurship,[17] and creativity are the aims of collaboration. Teams generally have cooperation as their goal. Teams also typically develop some form of social identity: cookouts, team names, special T-shirts, and the like. Most collaborators would shudder at the very idea. Read James Watson's story of how he and Francis Crick collaborated in the breakthrough

---

17. This is the phrase used by Fernando Flores and his colleagues to describe entrepreneurship as how ordinary groups of citizens live at their best.

discovery of the double helix base of DNA, a key scientific achievement of the past two centuries. Then read Crick's assessments of Watson's personality and behavior. The two shared little of anything, including liking each other, only plenty of shared drive. High trust does not have to mean commonality, except in commitment and respect for a particular range of abilities *relevant to the collaboration only*.

In reviewing work from many fields on trust, I sense that the everyday, commonsense view of trust as a value is most limiting in addressing collaboration in the pursuit of innovation and entrepreneurship. Because those are vital for the survival of many businesses, a rigorous and differentiated view of trust may help managers turn teams into collaborators and consensus into the search for innovation.

Telecommunications and Trust

The third force in the evolution of the trust advantage is telecommunications, the driver of so much of modern life: phones, fax machines, 1-800 numbers, with electronic mail and Internet commerce moving rapidly to the same degree of diffusion. The conflict between access and control in the use of telecommunications is fundamentally about opening up access to services, information, and communication. That means a loss of many traditional controls: audit trails, protection of databases and systems, documents and signatures, procedures to validate and authorize transactions, and so forth. In giving up controls, firms must learn to rely on trust. The Internet extends the access-control problem to customers as well. They cannot be sure of many of the basics that have historically given them confidence in relationships: the identity and location of the firm they are purchasing goods from; the validity of information; security against viruses, hackers, and intrusions on privacy; validity of the contract; or even the legal jurisdiction and applicable legal regime that apply when the buyer, seller, and the World Wide Web Home Page server computer may be, literally, anywhere on this planet.

The Internet thus demands new mechanisms of trust. The obvious example is the use of credit cards, briefly discussed above. Technically, making a credit card purchase over the Internet is far more secure than handing your card to a waiter who then disappears into the next room, giving it out over the telephone, or leaving it as a "signature on file" with your travel agent. Yet most people do not feel safe in using their card on the Internet. *The Internet is secure but not safe; people do not yet trust it.* (Security is the objective degree of risk; safety is the subjective sense of risk.) There are many efforts under way to build trust mechanisms for Internet commerce, including encryption, the Sears Encrypted Transaction (SET) Internet standard, authentication, nonrepudiation, digital signatures, eTrust certification (the equivalent of the Good Housekeeping Seal of Approval), third-party certificate authorities, escrow agents, private key holders, and other exotica. The variety and unfamiliarity of most of those indicate, first, that there is no consensus or established standard as yet for ensuring trustable electronic commerce, only a set of often competing candidates, and, second, that this is a truly massive issue.

Those two reasons are why I link trust and telecommunications in general and trust and the Internet in particular. If trust is at present mainly discussed in terms of personal interactions and relationships, within the next few years the primary focus will be on terms mediated by telecommunications. Business managers need briefing on the issues, on the proven tools, and on emerging principles since this is an area in which major new types of relationships are being built and which is already a major part of mainstream business and can only become more so. The trust topics raised by telecommunications are complexity, interdependency, and the evolution of the trust economy. Apart from customer safety and protection, these include privacy, copyright, and the nature of documentable reality. Essentially, no photo, piece of information, or claimed identity can be fully trusted at present, but they can largely be made so through a combination of technical skill and business manager priority. I won't go into the technical details here. My goal is to brief readers on the trust parameters of networked relationships and remind them of how much intellectual capital and intellectual property will depend on telecommunications and multimedia.

Desquishing the Concept of Trust

Together, the forces of complexity, interdependency, and telecommunications networks move trust right to the top of the management agenda. But the everyday, commonsense view of trust gets in the way of it as the basis for practical management action. Trust as a truism is about as useful in this regard as many of the employee-derided mission and value statements, however much they are the pride of the corporate head office.[18] They sound good but don't lead to solid managerial judgments. Start off with bad common sense about trust, and the result will be the same.

Here are just a few examples of how common sense doesn't apply in business and in personal life:

- Nice guys can't always be trusted: Common sense says that trust is about values. As one chief executive told me (as a direct rejection of my main thesis—that trust is as much a

18. The comment by Thomas A. Stewart ("Why Value Statements Don't Work," *Fortune*, June 10, 1996, p. 137) is one that many employees will agree with: "Nearly all the employees were aware of the company's value statements, but only 60% believed the company actually meant it. I described the survey to a consultant who specialized in employee-attitude surveys. What he said shocked me: 'Those are really high scores.'"

competence and a discipline as a value), "All I have to do is get to know someone and be sure he's honest, and then I can trust him." Yes, but . . . My dentist is one of the most decent people I know. By every measure of personal values, he scores high. But I would not trust him to repair my car. I hope I'm a sincere and honest person, too, but I would never trust me to navigate from point A to point B even if it's just three blocks away. (My friends and family endorse that comment.) *Trust is domain-specific.*

- Nasty guys *can* be trusted in certain domains: Al is a bookie who operates out of a porno store near Stanford University in California. Here's a comment made about him by Professor Eugene Webb at a conference on trust in organizations: "Al the bookie has written no scholarly books or articles, but he has been thoughtful of the same topic. His precarious occupation generates a continuous sense of crisis and near-crisis. On each day's table is a new and full plate of risk, uncertainty, and potential wealth. And in that crisis milieu, he asserts, is the centrality of trust. It is not by accident that among the most trustworthy and scrupulously honest occupations is that of an illegal bookie. Those who conduct such illegal business over the telephone are out of business unless they are absolutely trustworthy . . . A laconic restatement of this came one day when I asked the bookie about his scrupulous honesty and trustworthiness. He answered, avoiding any invocation of moral element of trust, 'Hey, how else could you do business?'"[19] Indeed, how else?" *Trust is about preserving the possibilities in future relationships.*

- You can't trust a car salesman but you can trust Earl: "In my ethics classes, no person is viewed as more untrustwor-

19. Kramer and Tyler, eds., *Trust in Organizations*, p. 288.

thy than a car dealer. But Earl, a car dealer in my hometown of 800 residents, was one of the most trusted persons in the community. Earl did not negotiate price. You told Earl what you wanted and he told you the price for which he could sell it. End of negotiation. Earl had every reason to be trustworthy. That is the kind of person he wanted to be. More cynically, if he did start cheating people, the news would be the talk of the greasy spoon located one hundred yards away and his reputation would be lost. No doubt there was a connection between these two motivations, but the point is that Earl would not be dishonest and therefore people reposed tremendous trust in him."[20] *Earl has made trust his brand.*

The commonsense perspective muddles trust as goodness and as making relationships work. In many domains of life, making relationships work does depend on values, but values generally aren't enough in themselves. I want to show that trust is the building block of sound business and management, that it can be engineered and made a skill and a currency. If it also generates a moral and ethical climate, that's a wonderful extra. I certainly believe that a trust economy betters society and that trust is an indicator of well-being for the trustor and trustee. But trust is not a soft virtue. As I stated earlier in the chapter, it's a hard-won advantage.

That said, although I stress what might be termed *tough trust* and try to show that trust is a matter of performance, I do not in any way diminish the importance of integrity, caring, honor, fairness, and kindness. But these are personal choices and attributes. They facilitate trust in many instances but they are not equivalent to trustability. I distinguish here between trustworthiness (a value)

20. Timothy Fort, "Trust and Law's Facilitating Role," *American Business Law Journal*, no. 1 (winter 1996).

and trustability (a skill). To be trustworthy but unreliable may leave you with a warm inner glow but make it very hard for others to work with and rely on you.

Having said that, I believe that one of the byproducts of trust as a formal element in business design is a moral environment and a joyous sense of living. Distrust can paralyze the individual and the company. Trust in all its dimensions is closely linked to personal dignity and sense of well-being; to be autonomous and effective human beings, we must be able to trust, earn trust, know the limits of trust, and share trust. Distrust carries a high cost of surveillance and closes off many opportunities in relationships. Breach of trust, whether intended or accidental or whether a failure in trustworthiness or trustability, hurts. Working for a company that establishes trust as part of its brand and skill base and makes it an integral part of its everyday organizational way of life means that company is profitably well positioned in the emerging mainstream of the trust economy and thus likely to be a good place to work.

President Reagan left us with a profound insight, "Trust, but verify." The noble Vulcans of *Star Trek* greeted the human race with the wish that we all "Live long and prosper." I believe that trust is vital to living well and that firms can and will prosper by cultivating and harvesting their fruits. But Reagan's message about nuclear disarmament can be adapted to business; trust has to be earned before it can be granted and once granted must continue to be earned. My additional message is that trust is a good deal— financially for your business and good for *everyone* involved in its relationships.

Trust is just one of the factors you and your company must address every day, along with the pressures of competition, the latest internal crises, operations, and customer phone calls. But trust is so much at the core of much of what we do in business that the more rigorously managers can reflect on it, observe its nature and mechanisms, pull it from the background of their mind to the foreground of planning and action and consciously regard it as a business *design* issue, the better they will be able to handle the demands and opportunities of complexity, interdependence, the trust economy and the networked age. These forces are not going to slow down. Live well and prosper.

Conclusion: Trust and Intellectual Capital

I wish I could offer a solid guide to the mechanics of designing trust. I can't. Here, though, are my tentative recommendations, derived from my reading, thinking, discussion, and work as an adviser in many organizations. First, the issue is to identify the relationships you want to or need to build and ask what are the trust enablers—professional, social, and economic values—and disablers. You need to distinguish carefully between *trustworthiness* and *trustability*. You need to become a skilled observer of relationships and of yourself. Where are the trust breakdowns? You must avoid the squishy conception of trust, too, and not think that trust is a matter of a good dinner and lots of promises.

Second, you must keep promises. What I observe in company after company is that we assess what's happening in relationships largely by assessing the promises made and kept. I think people often muddle the value and competence elements of trustworthiness and trustability, seeing insincerity where the real problem was incompetence or seeing a promise where there was just a maybe.

Finally, and most relevant for intellectual capital in the most competitive, fast-moving and intellectual property–dominated industries (Silicon Valley, most obviously), I want to point out that, where there is no trust, there will be lawyers. At the conference on which this book is based, I was an outsider from the East Coast. I felt at times that I was in a new and very strange land. I heard a stream of arguments about IP, protection, licenses, and litigation.

The debate was around the most appropriate legal mechanisms and the role of the legal profession and legal system. My conclusion was a simple one, that I stated in my presentation: the valley talks only in terms of its legal problems, but it has a trust problem, and you don't solve trust by law; law is the mechanism for ensuring cooperation when there is mistrust. But the valley lives by creating intellectual property that can be turned into intellectual capital through collaboration. Mistrustful collaboration is almost an oxymoron.

The automotive, retailing, and banking industries have shown how to cooperate in the morning in order to compete in the afternoon. Perhaps there is a lesson here for executives in the valley. Electronic commerce in business-to-business relationships is the spearhead of the new phase of the trust economy. Just as the Automotive Industry Advisory Group used collaboration in supply chain management as a major weapon in the U.S. automakers' recovery from near death, the industries that depend on intellectual capital can work together to define the collaborative arrangements and agreements that are the equivalent of the trading partner agreements (TPAs) in electronic commerce that are replacing liability-centered formal contracts. Those contracts assume that something will go wrong and that one of the parties is then at fault; the art form is then to cover every possibility in the legal fine print. TPAs are designed with the idea that things work out. They are explicit on responsibilities and accountability (promises) but they are designed to create an effective relationship space for the future, not a blame-and-shame look back at the past.

Michael S. Malone

<table>
<tr><td>

(**2**)

</td><td>

Reflecting a
New World of Business

</td></tr>
</table>

As a high-tech journalist, I've spent my career charting the development of revolutionary ideas as they emerge from the minds of a few creative individuals (often in the most unlikely places), spend several years in the wilderness of experimentation and debate, then suddenly sweep across the landscape, flaring up in the public's imagination as if from thin air.

That is precisely what is happening right now with a new/old idea called *intellectual capital*. If you listen closely to the words of our business leaders, read between the lines of industry journals, and watch the behavior of the best corporations, you can feel the distant rumblings of a great change approaching. The intellectual capital movement, often disguised with other names, is bursting out everywhere.

But appearances aside, movements never arise spontaneously.

Rather, they are born from a deep, but unspoken, dissatisfaction with the status quo.

The balance sheet has been the sacred text of the industrial world now for four centuries. But in the last thirty years, as one by one each sector of modern life has been transformed by technology, there has been a growing sense that our measurement systems too—not the least of which are the balance sheet and the rules of accounting that stand behind it—no longer serve their appointed task. And that task is to determine the real value of an enterprise.

During these times of rapid, unremitting change, new factors and forces within companies have taken on a vital role in creating success. And none of these critical factors fits into the old categories of assets and liabilities, revenues and expenditures, profit and loss. They are too evanescent, too intangible, too subjective—too embedded in transience of time—to fit the timelessness of the rules of accounting. Yet such characteristics do not make these factors less important, but more, because they accurately reflect the complexity and the continuous change of modern life. Unlike traditional accounting, these new measures look forward instead of backward; toward qualities that create future competitiveness, not transactions that created past profitability. Needless to say, in the fast-moving world of a modern, global, Internet-based commercial world, so do we.

Still, knowing the existence of these other factors doesn't automatically mandate their use. There are some good reasons for not attempting to measure the intangible assets, the "intellectual capital" of companies and other organizations. Such a measurement will be difficult, imprecise, and it will open the Pandora's box of politicization and hype, fad, and fraud.

But there is also one compelling reason for doing so: we have no choice. And for that reason, we must move forward . . . but carefully, lest we do as much damage as good.

Anyone who follows the stock market—and these days that's everyone—knows that there is a widening gap between the value of a company's balance sheet and the value bestowed on that company by the market. Even if we strip away the distortions of a bull market, those differences are still there, and they are decisive. The average value of companies today on the world's stock exchanges is two times book value. In the United States, especially among knowledge-based companies, that multiple can be as great as nine.

Clearly, this represents a serious problem. Traditional accounting gives us half or less of the information we need to make an intelligent judgment about corporate value. As for the rest, we are on our own. We don't even have a language to describe the rest, much less a yardstick. Instead, we rely on rumor, inside information, auguries, and gut instincts.

And that is both unfair and dangerous. Unfair because it distorts the free flow of capital and tilts the field against the small investor. Even the best analysts are still half blind to the firms in which they are making buy and sell recommendations. And they have almost unlimited access. The small private investor, with a pension and a few shares, is left to divine a company's real value from the obscure footnotes in the back of the annual report and from rewritten press releases in daily newspapers. The result is not only an extraordinary volatility in valuations, driven by the unexpected eruptions of hidden strengths and weaknesses, but also a massive inefficiency of investment, as good money flows into bad companies with great media savvy, while good but less-noticed companies pay more for the capital they rightly deserve. Even more serious for the long-term strength of our economy is that we reward companies with good balance sheets but no future and punish companies that are compromising their balance sheets now for what would have been a bright future.

As I said, this blindness is also dangerous because it is the business equivalent of driving looking only in the rearview mirror.

And these days we are all driving at breakneck speeds. Traditional accounting is brilliant at telling us where we've just been and pretty good at telling us where we are right now, but it does a miserable job of telling us where we are going. That kind of static measurement was efficient enough in 1876 or even 1976. But, thanks to the technological revolution, we now live in a world in which perpetual, revolutionary change is the status quo and in which tomorrow is often more present than today. It is the rare company that can operate the same way it did a decade ago or build a business strategy based upon incremental change. More often, the best we can do is try to build an organization with enough resilience, with enough openness to new ideas, and, most of all, with enough intelligence to react swiftly and decisively to radical change coming from unexpected directions.

You won't find the capacity to cope with profound change on the traditional balance sheet or in inventories or accounts receivable or equipment. Instead it lies within that odd little catchall category of traditional accounting called *intangible assets*. Today we call it *intellectual capital*, and it includes everything from intellectual property to customer satisfaction to employee training to corporate information systems. Our challenge is how to identify intellectual capital, codify it, and measure it—in other words, to make it as accurate and informative as the balance sheet itself.

In the old economy one didn't need to worry about these intangible assets until the day the company was sold. Now CEOs worry about them from the moment they awaken in the morning until the moment they fitfully fall asleep at night. Is my company prepared for what's coming? Do we have enough information, and are we distributing it properly? Are my people smart enough? Am I smart enough? Should we be training more? And if so, what should we be learning? What is the intellectual capital of my company, and how can I increase it?

More than a decade ago, Walter Wriston in his book *The Twi-*

light of Sovereignty set into motion the intellectual capital debate by stating, "The new source of wealth is not material, it is information, knowledge applied to work to create value."

Five years ago, the consensus was that intellectual capital had indeed become the decisive factor in the long-term success of a growing number of companies, but that as an asset it was so ineffable—indeed, so intangible—that it could never be truly identified, much less measured.

But, during the past few years, as the role of intangibles has grown evermore dominant in modern economic life, several companies have made pioneering efforts to make intellectual capital an empirical discipline. The first of these, by my *Intellectual Capital* coauthor Leif Edvinsson of Sweden's Skandia, broke new ground in 1995 with the publication of the world's first intellectual capital annual report. Others have followed, such as Gordon Petrash of Dow Chemical, currently preparing the first IC report by a U.S. company. Dozens, perhaps hundreds, of projects of similar or lesser scale are in the works throughout the world. The number of IC Web sites grows by the week. And, in that barometer of hot business trends, most of the top consulting firms, such as Anderson Consulting and Ernst & Young, have started up their own IC practices. Clearly, we are at a turning point.

The ultimate test, of course, is the accounting profession. But even here we are beginning to see thoughtful accounting firms coming to recognize that intellectual capital measurement and reporting is not a threat to traditional accounting but an adjunct to it. IC measurement, done right, is the leading indicator of tomorrow's earnings statement.

What is likely to come out of all this activity is both a philosophy of intellectual capital and a body of metrics that will slowly codify into a standard IC reporting format comparable to that used by traditional accounting. It is no longer outrageous to predict that by the early years of the twenty-first century, intellectual capital annual reports will be as common as traditional annual reports and that, indeed, today's balance sheet may in time be an appendix to a larger body of IC measures.

It is a thrilling idea, but a disconcerting one too. One of the best ways to win any game is to write the rules. And with intellectual capital we are entering an era in which the most fundamental financial rules are about to be up for grabs. Already we are seeing the first signs of two extreme and opposing camps emerging to define just what metrics we shall use.

On one hand there are those who believe that intellectual capital is the best way to sneak into the back door of the modern corporation. That camp would love to see the IC reporting metrics weighted toward measures of diversity, community outreach, and all of the *-isms* that hold sway over modern life. They believe intellectual capital will finally bring justice and enlightenment to the corporate world. This is IC as PC, as a tool for social activism.

The second camp believes that IC should only measure the most tangible of the intangibles—that is, systems, the ability of the company to process and use information. This is intellectual capital as diagnostic software. That camp, understandably, fears opening the doors to wild-eyed activists. And, to keep those doors tightly shut, that group is willing to destroy intellectual capital by reducing it to a meter on the front of a computer.

But there is a third approach—one to which most of us will eventually belong and from which the real IC revolution will spring: intellectual capital as a dynamic filter. Let's take all the metrics devised by the many different camps, from the number of nodes in the client-server system to the number of minority women in executive positions, and *test* for their true contribution to a company's value. Let's see which actually converts over time to dollars and cents on the balance sheet.

Each of us has our own opinion about what makes a company successful, as does every politician, stock analyst, union organizer, and corporate executive. Now is that once in a half-millennium opportunity to put them all on the table and see which really do matter. Let's begin that process right here, today.

We have time. It took four hundred years to perfect double-entry bookkeeping and the principles of modern accounting. We don't have that long, but a few years of serious debate won't cost us much and may ultimately save us. We now have the best minds at work on intellectual capital, and the experiences of a growing number of companies.

If we do this right, we can construct a value system that will make companies more efficient, more competitive and ultimately more valuable. Even more than that—because intellectual capital measurement is not confined to business but is likely to be the first universal measurement tool for *all* human institutions—we will be able to construct a more valuable society.

That, of course, is the hope that emerged last out of Pandora's box. Intellectual capital is indeed our best hope for continued prosperity into the twenty-first century. And learning how to measure it is the only path for getting there.

Robert J. Barro

Ideas and Intellectual
Property Rights in the
Determination of
Economic Growth

From 1986 to 1989, Paul Romer revolutionized growth theory by including an analysis of technological progress in the form of the creation of new ideas. These ideas were modeled as new varieties of products, but they can also be viewed as better-quality products or superior methods of production.

Since the ideas were fundamentally public goods in the sense of being nonrival—that is, usable by many producers without compromising the physical usefulness to others—there was a basic conflict between *ex post* and *ex ante* efficiency. *Ex post* reasoning, such as that advanced by Hillary Clinton for pharmaceuticals, would argue for low prices on goods or ideas that had already been discovered. But such a policy provides no incentives for future research and invention. Thus, as is well known from the patent literature, efficient outcomes require some kind of property rights over past discoveries. These rights may be sustained to some extent through formal legal protection, but they also involve secrecy and the benefits from being the first entrant into a new area. If these intellectual property rights are too weakly maintained, then the incentives for research are small and economic growth will be sluggish.

Proper policies for maintaining intellectual property rights are difficult to design because these rights can be too strong as well as too weak. When the rights are too weak, the incentives for the creation of new ideas and products are insufficient and the rate of technological change will be too low. The incentives to copy existing technologies—by rival companies and countries—will be correspondingly too great. That is, too much effort will be expended on technological diffusion and not enough on technological advance.

Intellectual property rights can, however, also be too strong. For example, the development of a new product or idea sometimes allows the inventor to acquire the monopoly rents that had been accruing to the previous technological leader in a field. This rent transfer has no social value and, therefore, provides an excessive incentive for research and discovery. Similar effects arise if competing inventors use up resources to race for the next innovation.

In principle, outcomes can be improved if an inventor has to compensate the previous technological leader for the loss of rental income. Partly this is because a potential inventor knows that future compensation will be forthcoming when the next innovator comes along. But it is hard to imagine how such a compensation scheme could be reasonably implemented, especially by some government bureaucrat! So any realistic form of legal protection has to make compromises, such as having patents last for a while and not forever.

The initial promise of the new ideas-based growth theory was that it would supplant the existing theories by virtue of being a better empirical model of growth. The existing framework was mainly the neoclassical growth model, as developed by Frank Ramsey in the 1920s, Bob Solow in the 1950s, and other economists in the 1960s. This model focused on the accumulation of capital—which can be broadly interpreted to include human, as well as physical, forms—as a source of per capita growth. Diminishing returns to capital were a key feature of the model. This feature led to the prediction that poor countries would tend to converge toward rich countries. Although the role of technological progress was recognized, this model did not explore the sources of this progress. Whether or not the neoclassical growth model has been supplanted depends a lot on the empirical question one wants to ask.

One key issue is why some countries grow much faster than others over long periods. For example, why has South Korea done so much better than Mozambique during the last thirty-five years? For this purpose, the neoclassical growth theory has proven to be much more useful than the newer ideas-based theory, especially if the neoclassical model is extended from the literal form developed by Ramsey, Solow, et al. to incorporate elements such as government policies and institutions and the accumulation of human capital.

The augmented neoclassical framework has provided the basis for empirical work that isolates growth determinants such as institutions that maintain property rights and the rule of law, policies that promote free markets domestically and internationally, macroeconomic stability, and high investment in human capital. Given these kinds of factors, the international data reveal a strong (conditional) convergence force—the hallmark of the neoclassical model—whereby countries grow faster if they start out poorer. Thus, as I have argued elsewhere, one irony of the new ideas-based growth theory is that it stimulated empirical work that demonstrated the great explanatory power of the older type of growth model (at least in extended versions). This development was particularly important because the neoclassical model had previously been mainly theory without empirical implementation.

In contrast, it is pretty clear that differences in growth rates between, for example, South Korea and Mozambique have little to do with one place inventing a lot of new ideas and the other inventing few. The key to South Korea's growth is that it was able to use technologies developed elsewhere, to accumulate lots of human and physical capital, and to get people to work hard. None of this has much to do with Paul Romer's elegant modeling of basic discoveries and the intellectual property rights that would motivate such discoveries.

However, one can ask a different question, namely, how is it that leading-edge countries, such as the United States, can continue to grow for a long time without a strong tendency for growth rates to slow down? (Whether a sustained drop in the rate of productivity growth has occurred in the United States and other leading countries is a controversial matter.) In this context, basic technological change—new products, better products, and superior methods of production—must be the key. Otherwise, the economy would have encountered more obviously diminishing returns with respect to the accumulation of physical and human capital. In the long run, this perspective also applies to the world. That is, the world as a whole can continue to grow at high rates per capita only if new things are continually discovered. Thus although South Korea was able to exploit technologies developed elsewhere, the whole world does not have this option.

It would be nice if there existed empirical work that documented this key role for technological progress and intellectual property rights in the long-term growth performances of the United States and other advanced countries. That is, it would be nice if this type of time-series evidence were as convincing as that available from a cross section of countries supporting the convergence-type implications of the neoclassical theory. At this point, interesting case studies of innovations and some aggregate evidence related to the role of expenditures on research and development are available. But the total of the evidence currently available in this area at the macroeconomic level is not impressive. Probably we need more evidence of this sort, rather than more stories about particular innovations or more formal theorizing about the growth effects of ideas and intellectual property rights.

Intellectual Capital and Intellectual Property: Issues of Protection

4

Overcoming the Legal Behemoth: The Urgent Need for a Private Legal System in Electronics

Consumers are opening their arms to technology as they never have before, and the electronics industry is poised to become the single most influential industry on earth. At the core of the electronics industry growth is the capability of advanced silicon manufacturing processes. Specifically, the ability to integrate entire systems onto a single silicon chip, or system chip, is the technical innovation that will enable the consumerization of electronics. Since no single company will own enough intellectual property (IP) to populate complex system chips, however, companies will need to exchange building blocks of IP on a regular basis. Looming more ominously than the technical challenge is the fact that the existing legal system in the United States fails to support the effective exchange and reuse of IP building blocks. The legal system that once gave America its strategic advantage is now constraining the U.S. electronics industry and threatening to undermine its global competitiveness.

The existing legal system lacks both the technical knowledge and the speed to facilitate effective IP protection and exchange. Rather than outsource the enforcement of something as critical as IP exchange to a besieged public legal system, the electronics industry should form a private legal system to meet its needs. Establishing basic IP exchange guidelines and enlisting knowledgeable industry insiders to resolve disputes would allow electronics companies to better leverage their IP assets, reduce legal expenses, and, most important, deliver new and exciting products to market faster than ever before. Forming a private legal system for IP exchange is both a necessary and a realistic proposition. Given a logical approach and simple objectives, electronics companies can create an efficient legal system that fosters industry growth.

One potential starting point for creating a private legal system is the Virtual Socket Interface (VSI) Alliance, a coalition of more than 125 companies dedicated to the shared vision of the system chip. Although the VSI Alliance currently focuses on the technical issues of IP mix and match, the organization could be expanded to address legal issues. The VSI Alliance provides the critical mass of companies necessary for legal reform, as well as an infrastructure on which to build a private legal system. Ultimately, the electronics industry must take responsibility for eliminating the barriers that threaten to stifle its growth. If a better legal mechanism for IP exchange is not created, the United States risks losing valuable electronics business to other countries where existing legal environments are more conducive to success or are at least more flexible and adaptive in the face of needed change.

Consumerization Drives Growth and Change in Electronics

The electronics industry has grown tremendously over the last few decades by selling electronics-based innovations to the industrial world. Electronics is now one of the largest industrial segments worldwide, surpassing one trillion dollars globally. Until recently, the primary customers for electronics companies were sophisticated technical and business users. Although opportunities remain in the business-to-business market, technical and business markets for electronics products are beginning to reach the saturation point. The only market large enough to drive significant new growth in the electronics industry is the consumer market; only by expanding to serve the largely untapped consumer market can the electronics industry realize its enormous growth potential.

Already today, silicon is embedded within a wide variety of consumer products, from cellular phones, pagers, and electronic organizers to video games and even running shoes. The exciting part, though, is that the consumer revolution in electronics is just beginning. Analysts predict that consumer expenditures on products containing silicon will increase significantly over the next decade, as electronics companies scramble to deliver a wider variety of products to market. The companies that master the nuances of the consumer market will become the powerhouses of the next millennium.

Meeting the demands of fickle consumers, however, requires a change in the way companies conceptualize, design, and manufacture products. Tomorrow's technology business will have more in common with the fashion industry than with the traditional model of selling big iron (large computing systems) to corporate enterprises. Consumer preferences and desires change rapidly, creating a market characterized by brief windows of opportunity and constant churning. Fortunately for electronics companies, it is often the external attributes of consumer products (color, size, etc.) that come in and out of fashion most rapidly, leaving the opportunity to deliver a broad assortment of products based on a core set of internal, functional components. Still, no single company will be able to develop all the necessary components. Rather, a range of companies, large and small, will develop the building blocks of intellectual property required for complex electronic designs.

The System Chip and the New Age of IP Exchange

Indeed, the technical ability to integrate numerous functional blocks onto a single piece of silicon promises to revolutionize the electronics industry. Rather than creating a new product by combining many chips from different manufacturers onto a single printed circuit board, electronics companies of the future will mix and match numerous functional pieces of IP into a system on a chip, or system chip. The system chip provides the benefits of reduced product costs, improved performance, and faster time to market when compared with traditional circuit boards. In essence, the system chip model meets all the important criteria for companies to deliver an ever-changing array of low-cost consumer products.

Although the benefits of the system chip are powerful, the industry must overcome several obstacles before the new design paradigm becomes a mainstream reality. Perhaps looming larger than the technical challenge is the hurdle of creating a business environment where companies can mix and match IP building blocks from multiple sources. The move to system chip electronic design requires critical action on the part of both individual companies and the industry as a whole. First and foremost, individual companies must be willing to play in the new game of IP mix and match. They must reformulate their corporate IP strategies to leverage their intellectual assets, their intellectual capital, while incorporating principles of exchange and reuse.

In the traditional approach to IP management, electronics companies sought to develop as broad a technology portfolio as possible and to register the largest number of patents to protect those technologies. Throughout the 1970s and 1980s, companies increased market share by leveraging patents to barricade rivals out of market niches. The more patents a company owned, the more niches it could dominate. Patenting both important and trivial technologies enabled large companies to intimidate potential market entrants who, with fewer financial resources, would likely shy away from costly legal battles with dominant corporations. Until recently, the primary purpose of a corporate IP portfolio has been self-protection. On relatively rare occasions, companies have exchanged IP through cross licensing wherein both companies think they can leverage their IP for financial gain. It has been the exception, not the rule, however, for companies to gamble their IP building blocks through cross-licensing agreements.

Today, more and more electronics companies are realizing that they will never own enough IP building blocks to construct the broad range of products consumers are scrambling to purchase. Rather than protect their entire IP portfolio, companies are now beginning to make important distinctions between technologies that provide real competitive advantage worth protecting and technologies that can be commercialized for the good of the industry without negative financial repercussions. The electronics industry is starting to realize that it has outgrown its IP management paradigm and that each company will need technologies from the others to engineer great products from great ideas. *Co-opetition*, the act of simultaneously competing with and partnering with other companies, is fast becoming standard business practice as electronics companies embrace the concept of the system chip.

Adopting the IP exchange business model and developing the underlying technology are critical steps to making the system chip a reality. Fortunately, those two steps are well under way. The third and final step to success is creating an effective mechanism for the exchange and reuse of IP building blocks. As individual companies reformulate their IP strategies to incorporate principles of reuse, the industry as a whole must lay the foundation for exchanging IP in an efficient and timely manner. Currently, electronics companies outsource their morality to the U.S. public legal system to create IP exchange contracts and resolve IP-related disputes. The reliance of electronics companies on an external and overworked legal system to facilitate the critical exchange of IP is, as indicated, one of the most pressing problems facing the industry today.

Existing U.S. Legal System

The U.S. legal system was designed to deliver basic law and order to a growing society, and in that respect, the system is one of America's crowning achievements. Faced with the daunting task of protecting our society from crime, drug abuse, and other societal evils, however, the existing public legal system in the United States lacks the capacity to keep up with the rapid progress of the burgeoning electronics industry. Outsourcing such a critical function as IP exchange to an already overburdened public system is a grave mistake on the part of the electronics industry.

The essence of the problem is that, whereas law is rooted in the past, business, and particularly technology, is focused on the future. The electronics industry, where constant change and innovation are the norm, needs new rules and standards. Most patent laws were designed to protect physical, industrial designs, not the highly conceptual designs at the heart of today's electronics products. In many cases, there are simply no past precedents that apply to the modern, high-tech business world. Besieged with other problems to solve, the existing legal system in the United States cannot provide an efficient mechanism for facilitating IP exchange and reuse.

Specifically, today's legal system falls short in two critical areas. First, the majority of people involved in the legal process lack the depth of technical knowledge required to create effective IP exchange contracts and settle IP-related disputes. Second, the existing legal system lacks the speed to deliver contracts and dispute resolution in an acceptable time frame. Each of these shortcomings on its own is capable of stunting the electronics industry's growth. Put them together and the industry faces a substantial barrier that needs to be toppled.

Lack of Technical Knowledge in Existing Legal System

Intellectual property today is complicated business. During the past thirty years, the electronics industry has succeeded in packing more and more functionality onto smaller and smaller pieces of silicon. Building blocks of IP have grown smaller, and the ways in which they fit together now are more intricate than ever before. Only a small percentage of people within the electronics industry truly understands the technical intricacies of IP mix and match. Within the broader context of the business and legal community, that technical knowledge is all but nonexistent.

With relatively few exceptions, legal professionals and judicial officials are trained in the process of law and justice, not in deep submicron design or interface logic. Writing a meaningful contract between two companies that are collaborating on a system chip design, however, requires a certain comprehension of the technologies involved. If two companies are lucky, in-house attorneys with a knowledge base spanning both law and technology can negotiate such a contract in a reasonable time frame. But as the number of parties to a collaboration grows, as will inevitably happen in the age of the system chip, the likelihood that everyone involved in the contract creation possesses sufficient technical knowledge decreases.

Nowhere is the lack of technical knowledge more evident than when IP-related disputes go to court for resolution. When companies decide to litigate an IP dispute, they outsource all responsibility for determining a solution to a judge or jury unfamiliar with the key concepts and technologies. The American legal system was founded on the principle that one side have the opportunity to tell its story, the other side its story, and a wise person sit between them and come to a conclusion. Given the vast complexity of technology today, particularly in the area of intellectual property, who can serve as the wise person? To expect judges and juries of the public courts to adequately understand IP disputes is increasingly unrealistic.

Another fundamental principle of the U.S. legal system is that judges and juries are selected at random to hear cases and pass judgment. For a case involving complex technical issues, a judge often receives a brief tutorial before the trial, but this amounts to a weak bandage over a gaping wound. Without significant and ongoing training, no judge could hope to stay abreast of such a fast-moving industry as electronics. Rather than assign the individual most likely to make an informed and fair decision, the U.S. legal system in effect ignores the importance of technical knowledge by assigning judges and juries randomly.

Add to this scenario the fact that the parties most likely to understand the key issues—the corporate attorneys—are the ones trained to leverage selective evidence to win the case for their employer. The two advocates present one-sided accounts of the story and call on the testimony of expert witnesses, who often overwhelm the judge or jury with gratuitous technical jargon. Some studies have found that jury members are more likely to be influenced by external attributes, such as the attractiveness or presentation skills of attorneys and expert witnesses, than the content of the argument.

Ultimately, the existing legal system in the United States is akin to providing a blind judge for a beauty pageant, and giving each contestant an advocate to describe their beauty. "Isn't she lovely, judge? She looks absolutely fabulous today." The judge listens to the comments from both advocates and determines the winner. With so much at stake in the market for IP exchange, electronics companies need a more reliable forum for contract creation and dispute resolution. The lack of technical knowledge in the U.S. legal system is understandable, but, given the increasing complexity of IP-related agreements and disagreements, the system is quickly becoming an insurmountable obstacle for the electronics industry.

Slow Existing Legal System

The second major problem with the existing legal system is that it works too slowly to facilitate the exchange and reuse of IP in a relevant time frame. In an age where design schedules for consumer electronics products are condensed from years to months, companies need to exchange IP building blocks quickly and efficiently. Today, a fine line separates the winners from the losers in the consumer electronics marketplace. The company that executes its strategy and delivers a product to market on time reaps great rewards. Conversely, the company that misses that window of opportunity by even a few weeks or months has wasted precious development resources. A legal system that delays a company from using IP from a willing supplier can spell financial ruin.

Most delays in the legal system seem to derive from the system's focus on history and process rather than on results. The system has grown over hundreds of years from a set of basic rules and guidelines to a complicated labyrinth of statutes, precepts, and arcane case law. Given the sheer volume of rulings now in existence, it is no wonder that reaching a conclusion requires so much time. The judicial process requires a thorough analysis of each party's argument in the context of past decisions. The growing volume of case law means that the legal system's obsession with process and historical precedent is making it slower, not faster, with each new decision on the record.

Although the original goal of the legal system was to give both sides a chance to tell their stories fully, it has extended those privileges by granting each side seemingly endless opportunities to stall proceedings whenever it becomes convenient to do so. In addition, legal professionals are taught to cover all possible loopholes in closing cases, so that the opposition is less likely to win an appeal. Indeed, the opportunity for the loser to appeal a decision injects further and often unnecessary delay when most technology companies simply want fast justice and the opportunity to move ahead quickly. Not that legal professionals are to blame. How could they be, when in fact most companies regularly encourage their legal representatives to manipulate the nuances of the system when it suits them? This behavior by technology companies and their executives is a major contributor to the slowness of the legal system.

Among the most highly visible examples of the legal system's slowness is the case between chip-maker rivals Advanced Micro Devices (AMD) and Intel Corporation. After AMD began cloning Intel's 386 chip, the two companies engaged in what escalated to be a seven-year legal battle. Over the course of the seven years, charges included copyright infringement and patent and antitrust violations. In the end, the California Supreme Court upheld an arbitrator's authority to allow AMD to continue cloning the Intel chip. Multiple lawsuits, arbitration hearings, and appeals ultimately outlasted the useful life of the technology under dispute. Both companies reportedly spent millions of dollars on the legal battle and, after becoming increasing frustrated by constant delay in the proceedings, turned to an outside mediator to resolve the conflict.

Although full-scale litigation provides the most striking examples of the legal system's shortcomings, intolerable delay is not isolated to court cases. With time-to-market pressures becoming ever greater in the consumer electronics business, even the nonlitigious act of creating an IP exchange contract can derail a project. In a recent case, lawyers representing a supplier and a consumer of IP required a full year to put in place a contract between the two companies collaborating on a new product. The life cycle of the product itself was only six months. Clearly, the existing legal system is paralyzed by an obsession with process.

Alternative Dispute Resolution

Discussion so far has focused on the legal system as a bottleneck when IP disputes go to trial and has not specifically addressed existing alternatives for dispute resolution. This is because the most clear-cut examples of the legal system as a barrier to progress arise from circumstances where companies choose to litigate. No doubt many interested readers, especially those trained in the legal profession, are now asking, "But what about alternative dispute resolution?" Although alternative dispute resolution (ADR) tactics such as arbitration and mediation can lead to faster and more cost-effective results than litigation, ADR still falls short as a solution for effective IP exchange.

As its name implies, alternative dispute resolution is a reactive measure invoked only when two parties have reached the point of disagreement. ADR is not a proactive solution with the built-in goal of facilitating IP exchange and reuse; it is simply a mechanism for avoiding the frightening prospect of full-scale litigation. Whatever the specific method, ADR is an attempt at tweaking the existing legal system to speed dispute resolution. ADR can help companies out of a damaging hole, but it will never fill the hole to prevent companies from falling in again. To meet the challenge of IP exchange and realize the benefits of the system chip, the electronics industry requires more drastic legal reform than ADR delivers.

Forming a Private Legal System

The shortcomings of today's legal system are no secret. Unfortunately, most technology companies and executives seem to have blindly accepted the notion that the existing system, despite its flaws, is the only possible forum for IP exchange and dispute resolution. What the electronics industry needs is a new system that allows fewer excuses for disputes and provides a smooth and efficient mechanism for companies to exchange IP building blocks. By first believing that a private system is both necessary and realistic, and then by working together to establish a basic set of IP exchange guidelines and to police the behavior of companies and their legal representatives, electronics companies can create and maintain a legal environment conducive to industry growth.

Step One

The first step to solving the problem is for electronics industry executives and legal representatives to believe that establishing a private legal system is both necessary and realistic. Given the widespread delays in IP proceedings and the excessive amounts of money companies spend on litigation today, it is difficult to fathom that anyone within the industry does not see the pressing need for reform. In addition, many prominent economists, legal experts, and opinion leaders outside the industry agree that a better mechanism for IP sharing is needed. More challenging, perhaps, is convincing those involved in the day-to-day business of IP contracting and dispute resolution that forming a private legal system is a realistic undertaking.

Implementing reform can be a daunting proposition. On first inspection, it often seems much easier to replace a few faulty shingles and floorboards than to build a new house. The problem in trying to amend the past is that a transition period inevitably results. During that transition period, the parties that rely on the system to deliver results are stuck in no-man's-land. As business leaders worldwide will attest, achieving success often requires making new rules rather than trying to play and win by the old rules. The right thing to do is to establish a new business model for exchanging IP building blocks. There is little sense in building a new roof atop a house with a crumbling foundation.

Fortunately, there are proven methods of implementing reform and establishing better ways of doing things. The easiest way to build a new house is to use existing blueprints. A brief examination of other industries demonstrates that creating a private system for conducting important transactions is not a new or radical idea. For reassurance that forming a private legal system is a realistic goal, electronics industry insiders would do well to consider the real estate business.

In the old days of real estate in the United States, owners wishing to sell a property hired a lawyer to manage the sale. Likewise, the person wishing to purchase the property hired a lawyer, and the two attorneys negotiated a contract between the buyer and seller. In an effort to speed transactions and to extend the real estate business to the masses, somebody pioneered the system of using brokers to facilitate property exchanges (at least in my state, California). Rather than involving lawyers to negotiate a new contract for every sale, the industry adopted and standardized on a basic set of legal guidelines for the exchange of property. With those guidelines in place, and with the buy-in of real estate practitioners (i.e., broker certification), the exchange of property between individuals became a much more efficient process.

Although legal professionals will no doubt continue to play a crucial role in IP exchange, the real estate analogy is a good one for the electronics industry. Whether trading houses or IP building blocks, the goal of a private system is to facilitate vital transactions. The U.S. real estate industry succeeded in establishing an efficient private system even given the millions of properties nationwide to be bought and sold by a population of buyers and sellers almost as large. The electronics industry, growing to be one of the world's largest, enjoys the benefit of having fewer players with pieces to trade. Thus although trades will become increasingly frequent, the prospect of forming a private legal system for IP exchange is still realistic today.

Step Two

Once a critical mass of companies has bought into the concept of forming a private legal system, the industry will need to establish a basic set of guidelines for IP exchange and reuse. The most important objective is to keep it simple. The existing public legal system in the United States began simply but evolved over hundreds of years to encompass the myriad rules and regulations in effect today. A good piece of advice is "walk before you run." Likewise, the electronics industry would benefit from simple guidelines that define a general process for IP exchange as well as what behavior is acceptable from participants in the process. By working together to establish guidelines and agreeing to abide by them, electronics companies can lay the foundation for a self-governing, private law that fosters the growth of the industry.

Guidelines for exchange and reuse must be broad enough to apply to a wide range of intellectual property yet specific enough to yield predictable results in a timely manner. Making the rules will require the input of many participants, so that each company joining the new system feels that the rules are applicable to their specific IP portfolio. The last thing the industry needs is a system that effectively rejects certain types of IP from the exchange mechanism; such a system would give some companies unfair competitive advantage while locking out others. At the same time, rules cannot leave the door open for long and inconclusive disputes. The decision makers for dispute resolution within the new system should be industry insiders who bring some expertise to bear. In addition to knowledge, however, those experts will need some specific guidelines to make the right decisions. Without clear direction, they will be reduced to making arbitrary and unpredictable rulings. Striking the balance between inclusiveness and specificity will be an important charter for the companies that band together to form the new guidelines for IP exchange and reuse.

Finally, when companies are establishing guidelines for IP exchange, they need to protect the interests of companies that will participate in the new system. The only sure way to engage corporations in an industrywide effort is to provide financial incentives to those that participate. Like members in any private club, electronics companies that join the new IP exchange system should enjoy benefits. Currently, companies that enter into IP exchange contracts must protect themselves from expensive lawsuits or other damage, such as trade secret theft, that can result from IP sharing. The new system should build that protection into the rules, so that participating in IP exchange automatically affords companies some level of insurance against frivolous lawsuits or other undeserved financial loss. Without such incentives, companies will be reluctant to join in the industry effort.

Step Three

The final step to implementing a private legal system for IP exchange will be for the industry to police the behavior of electronics companies and their legal representatives. Indeed, much of the problem in today's system is that companies openly engage in counterproductive behavior when it suits them. Given that they are involved in a complex and flawed legal process, companies encourage their legal representatives to exploit the system's nuances to their advantage. Electronics companies haggle over obscure contract clauses, conceal critical evidence during trials, manipulate countless opportunities for delay, and file lawsuits with the intent of intimidation rather than self-protection. Then they complain about the system. Although this counterproductive behavior has become routine within the existing legal system, the industry must eradicate it within the new private system.

Reform must be brought about in action as well as in word. Once a basic set of guidelines for IP exchange is agreed on and put into place by electronics companies, the industry must police itself carefully. For starters, each company must take responsibility for its own behavior. Executives should no longer encourage their legal representatives to manipulate the system, and, likewise, lawyers should seek the most effective and expeditious contracts possible within the industry's guidelines. When companies routinely fail to channel their energy into forward progress on IP exchange, the industry will need to punish that behavior. Perhaps the new system should feature an unbiased commission that disciplines companies that fail to live up to industry standards for productive behavior related to IP exchange. Much like the United Nations, the enforcing body would represent the interests of all companies that participate in the new system.

Whatever the specific model for enforcement, the electronics industry will need to improve its behavior to make the private legal system a success. By first believing that a private legal system is a realistic goal, and then by establishing basic guidelines and eliminating counterproductive behavior, the electronics industry can drastically reduce the effect of the public legal system as a barrier to progress. In cases where disputes extend beyond the capacity of the private system, the existing public legal system in the United States will no doubt come into play. But as long as executives are frustrated enough and industry growth is stifled enough by the existing system, and as long as the new private system is functioning well, the instances where electronics companies outsource to the public legal system will be kept to a minimum.

Getting Started

After every important discussion of reform, the question begs, "Where do we go from here?" When faced with a task as significant as forming a new legal system, the temptation for electronics companies to succumb to inertia will be great. It is true that the longest journey begins with a single step. That first and most difficult step is pulling many competing companies together to work toward the common goal of IP exchange and reuse. Fortunately, the electronics industry has already taken that step with the formation in 1996 of the Virtual Socket Interface Alliance mentioned earlier. The mission of the VSI Alliance is to establish a unifying vision for the system chip industry and the technical standards required to enable the mix and match of IP building blocks from multiple sources. At the time of its formation, the VSI Alliance included more than thirty-five companies representing a cross section of the electronics industry.

Although the VSI Alliance, which my company helped spearhead, is dedicated to solving the technical issues associated with IP exchange and reuse, the organization might be a logical starting point for legal reform as well. Not only does the VSI Alliance represent the industry's coming together to achieve the system chip, a goal at the heart of the legal reform movement, but it also provides a ready-made infrastructure on which to build a private legal system. Since the VSI Alliance is already working to overcome fundamental obstacles that stand in the way of the system chip era, the organization could be extended to address legal reform. The private legal system could ultimately remain an out-growth of the VSI Alliance or become a separate entity altogether.

Conclusion

The legal problem in the electronics industry is quickly reaching the point of crisis. As companies shift their strategies to embrace the concept of the system chip, the legal process of exchanging intellectual property and resolving IP-related disputes looms as one of the greatest barriers to industry growth. Rather than outsource a function as critical as IP exchange to a besieged public legal system in the United States, the electronics industry should take back the responsibility for IP exchange and form a private legal system to meet its needs.

The benefits of forming a private legal system for IP exchange are numerous. Establishing basic IP exchange guidelines and enlisting knowledgeable industry insiders to resolve disputes will allow electronics companies to better leverage their IP assets, reduce legal expenses, and, most important, deliver new and exciting products to market faster than ever before. Rather than shy away from the challenge and continue to accept the losing terms and conditions of the existing legal system in the United States, the industry should create a new set of rules by which to succeed.

Success in this endeavor can be attained by following three sequential steps. First, a critical mass of companies must believe that forming a private legal system is both a necessary and a realistic undertaking. That critical mass of companies already exists in the form of the VSI Alliance. Second, the companies that agree to join the system must establish a basic set of guidelines for IP exchange and reuse. These guidelines will govern how companies trade IP building blocks and resolve IP-related disputes. Third, the electronics industry must police itself carefully to prevent counterproductive behavior from spoiling the success of the new system.

Companies that misbehave should be punished, and companies that play fairly should be rewarded and protected.

By following these three steps and by making a conscious effort not to get embroiled in too many details too soon, the electronics industry can create an efficient mechanism for IP exchange. If the industry remains reliant on the public legal system in the United States, however, it risks the possibility of companies moving operations to other countries in search of a legal environment more conducive to success. The age of the system chip and its benefits is dawning, and companies will locate where the sun is most likely to rise first. The time is now for the electronics industry to knock down the barriers that threaten to stifle its growth.

Margaret Jane Radin and Erin Sawyer

The Role of Nonproprietary Technologies

5

The growth of the technology sector both in terms of sheer size and in terms of product diversity has led to debate about the optimal level of intellectual property protection. At the same time, firms whose major assets are intangible trade secrets and the collective brainpower of their employees are trying to formulate strategies to protect and accurately value their intellectual capital. Implicit in these discussions is the question of how intellectual property and intellectual capital relate to each other. Clearly, intellectual capital and intellectual property are not synonymous terms. The key question for industry analysts and participants is how the two concepts map onto each other. In

The authors wish to acknowledge the generous support of the John M. Olin Program in Law and Economics.

particular, how can intellectual property be used both to protect established intellectual capital and to encourage growth and future innovations? When is intellectual capital best fostered by a property regime and when does it require the free-for-all of the public domain?

These questions raise the issue of how to locate the boundary between what is and is not property. Defining a realm of technologies to be protected as property necessarily involves creating a residual realm of nonproperty items. More than just a definitional exercise, the designation of property/nonproperty is essential to the task of balancing the need for current protections and future incentives. Creation of value may be stifled if too many resources are tied up in property, but creation of value may also be stifled if too few are.

In this chapter, we review traditional economic narratives that balance present and future interests and describe the expansion of the computer industry in terms of those narratives. We then look to a continuum of technologies and market strategies ranging from proprietary to nonproprietary. We consider Microsoft on the strong proprietary end and the Linux operating system on the nonproprietary end. As a hybrid between the two, we analyze Sun's Java language and its potential impact on the computer industry as a whole. Our analysis suggests that many nonproprietary technologies will be part of a larger package with proprietary interests at the core. The proliferation of nonproprietary technologies, albeit in varying degrees, will continue to provoke discussion about how intellectual property protections can be shaped to encourage competition in the present and innovation in the future.

Traditional Economic Conceptions of Intellectual Property

The most basic economic understanding of intellectual property supposes that, in order to produce an optimal amount of information, incentives to creators are required in the form of limited-duration monopolies to internalize benefits to those creators. These limited-duration monopolies serve to internalize benefits to those creators, but they have costs of their own. Thus, intellectual property theory consists of a giant hypothetical cost-benefit analysis attempting to maximize the difference between (1) the added benefits drawn forth by intellectual property rights and (2) the costs of protection. This involves the messy (hopeless?) practical task of trying to plug numbers into this complex hypothetical equation. At issue is not only the "correct" number of years for the monopoly, but also the "correct" delineation of rights.[1]

At best the giant hypothetical cost-benefit analysis is a story that resists definitive actualization. The balance shifts between what is appropriately designated intellectual property (for present creators) and what is appropriately left in the public domain (for future creators). In the realm of intellectual property, propertization (of some things in the world) always implies nonpropertization (of other things in the world). Therefore, in studying intellectual property both theoretically and in real-world implementations, it is important to consider areas of nonpropertization equally with areas of propertization. It may be costly not to have property, but it is also costly to have property.

A more subtle economic understanding of intellectual property, which has recently become part of the standard story, takes

---

1. Should follow-on innovation give rise to a blocking situation, as in patent law, or should the original creator simply be able to enjoy an unlicensed follow-on work, as in the way copyright law treats derivative works? And how should we treat reverse engineering? And should competitive concerns give rise to exceptions in the form of fair use or compulsory cross-licensing? Moreover, the "correct" number of years can hardly be thought to be the same for movies, music, books, computer programs, and so on, so the cost of the error introduced by making all industries the same in each field of IP must be balanced against the gain of having a more implementable general rule.

note of lock-ins and network externalities.[2] Lock-ins can extend the owner's market power by imposing significant learning costs on buyers who might otherwise shift to better technology, which explains why almost all of us still use the slow QWERTY keyboard on word processors. Network externalities raise the value of a product when more people use it. For example, a particular Web browser increases in value as the number of sites with which it can interconnect rises.

The two phenomena of lock-in and network externalities have resulted in three characteristic market strategies: Firms will (1) sacrifice product quality in order to be first to market; (2) sacrifice current revenues (in some cases even distributing products for free) to achieve a widespread installed base for future revenues; and (3) count on their installed base and the revenue it generates to spend less on cutting-edge development. Microsoft is a prime example of the third strategy, Netscape of the second. The first strategy—sacrificing product quality to be first to market—applies to almost any early software release.

Of particular note for nonproprietary technology is strategy #2. Given the phenomena of lock-in and network externalities, under some circumstances it will turn out to be profit maximizing for your firm to give away product X. Roughly speaking, those circumstances obtain if you also own Y and X plugs into Y to form an operative unit. Thus a firm may elect to make X "nonproprietary" for perfectly straightforward proprietary reasons (i.e., maximizing the proprietary value of Y to the firm). This situation should

2. A large body of economic literature documents the effects of direct and indirect network externalities on product introduction and interfirm competition. See Michael Katz and Carl Shapiro, "Product Introduction with Network Externalities," *Journal of Industrial Economics* 40, no. 55 (1992), Katz and Shapiro, "Systems Competition and Network Effects," *Journal of Economic Perspectives* 93 (1994), and Katz and Shapiro, "Technology Adoption in the Presence of Network Externalities," *Journal of Political Economics* 94, no. 822 (1986).

be contrasted with a true nonproprietary situation in which goods are held nonexclusively and benefits are not internalized to an ownership entity.

A Proprietary Spectrum

To elaborate the distinction in the realm of computer technology between a nonproprietary good, which is part of a larger strategy of marketing (strategy #2 above), and a good that is nonproprietary in a more radical sense, we consider three points on a proprietary continuum represented by Microsoft, Sun Microsystems' Java, and Linux (see chart 1). In each of these cases we consider a computer *system* to be what is often called a *platform*— roughly the entire package of goods that users need to make the system function. The classes of platform components include hardware (silicon printed circuits) together with an operating system (software programs that function together with the hardware to run the computer) plus application programs that run on the system (accomplishing tasks for the user such as word processing, spreadsheeting, or sending documents to a printer).

The Microsoft platform is an example of a strong proprietary system, by which we mean that Microsoft controls all the interlocking parts that users need for the system to accomplish tasks. (This situation could be considered *full bundling*.) Applications will generally only work on a single platform and may have varying degrees of compatibility both with other applications and with prior and future versions. If software developers want to write applications for a proprietary system, they must enter into contractual arrangements to obtain enough source code for their products to interact seamlessly with the operating system software. Developers are then restricted from distributing the source code or disclosing its terms to others. In the parlance of the software industry, Microsoft is strongly protective of its store of intellectual

CHART I

The Proprietary Continuum

Proprietary Systems	The Middle Ground	Nonproprietary Systems
Microsoft	Sun's Java	Linux
Closed architecture and secret specifications	Open architecture and published specifications	Published specifications
Source code not publicly available	Source code available through commercial license or for noncommercial use	Source code freely available and redistributable
Strong IP protection through licenses, patents, trade secrets, and nondisclosure agreements	IP protection through confidential commercial licenses, noncommercial licenses, and strong trademark policing	IP protection through the General Public License, allowing freedom to copy, alter, and distribute
Emphasis on acquiring a large installed base and protecting this market share	Emphasis on widespread incorporation of the Java VM—real potential in cross-platform possibilities	Emphasis on freedom and the public domain
Tight control over application development, distribution, and marketing	Less control over application development, but 100% Pure Java is an effort at quality control	No centralized control over application development

capital, such that the control over development and marketing is seen as a way to safeguard its economic success.

Proprietary systems also have strong intellectual property protection combining patents, trade secrets, and licenses with original equipment manufacturers (OEMs), chip manufacturers, and software developers. Because of these matrices of confidential licenses and contractual development arrangements, firms that control proprietary systems can carefully orchestrate releases of applications and operating systems. Developers are not free to alter proprietary applications by contributing code. Rather, users must wait for the next upgrade or version to be released by the controlling firm.

Using strategy #3 above, proprietary firms rely on their installed base for continued profits in the hardware and software sectors. The fact that 97 percent of computer users are on the PC platform gives Microsoft an enormous market share in the operating system market as well as in the applications market due to the high degree of bundling and the direct and indirect network externality effect conferred by having a large number of users on one system. Thus, revenue comes both from supplying the existing installed base and from attracting new users to the system. As the market share becomes larger and larger, a proprietary firm such as Microsoft can depend on the phenomena of excess inertia and market tipping due to network externalities. New users will choose the platform with the largest combination of available software and technical support.

Java, a relatively new programming language developed by Sun Microsystems, is an example of the middle ground in the proprietary continuum. Java plugs into a software virtual machine, the Java VM, that allows programs written in Java to run on any operating system.[3] The Java language represents a high level of abstraction; as a cross-platform device, it is not inextricably intertwined with any particular hardware arrangement or operating system software. The Java VM, implemented separately by Sun for each different operating system, acts as a universal translator of sorts, creating an operational environment (the Java run-time environment) separate from the user's particular computing configuration. The Java tools themselves are bundled in the sense of being interconnected in functionality, but their actual operation is intended to be transparent to the user. Thus, for the user, the bundling of hardware, operating system software, and applications

---

3. For descriptions of Java's business plan and technical abilities, see generally the materials available both at Sun's main home page (http://www.sun.com) or at Java-Soft's home page (http://java.sun.com).

found in the strong proprietary model no longer exists in this cross-platform environment.

Sun initially released the specifications to the Java language and continues to release versions of the Java Developers Kit (JDK), which contains all the information necessary to write applets and applications in Java. Any developer with Web access can download the JDK to write applications in Java.[4] Because the technology exists to alter these Java applications so that they run on only one platform—a strategy of considerable interest to Microsoft—Sun has introduced a program of "100% Pure Java" to ensure the quality and purity of Java applications and to preserve their cross-platform capabilities.[5]

Although the Java language is given away (nonproprietary), the VM is proprietary (that is, licensed under strict conditions of secrecy). Sun protects its Java technology through various levels of licensing arrangements. It keeps its source code under control through confidential commercial licenses (e.g., the license that allows Netscape to incorporate the Java VM into its Navigator browser). Sun states that its source code is available for academic study and other noncommercial uses as long as a license is signed that restricts the recipient's ability to disclose, distribute, or incorporate the source code.[6]

This mixture of proprietary and nonproprietary treatment is an example of the second strategy we described above and responds to the presence of lock-in and network externalities. If widespread use of the free Java language creates demand that

---

4. The JDK can be accessed through http://java.sun.com/products/jdk/1.1/.

5. For an informative discussion of "100% Pure Java" in terms of its marketing strategies, development goals, and industry position, see http://java.sun.com/features/1997/may/100percent_qna.html.

6. For descriptions of Sun's licensing policies, both commercial and noncommercial, see the licensing pages at http://java.sun.com/nav/business/source_form.html and the Licensing FAQ at http://java.sun.com/nav/business/license-faq.html.

OEMs respond to by seeking to include the Java VM in their systems, then Sun profits by licensing its proprietary source code to those OEMs. If, in contrast, Sun had attempted to enter the market by introducing and exercising control over an entire new system of interlocking parts in competition with Microsoft, it would have faced an impossible battle because of lock-in and network externalities already accrued to Microsoft's installed base. A more feasible strategy was to give away something that could be used by Microsoft users (as well as others) with minimal retooling (i.e., the Java language) while making sure that that something would function in a necessarily interlocking way with a product that Sun retains control over, a product whose value increases as the installed base increases (i.e., the VM).[7]

At the far end of the proprietary continuum, consider Linux, a complete nonproprietary system in a more robust sense than the nonproprietary portion of the Java system. Linux is basically a version of the Unix operating system that is freely distributed under the terms of the GNU General Public License (the GPL), which attempts to ensure that the system and its source code will remain freely available to everyone and that the system is nonappropriable.

There is little or no centralized control over the Linux development effort. The sociology of Linux development is comparable to the governance of the Internet, which was developed by a loose volunteer group of engineers whose motto was "rough consensus and running code." Developed by a worldwide group effort of volunteers connected through the Internet and the Web, Linux

---

7. Brent Schlender, "Sun's Java: The Threat to Microsoft Is Real," *Fortune* (November 11, 1996), discusses Sun's overall corporate strategies and goals for revenue generation from the Java products. Tom R. Halfhill, "Today the Web, Tomorrow the World," *Byte* (January 1997), gives an excellent technical description of how Java works and where it needs to improve.

owes a great deal to the Free Software Foundation in terms of both its development and distribution philosophy and its package of utilities. Most of the key Linux utilities (e.g., the C compiler, make and awk, shells, and the editors [EMACS]) come from GNU (GNU's Not Unix) developed by Richard Stallman, founder of the Free Software Foundation.[8]

Coordination problems in Linux development have been largely overcome through the open architecture of the Internet, which allows for sharing code and distributing modifications and adaptations. There is no single organization that dictates the development path and goals; rather, developers and users communicate through mailing lists and news groups. The open-ended system is focused on adding new features and correcting problems. Linux developers focus on technical excellence over market returns and on creating a free implementation of Unix for developers rather than for end-users or a third-party target market. Developers argue that this process of expanding Linux is the most efficient model for constantly developing a free system and porting free software to the Linux platform.[9]

There is a split in the Linux community between developers and nondevelopers. Developers program and support the system primarily for their community of developers rather than for commercial or corporate customers. The role of end users, in constrast, is to promote the widespread use of Linux. Although some view the developer–end user relationship as a vertical hierarchy of knowledge and ability, others see it as flat, with each group fulfilling a valuable role. Still others envision the Linux

8. Arnold Robbins, "What Is GNU?" in *The Linux Sampler*, ed. Belinda Frazier and Laurie Tucker, 1995).

9. See the Linux International page at http://www.iinet.com.au/~pdcruze/. For a statistical report of Linux usage worldwide, see the Linux Counter at http://counter.li.org/.

development process as a random puzzle where people add bits and pieces to a common system, which then expands and grows in a chaotic fashion.[10]

Unlike either Microsoft or Java, Linux is nonproprietary in five senses: (1) the source code is not secret; (2) anyone can use the source code and build on it; (3) the operating system is freely distributed to anyone who wants it; (4) no one person or firm is unilaterally reaping a profit because of the system's value to its users; and (5) improvements in the system are not controlled by any one user but instead accrue to the benefit of all users. These five indicia are the characteristics of a true nonproprietary system.

Yet even Linux is proprietary in that it relies on the property system—specifically a version of copyright—to accomplish its nonproprietary structure. We next consider this apparently paradoxical situation, which underlines the importance of considering property and nonproperty together.

Reflections on the Interaction of Property and Nonproperty

Why does Linux rely on the property system? Because of the problem of appropriation. If Linux were released into the public domain, nothing would stop individuals from attempting to appropriate it for themselves by attempting to keep the source code secret; at minimum nothing would stop individuals from keeping any improvements they invented secret and proprietary, so that over time as the system improved it would become proprietary. In other words, the intellectual capital generated by Linux development which currently inures to the benefit of all users would become fractionalized and absorbed by larger firms focused more on the financial bottom line than on the technical bottom line.

10. Matt Welsh, "Guerilla Unix Development," in *The Linux Sampler*, ed. Frazier and Tucker.

Hence, rather than releasing its system into the public domain outright, the Linux group uses the General Public License (GPL) developed by the Free Software Foundation. The GPL is an attempt to use copyright to overcome these possibilities of appropriation and to keep software nonproprietary in the five senses stated above.[11] (Perhaps for obvious reasons the GPL is known as copyleft.)[12] The GPL gives users the right to obtain the source code, make modifications, and freely distribute the software (and the modifications) as long as the rights of free distribution and modification remain in effect no matter who possesses the program. The best analogy is to "covenants running with the land" in real property law. The GPL uses the property regime of copyright to try to carve out a realm of nonproperty that "runs with" the program, in the interest of creation and wide distribution of intellectual capital.[13]

The GPL was created by the Free Software Foundation in the context of its GNU project, which is part of an ongoing effort of the Free Software Foundation to create a complete and freely redistributable software development environment for operating systems and utilities. Free, often misinterpreted as free from cost, refers to the freedom to distribute and modify the software. It does not prevent anyone from making a profit from the development or distribution of free software; rather, it prevents developers from

11. See Richard Stallman, "Reevaluating Copyright: The Public Must Prevail," *Oregon Law Review* 75, no. 291 (1996).

12. For the text of the GPL, see http://www.gnu.ai.mit.edu/copyleft/gpl.html. For a description of copyleft generally, see http://www.gnu.ai.mit.edu/copyleft/.

13. As this chapter goes to press, Netscape has released the source code for its browser, Communicator 5.0 Standard Edition. To protect the rights and interests of all developers, the source code has been released under the Netscape Public License, which builds on the form and philosophy of the GPL. Information on the NPL can be found at http://www.mozilla.org/NPL/index.html. Some say Netscape's move is a strategic ploy to get OEMs to install its browser. Others say this move may help to demonstrate the superiority of a distributed model for software development.

restricting the distribution and use rights of others further down-stream. Thus, it should be clear that GPL-licensed software is unique in the sense that it does not fit into several of the common categories of software such as shareware or software in the public domain.[14]

To date there have been no publicized legal challenges to the GPL. The GPL, however, raises important questions about how contract can be used to alter traditional copyright rights and whether this contractual scheme is a legally viable way to preserve the freedom of the public domain as the Free Software Foundation hopes. One central question is whether the package of rights granted by the copyright statute can be treated as merely a default starting point, subject to contractual alteration by the parties. In legal terms, the issue is under what circumstances federal copyright law will preempt state contract law.

"Copyright maximalists,"[15] no less than proponents of copyleft, want contract to prevail. But unlike copyleft proponents, who use contract to diminish copyright rights, maximalists would like all copyright law to be treated merely as a default rule between the immediate parties. For example, maximalists would like to contract around reverse engineering where copyright law would otherwise permit it or cover databases not protected by copyright law.[16]

---

14. Shareware is copyrighted and owned by the author, but the author requires users to send in money for use and distribution, whereas the GPL places no such restrictions on users. Correspondingly, public domain–ware belongs to the public and is not under any sort of copyright.

15. The term is Pam Samuelson's from *The Copyright Grab*, available at http://www.wired.com/wired/4.01/features/whitepaper.html.

16. Maximalists dislike the result in *Sega Enterprises, Ltd. v. Accolade, Inc.*, 977 F.2d 1510 (9th Cir. 1992). In *Sega*, one-time copying and decompilation of object code was permitted as fair use under circumstances where it was the only method open to Accolade to create a product that could interoperate with Sega's console. Interoperability was understood to be a necessary feature underlying the competitive market for video

Like copyleftists, maximalists would also like to make those contractual expansions of property stick as the objects of the right change hands. That is, by using contracts that "run with" a copyrighted program or document, maximalists want to alter the underlying entitlement structure for everyone.

There are important arguments against allowing statutory propertization to be flexible in the hands of individuals and firms. Recall that the area of propertization is supposed to be determined by a cost-benefit analysis that considers the gain to society as a whole. (In fact, the constitutional clause authorizing Congress to establish patent and copyright limited-duration monopolies is read to require it.) It is at least not an obvious or foregone conclusion that allowing individual parties to alter the balance struck will be beneficial to the public as a whole. For example, the rationale for interpreting copyright law to permit reverse engineering where required for interoperability is based on competition; permitting parties to restrict competition by contracting around this legal rule is not prima facie welfare enhancing. On a deeper level, the area of nonpropertization of knowledge is related to freedom of expression and political freedom. These democratic principles are

---

games. The decision can be interpreted as a curtailment of the scope of property rights granted under copyright law.

In this context there arises another important issue: Even as between party A and party B, can a shrink-wrap or click-wrap license be considered a valid contract? The question of validity of such "contracts" involves important legal doctrines involving contracts of adhesion. In *ProCD, Inc. v. Zeidenberg*, 86 F.3d 1447 (7th Cir. 1996), a license contained within the product box extended protection to a database, otherwise unprotected under *Feist Publications, Inc. v. Rural Telephone Service Company, Inc.*, 499 U.S. 340 (1991) (holding "sweat of the brow" works outside the realm of copyright protection because of their unoriginality). The license was upheld against a challenge that copyright law would preempt such protection for factual compilations. Although the *ProCD* decision gives comfort to copyright maximalists, the result is controversial.

not prima facie best implemented by being left to the individual decisions of market actors.

In this chapter we do not pursue these important issues further. For now we simply note the interesting point that an expansion of contract is needed both by those who want to diminish the realm of the public domain vis-à-vis the realm of private property and by those who want to enlarge it. In this sense, copyright maximalists and copyleftists are in league. Should copyright maximalists prevail in the real world, copyleftists may be given a boost as well.

Many questions suggested by our analysis remain unanswered precisely because the answers lie in the future evolution of the technology industries themselves. The boundary between property and nonproperty is constantly being redefined as circumstances change. Currently, Microsoft holds a dominant position in the market for operating systems and, as a consequence, in the market for applications software as well. Microsoft is the prime example of a firm that uses the battery of intellectual property protections to the fullest extent to protect its valuable store of intellectual capital. The question is whether, as a result, the creation of even more valuable intellectual capital has been foreclosed and will continue to be. The advent of cross-platform technologies such as Sun's Java language threatens the Microsoft stronghold by countering the effects of network externalities and lock-ins as users invest in computing technology, including the large financial and learning costs to switch. If programs evolve to run on any platform with sufficient speed and accuracy, users would not be tied to their particular hardware/operating system configuration and "minority" platforms such as Apple and Linux would be able to compete against firms such as Microsoft. The loss of control over intellectual capital that results from nonproprietary technologies could lead to more-robust competition and higher-quality product in the computer market as a whole.

Richard A. Epstein

6

Intellectual Property:
Top Down and Bottom Up

All too often, lawyers receive bad press for their role in a modern commercial society: They are regarded as the fount of all obstacles to innovation and improvement. Oftentimes I am happy to join a growing fifth column against the excesses of law, notwithstanding my own training and credentials. But although those charges are often warranted, sometimes they are not. What I hope to do in this short chapter is to dispel the illusion that all lawyers are necessarily pitted against productive labor. Accordingly, I want to address the positive legal contribution to setting up the framework in which commercial transactions, especially those in the information age, take place. I shall outline my themes in a somewhat broader context than is appropriate for the technical panels that rightly dominate academic conferences and publications. My self-appointed task therefore is to view intellectual property as part of the broader species of property rights.

False Utopias

I want to begin with one note of caution. When people get together to talk about their common problems, they tend to make gloomy assessments of their shared future. In many ways, the intellectual property business is booming. Ironically, however, people within the industry dwell not on its successes but on its problems; then, to highlight their angst, they feel compelled to construct some alternative utopia, which from a distance looks so pure and so rhapsodic that we can only dare hope that intellectual property will reach that same level of coherence, simplicity, and rationality. To carry out this program, intellectual property takes as its benchmark the law of property as it relates to land and commodities such as wheat. We have heard that this area displayed a remarkable simplicity in which all the major economic problems had been solved. Our task therefore is to figure out how to make the law of intellectual property resemble the law of property in land.

This approach suffers from a bit of short-sightedness. The history of land law, for example, shows that this subject has been heavily contested from the beginning of time. Fortunately, understanding those disputes helps explain why the law of intellectual property (IP) will always contain certain irreducible uncertainties that no amount of legal reform can dispel. The frictions that inhabit any dynamic system block the creation of any utopia in human affairs.

Once it is understood that these utopias are not obtainable, incremental improvements should become more acceptable than they sometimes are. To set the frame of reference, it is useful to view the world as a piston engine. Primitive engines generate more heat than motion; our job is to change that ratio. It is in that spirit that we should examine empirical propositions. In life, unlike logic, a single counterexample or counterargument needn't defeat a long-standing proposition. Rather, the question is whether the defects identified in a new proposal are greater or less than those of some alternative, including the status quo. The anti-utopian flavor is designed to introduce a certain degree of humility in discourse; it is not designed to deny our striving for improvement.

Do improvements matter? Think of what small improvements do from a large base. One brand name, Coca-Cola, has been said by its enthusiasts to be worth sixty-nine billion dollars. Perhaps that number is high or even low. But, whatever the precise figure, just think of it this way: If one brand name is worth billions, then this country has several trillion dollars worth of assets tied up in IP. On that base, even a 5 percent improvement along a single margin generates hundreds of millions of dollars in social benefits. Let us rejoice in those "small" improvements even if untold billions are, at this point, still left untapped. And those opportunities are always there. I can't think of a single property regime that has ever been bulletproof against the worst outcome in the worst-case scenario. Every system is going to fail under some circumstances. Our task is to "rig," or better, to "organize," the system so as to improve the odds. With land, an intuitive appreciation of the sanctity of property goes a long way toward delineating the correct system of rights. With intellectual property, that intuitive natural law appreciation counts for less. A more rational and instrumental approach is needed to put the system together. Natural law theories must be more explicit about their utilitarian foundations, and economists must (and will) play a greater role than the philosopher in organizing the law. Wise philosophers will educate themselves in the wiles and skills of another craft so as to join the parade instead of having to fight it.

The Origins of Property

To see how this theme plays out, it's instructive to think about property rights generally—how they're organized, how they're created, how they're justified, how they're protected, and so forth. With land, of course, these battles have been legion over time. Broadly speaking, two kinds of theories have been used to justify property rights in any kind of resource, land being no exception. One of these theories I dub (without claim to originality) the "bottom-up" theory, which claims that to understand a system of property is to understand how self-interested private actors organize and coordinate their activities so as to generate privately, as it were, property rights regimes over various kinds of resources. So it's the unilateral acts of private persons that first inspire and then organize the system of legal rights.

The opposition to this bottom-up view is a "top-down" approach, which claims that to organize complicated social institutions like property requires coordination and planning from the center because the impact of property is not limited to the owner but extends to the rest of the world. Thus the only way to form a coherent system is by direct state regulation from the top down, by regulation that parcels out and assigns the rights to various individuals to advance some larger conception of social welfare.

Which of these orientations do we prefer and why? Historically, the record on this particular problem is, to say the least, mixed. Anybody who starts with the standard textbooks on how rights in things are acquired, say for land, will discover that— under the common law system, under civil law based on Roman law, or under most tribal systems—the bottom-up approach prevails. More concretely, the basic maxim of property is that possession is the root of title. In practice property rights have been organized as follows: First, in the state of nature, nobody has any particular rights to any particular thing; second, by unilateral action the person who first occupies a particular parcel of land, in fact, becomes the owner of that parcel with title good against the rest of the world.

This position is subject to powerful philosophical criticism, which usually runs as follows: Since property is a social relationship between one individual and the rest of the world, why should the unilateral action of a single individual bind everybody else on the face of the globe without their consent? How is it, in effect, that we can impose these obligations without consent, when promises and agreements are ordinarily used to create obligations? To escape the aggrandizement of some, society has to resort to a top-down system, one whose political processes allow for wide public participation. Consent is used to obviate the difficulties of unilateral action. But, of course, even a quick romp through history leads to the conclusion that, although this theoretical objection has been frequently voiced, it rarely prevails. Virtually every legal system contains a heavy bottom-up component.

Lacking perfection, you should adopt the following frame of mind: For every particular rule on the assignment and creation of property rights, identify its correlative imperfection. If you imagine a world devoid of imperfection, you have backed yourself into a form of utopian thinking. What you must recognize is that, no matter how property rights are structured, so long as resources are scarce, people will have to be disappointed; so long as enforcement costs are positive, some scheming individuals can get away with breaking the rules. The task of the legal system is to minimize these imperfections. Given finite human resources and finite human intelligence, these untoward results cannot be eliminated, only reduced.

So, having identified the central problem with organizing the world from the bottom up, we must put our finger on the weak point of the top-down approach. It is quite simply this: If, in fact, individuals are treated as owning property in common, then how, even by agreement, will they allocate particular portions of that common property to various members of the group? Anyone who has ever co-owned a summer home with stubborn siblings will realize that these tasks of common ownership are often extraordinarily ticklish to discharge even within the confines of a single family that otherwise enjoys good relations. Seeking to allocate the planet earth among individuals who do not speak a common tongue and who do not live in similar communities leads you quickly to the result that John Locke himself identified with such great clarity. If we wait until we get unanimous consent to partition of the universe, we shall all starve first—a serious practical objection to common property regimes. The enduring advantage of a first-possession rule is, if you can eat what you grab, you won't starve, preserving any option to deliberate over our collective future to another day.

Land

Because both top down and bottom up are subject to powerful objections, neither can banish the other from the field. Therefore, we observe both systems working side by side simultaneously and often at cross-purposes. If that's true as a generic proposition, it's certainly going to be true for land. So, what would be an illustration of a top-down system in land? The most conspicuous illustration comes from our feudal English origins; after William the Conqueror took over England, he quickly partitioned much of the land among his henchmen turned lords in exchange for promises to supply an extensive feudal army. So the entire system of English property law started from the top down. Top-down systems have some real efficiencies, but in the end this natural historical experiment exposes its weaknesses.

Start with the positives. The great advantage of a top-down

system is that it puts your friends in the right places with the right resources at the right time. The initial conditions have a tidiness and rationality absent from the chaotic world of bottom up. But this top-down system is not likely to prove stable over time. By linking together service obligations with property ownership, death creates serious imbalances. It is easy for property to go to heirs but harder for those same heirs to assume service obligations to their lords. The entire effort to bundle land and services into a single contract becomes rickety and inefficient. Over long periods of time, the English constantly compressed the structure by eliminating intermediate layers of the feudal hierarchy. Sometimes land was abandoned or service obligations were neglected. Strangers could enter the land without any title at all. It could take five hundred years for ownership to collapse into a bottom-up system in which individuals become ordinary outright owners of land measured by metes and bounds.

Does that slimming down free us of all government regulation? The answer is, of course not. Land ownership is a much more complicated system to operate than ordinarily supposed. Whenever I attend land-use conferences, the wails and the moans of the various participants are at least as loud as those heard at IP meetings. What triggers these land-based wails? First off, boundaries aren't as clear or as dispositive as one might hope. In addition to occasional disputes about locations, protracted battles occur whenever activities on one plot of land negatively affect neighbors. Unhappily, conveyancing of land is often extremely tricky, as accretions to title build up over time. Stabilizing the entire arrangement required a top-down system—recordation—to combat the pervasive risk of double-dealing, whereby X sells the same plot of land successively to A and then to B. Having partial interest in land (life estates, leases, mortgages) creates immense cataloging problems as well. Easements and restrictive covenants give individuals ownership claims in the lands of their neighbors, as do certain customary rights to hunt or gather shrubs and wood. Future interests in land (i.e., those which will or might fall into possession at some future time) can clog commerce and prevent current development. Suddenly, various rules restrict the types of interests that can be created in land and the mode of their sale or disposition. Second, the system is not self-sustaining; real estate taxes must be imposed for general upkeep and for special projects. Taxation requires the formation of governance units, blessed with coercive powers, to decide which local improvements are needed and how they are to be financed. Water rights run through land, and manifestly a bottom-up water system does not feature separate ownership but complex forms of common ownership, with correlative rights and duties that vary from location to location by topography, technology, and custom.

So, even before zoning, modern land-use planning and environmental protection, seen from close up, is filled with glitches and warts. But if we step back a little bit to assess its overall achievements, our mixed system of rights in land is, in fact, highly successful, notwithstanding some serious errors at the margin. So from this quick trip I conclude that top down, bottom up is a false dichotomy introduced by an irresponsible speaker in order to intrigue his audience. For its part, the real world forces you to engage in mixed solutions. Nonetheless, the top-down/bottom-up dichotomy does not disappear. The results reached in seeking intermediate solutions are, to use a phrase from another line of business, heavily path dependent. If you start in the wrong place—usually top down—the errors are going to be larger and the corrections more chancy than by starting bottom up. In a near-perfect world, you could correct to the ideal, no matter what your point of departure. In a highly imperfect world, you'd best start at that corner closest to the ideal solution to make your journey shorter and less complicated.

The Spectrum

Now, another way to test my approach—and I'm moving a little bit closer to intellectual property—is to question a dichotomy that was presented by Paul Romer, who is not a lawyer, merely a world-class economist. Romer's thesis was that you could divide the universe into two sets, one of which is called objects and the other, ideas. Now, that's not a bad first approximation for how the world works, but many assets fall embarrassingly right between them. One of them is the broadcast spectrum. Do we call that an object? Well, not quite. Do we call it an idea? Not quite; indeed, not at all. But classification aside, how is it is to be allocated? The case is instructive because the spectrum forms a bridge between the easily understood, so-called tangible assets on the one hand and the more difficult intangible assets, of which intellectual property is one, on the other. Historically, I'm happy to report, both systems of allocation have been tried. The original allocations took place in a much shorter time frame, given the rate of technological advance between 1910 and 1930, but in fact the bottom-up system for the spectrum seemed to work fairly well in the brief period it was allowed.

What is this system like? It says that, just like land, you obtain ownership of a bit of the spectrum by occupying it. What does it mean to occupy some portion of the spectrum? Well, it requires more than just passing through a frequency while twisting the dials. You've got to sit on that frequency for a while, which means that you have to establish some kind of repetitive broadcast pattern that allows both users and rivals to understand that you have treated that bit of spectrum as your own. The moment that process begins it will be necessary to address physical interference between neighbors, just as there are spillovers between neighboring landowners from certain kinds of use. It thus becomes necessary to settle on some kind of a "live and let live" rule to determine the tolerable level of reciprocal interferences. Fortunately, by customary practice, broadcasters met that challenge in the period, say, between 1920 and 1926, before the whole bottom-up enterprise fell apart under the weight of federal intervention and regulation.

Note the key features of the bottom-up approach. Initially, it features acquisition by first possession, which is then protected against interference. Once the rights are protected, then the owners of the thing may subdivide it or use it in any way, shape or form they choose. The law replicates for this bandwidth the property rights system for land.

Enter the United States government. The key mover in the adoption of top-down regulation was none other than the then secretary of commerce, Herbert Hoover—a point that we shall pass over to talk about the larger issues. That top-down system holds that the world will look simply chaotic if private rights are acquired by individual grabbing; what is now required is government ownership of the spectrum, which is then allocated in feudal style by a system of grants. And that's the system that was basically forced on the entire spectrum with the Radio Act of 1927, which has survived various transformations to this very day.

Now, many of you might say, "Look, we've got the best radio and television and telecommunications system in the United States on broadcast. How could you complain?" The way you can complain is to ask, What are the defects of the system if you look at it up close? Let me mention just a couple of them for you. One structural problem is that government broadcast licenses don't have indefinite time horizons. In consequence the renewal process is enormously costly while fairly inviting protest groups to exercise political leverage for their own benefit. Property rights are indefinite; rent seeking takes place. Such a cycle applies to the spectrum as it applies everywhere else.

Then the next question, "Exactly how do you use the spectrum?" If you receive a license, you're not allowed freely to sub-divide the assigned spectrum as technology becomes more effi-cient. Under the present regime, no natural process pushes people to narrower bands for transmitting the same amount of informa-tion. Instead the lack of incentive, or even ability, to economize leaves huge amounts of waste inside the system. In addition, the initial central allocation rests on wild guesses as to what various sectors of the economy will require: so much spectrum to the military, so much spectrum to the weather service, so much spec-trum for private industry, and so on. Of course these property right divisions by central government allocation do not correspond with needed uses over time. The legislation needed to change frequency use takes place slowly, however, and with much discon-tinuity and intrigue. Worse still, central allocation favors the large battalions: minorities, however described, find themselves locked out of the business because subleasing of spectrum space at market rates turns out to be illegal. Broadcasters by statute must supervise the content put out over their frequency and can't be so vulgar as simply to lease out spectrum slices, however defined, to the highest bidder. By degrees the whole system becomes encrusted, unre-sponsive, and bureaucratic. The grants are rarely outright, and the strings attached often are designed to clamp down on dissent, controversy, and innovation.

Over the past seventy years the operation of the current top-down system has exacted a heavy price to overcome the problem of physical interference between neighbors. It was, in my judg-ment, vastly inferior to the bottom-up system that had spontane-ously evolved before federal intervention nipped it in the bud. In some cases it is all too easy to miss relevant historical patterns in seeking to assign property rights in some novel resources. But again it pays to be careful. There is nothing that says that a better top-down system could not have met all the objections I just raised against the current system of spectrum allocation.

In his celebrated article "The Federal Communication System" (*Journal of Law & Economics* 2, no. 1 [1959]), Ronald Coase elaborated on the proposal to auction off frequency allocations to the highest bidder. That auction system could create the same strong set of property rights that had started to develop in the 1920s and thus obviate many of the perils of repeated administrative allocation of property rights under the flaccid formula of the "public interest, convenience, and necessity." Once auctioned, those rights to use the spectrum are perpetual, divisible, assignable, and not tied to any particular end use. A well-designed system of top-down rights could thus converge with a sensible system of bottom-up rights.

Indeed in some cases it could outperform it. The slow pace of technology in 1920 allowed the first-possession rule to operate with tolerable efficiency. But that success could not have been replicated to assign a spectrum for the recent PCS (personal communication system) auctions, for any single determined entrepreneur could swoop down on the entire frequency in an instant. Having the state package the spectrum by frequency and auction does require some degree of planning at the center, albeit far less than is required for passing on the supposed merits of potential broadcast licensees. But it does result in more sensible frequency allocation (although even here, the apparent need to protect broadcasters limits the uses that can be made of frequencies once auctioned). So the true lesson is one that recognizes the regrettable necessity of some government role in defining property rights in the spectrum just as with other resources. Once again top down and bottom up coexist in uneasy equilibrium.

Intellctual Property at Last

Now how can our views of the spectrum carry over to intellectual property, the major focus of this volume? If we started and stopped with the original allocation of the broadcast spectrum, we should conclude that any top-down system has to be a mistake. But given today's rapid rate of technical innovation, public auctions of state-defined property rights might turn out to outperform a first-possession rule that works best for sparsely populated land and the broadcast spectrum. In this sense, the ultimate lesson might well be that the decisive test is where we end up with property rights, not where we begin. And so with intellectual property, the major danger is to have centralized government decide who owns what invention or literary work and why. And once that is done, then it turns out that intellectual property should be predominantly, but not exclusively, a bottom-up system. Private labor turns out to be the source of key intellectual property rights, not government fiat.

The analysis here, however, follows a somewhat different path from that used to analyze the spectrum. Here's why. The spectrum is a passive resource. It's a commodity. It is not, as it were, content. But once you deal with content and ideas, the institutions of property associated with their use will have to adapt to the changed subject matter. It may well be regrettable but true that we require a higher level of government intervention, including some top-down supervision, for this system to operate.

Let me just mention a couple of complications that call for caution in taking property rights regimes across different resources. The first question to ask yourself is this: How clear are the boundary conditions that separate the owner of the right from the rest of the world, that separate, as it were, me from thee? With respect to land, metes and bounds work pretty well most of the time. With respect to the spectrum, the system can be adapted by setting a permissible variation from some central frequency at some location and for some period of time. In intellectual property cases, stating the boundary conditions will be harder in some cases than in others. There's not much of a boundary dispute in figuring out whether or not some dialogue comes from Shakespeare's *Ham-*

let. But in addressing whether one song is a knockoff of another, the boundary conditions become more indistinct than the simple copying analogy would suggest. When dealing with the scope of patents, expect endless difficulty in figuring out the breadth of a valid patent for an invention that has yet to be brought to commercial realization.

The moment a mild bit of functionality is injected into the analysis, Epstein's Law (as it is now dubbed) exerts its tight grip: Every ideal solution is met with a decisive objection—which means that you always land in the soup. What do I mean by that? Well, one approach is to define patents broadly, which has the very desirable feature of encouraging the holder of a patent to invest extensively in the patentable resource. To define the patent too narrowly, after all, leaves its holder uncertain as to its future commercial uses. Why would you invest in the patent if its domain is tiny? So it looks like there is no resistance to the broad definition of patents. But scratch the surface and the trade-offs appear. Let the patent definition be too broad, and the patent's primary function is no longer opportunity for development; now it forms a blockade against development by competitors. So what emerges is a world that makes patents either too broad or too narrow. Somebody who wants to ignore one form of error because he's worried about the second misunderstands the nature of the problem. Working out these boundary conditions cannot be done in the obvious bottom-up way, as with a bunch of stakes and a piece of land. It's a much more difficult process.

The difficulty of this trade-off does not diminish when we confine our attention to so-called pioneer patents, that is, those that are likely to create opportunities for follow-on developments. Pioneer patents raise the stakes relative to incremental patents because follow-on inventions are by definition far more likely. But just because the stakes are higher, it does not follow that the relative balance changes either way; both blockade and expropriation risks increase, but it is uncertain what happens to their ratio. It seems therefore that we should be cautious about carving out some special rule for pioneering inventions, especially since it is easier to proclaim the distinction between pioneer inventions and ordinary ones than it is to draw it time after time. Although it's perfectly obvious (to some at least) what that distinction means in the first case that announces it, four cases later the term resides in obscurity. So, at least for the moment, I would favor a uniform interpretation and simplicity and shun some subtle common-law interpretation that enshrines different levels of patent protection for different types of inventions. As in all human affairs, every distinction has to earn its keep. Unless you can show some powerful reason for making a distinction, resist the temptation and incline toward simplicity; that of course is one of the themes of my book *Simple Rules for a Complex World*. (Its title is not *No Rules for a Complex World*; the rules are simpler than you might expect.)

Subject matter boundaries are not the only problem for patents. Duration, as is well known to intellectual property experts, also poses difficulties for patents, copyrights, and trademarks. And it's clear that the same solution won't work for all of them. The most vexatious disputes probably arise with the patent law, mainly because everybody understands that technical innovation, if not done by A, can be done by B shortly thereafter; whereas most of us think that a Shakespeare sonnet, if not written by Shakespeare himself, is not going to be done particularly well by an impostor. So that suggests that you have shorter time limits for patents than for copyrights, but it doesn't tell you exactly how long either period ought to be; it doesn't tell you whether or not patents ought to be renewed; and it doesn't tell you what to do with interlocking patents or follow-on patents.

In the end the problems with land reappear with intellectual property, but they are not amenable to the same solution. What do I mean by that? Define the rights too narrowly, and the lack of protection invites a second inventor to expropriate the labors of the first. Define them too broadly, and both the first and second inventors have blockade positions with respect to each other, which can make their negotiations both futile and protracted. It's just like land. Either you risk expropriation or you risk coordination failure. You cannot eliminate both risks simultaneously, and you don't know which interior solution minimizes the sum of these two defects. Once you understand that this pattern holds across the length and breadth of intellectual property, then you realize that it's not a single field, save in opposition to land and wheat. Within its own domain, further subdivision is required. Patents have to be broken off from other areas and then broken up into use patents, process patents, and perhaps other divisions of which I am unaware. Trademarks and copyrights will each require its separate regimes, subject to further subdivisions. Trade secrets present complex issues of their own.

Even when all the doubts are ventilated, the bottom-up elements still come out strong. The government may determine the boundaries of patents and their duration, but it does not hold the patents or decide how they should be used or marketed. Indeed within the basic parameters set by the law, private initiative drives the system. Use the patent of another, and you are liable for infringement, just as if you trespassed against land. Own the patent, and you can sell or license it to another, with or without restrictions on its use or resale. The ability to create by agreement complex divisions of right by territory, by language, and by end use increases the flexibility of the system. So notwithstanding the injection of strong doses of government control, the dynamism in intellectual property still comes from the bottom up. Yet it would be a mistake to assume that efficient use always requires the creation of intellectual property rights. As committed as I am to the institution of private property, it is easy to identify discrete contexts in which it is best to reverse field and assign certain things (e.g., ideas and mathematical theorems) to the public domain. Even though the law must create incentives for ideas and theorems, it has a still greater worry about the rate of their dissemination and use, which explains why intellectual property has wrinkles not found in the law of land and wheat, where it is relatively easy to embrace the proposition that he who sows shall reap because otherwise no one will plant at all. But what does it mean to reap when you leave the world of agriculture and enter the world of ideas? Once a great idea is out there, the marginal cost of its use by a second person is close to zero. Ideas are not like the crop, which can be eaten only once. Great ideas can be used over and over again, so that the agricultural metaphor fails to describe the intellectual landscape.

Now the basic difficulty is that, to set the right incentives for production, you have to distort the incentives on distribution. To get the proper incentives on use and dissemination after production, you must distort production. The theory of property law will not allow either of these problems to vanish. You will never reach a unique answer on the duration and scope of the rights as you can with land or wheat. The moment you accept the trade-offs, you acknowledge the errors. The moment you acknowledge the errors, you accept the necessity for estimating their scope and the inevitability of litigation in which both sides believe themselves correct. Once you recognize all this, you reluctantly accept the built-in undertow that no utopian vision can displace. It is part of the legacy of intellectual property.

Further Implications

Consequential Damages

This basic framework helps put into perspective some of the difficult current issues in dealing with intellectual property. One feature of intellectual property is how future advances depend on past achievements. Where the progress of knowledge is orderly and linear, these developments can take place with a minimum of fuss and bother. But sometimes the initial invention contains a serious mistake or flaw, which becomes apparent only after its use in new and different settings. Patent Number One, for example, may rest on some kind of a fundamental mistake—say, a faulty algorithm that has the decimal point floating the wrong way. Everybody incorporates this patent into their devices, and then, after all the damage is done, the situation is unearthed and everybody points the finger back to you as the original patent holder.

To what extent are you responsible for the derivative uses? Again there is no answer that satisfies everyone. To the extent that other individuals use a particular patent device under contract or license—which is the way it typically take place—the problem of error becomes a key point for negotiation. Indeed the issue comes up in every meeting on intellectual property: How do you deal with consequential damages, that is, those losses that flow in consequence of the use of your property by someone else, especially when the damages caused far exceed the purchase price or licensee fee. Does the agreement load on the consequential damages to the original holder of the intellectual property? Do users and licensees bear the loss? Do the parties adopt some formula to split the losses? If so, which one and why?

On these matters, I like the private analogies. Once the boundaries of a patent are defined both by time and by subject matter, let the owner wheel and deal by sale or licenses, exclusive or nonexclusive, parallel to subdividing land, leasing property, leasing the spectrum, and so forth. Since there's relatively good information, sophisticated parties should tend to the best solution by contract. So I don't want a collective, public solution. I want privatized solutions, perhaps more than one.

What might a typical solution look like? Here, almost categorically, the two corner solutions are likely to be unsatisfactory: One corner solution says that the user of this particular patent device takes the full loss himself. The other corner solution shifts all the loss back to the original patent holder. That solution is probably unworkable because even if the defect lies in the original patent, much of the loss prevention rests in the hands of the patent user or licensee. In the face of that divided control over loss prevention, you'd want at least to incorporate obligations to report imperfections back to the original patent holder, so that the information could be distributed to other users and licensees as quickly as possible to minimize the total size of the loss. In addition, in many cases the user or licensee can figure out what the defects are, even if he cannot identify their sources, by running cross-checks, tests, and so forth. So, given this capacity for mitigation, you want some of the losses to be shifted downstream.

But how much? There is no utopian answer here either. Essentially, any rule has to either give perfect compensation to the innocent party, which is hard to do when both parties could prevent the wrong, or make the liability of the patent holder sting enough to hurt but not destroy. So that sets the outlines for choice and leaves the details to experts who can craft more precisely with local knowledge. Does one use multiples of sale prices, fractions of total losses, third-party insurance with specific limits, and so on? The parties can figure out solutions that will be better and worse, though it's unlikely—and now we're back to our familiar theme— that they will hit some ideal solution. So it is back to our theme of making improvements that leave us short of perfection. Who would have it any other way?

International Protection

The same cautious blend of realism and optimism is necessary to get a handle on a second area of friction in intellectual property: Intellectual property has no obvious location and can be used anywhere in the world by people who understand how to manipulate the key programs. What legal system should be used to adjudicate their disputes scattered, as they are, across the globe? Here again the first temptation is to look to land law, where the answer is relatively easy. The conflicts of rules of law with respect to land (that is, the rules that decide which state law governs a particular dispute) basically lead to one outcome: the law of the place governs all the transactions over that land. So boundary disputes and trespass and mortgage laws are governed by local law as part of a single coherent system. That unified enforcement does not work for intellectual property because infringement doesn't require an infringer to come to the domicile of the original creator to commit the wrong. He can do it anywhere; in fact, the further one moves from the home base, the easier it is to infringe and hence the greater the temptation. Intellectual property by virtue of its idea base has a level of portability and international interconnections not found with land or, for that matter, even the spectrum.

Which way, then, do you harmonize? I think, in effect, the United States has been extraordinarily aggressive. We follow two policies. When our domestic behavior is at stake, we follow the territorial principles because we're sovereigns in the United States. When foreign policies are at stake, we follow the effects doctrine because anything a foreign nation does affects our territory. So we want our law to govern both ways. The difficulty with that approach is that it does not generalize; if the British follow the same path, our two systems will necessarily collide everywhere they come in contact. So we have a problem, which covers intellectual property but extends beyond it to international finance and international antitrust. Do we say that Lloyds of London is bound by the American antitrust law if it organizes a cartel in England to deal with American insurance firms? The United States Supreme Court has said yes. I think that the basic answer is that we want harmonization desperately in this area; it's in everybody's interest to back off strong nonterritorial claims. Because intellectual property contains a lot of hunch and judgment, you can't dogmatically insist that there's only one solution to all issues. You have to meet the other side halfway. In my judgment, in the intellectual property game compromise is the appropriate stance with other nations both as producers and consumers. But that also entails a harsh line to those nations who think that filching is okay because they have nothing worth stealing in international markets.

So, all in all, I fear that, being the biggest kid on the block, we try too often to impose our will on the rest of the world. And that attitude will run into rough waters now that the European Union rivals us in size. We should fundamentally rethink our attitudes to intellectual property and antitrust, worldwide. Perhaps the same is true for international securities transactions, about which I know less. But whatever the current practice, the lodestone for all these international service, financial instruments, and intellectual property transactions has to be a norm of reciprocity in which we say, "Look, once we're behind some rule we're going to do our best to enforce it, but we do not take the position that only we can play the tune to which everyone else must dance." In an area this fluid and uncertain, one nation cannot hope to impose its norms on everyone else.

Parting Words

So I end where I began. Knowing that some failures are the price of success, praise the success while seeking to limit the scope of the failures. And recognize that, no matter what view we take on the question of whether a patent should run for twenty or twenty-five years, the basic structure of the rights is, for the most part, as good as you're likely to get it; perfect agreement on necessary trade-offs is not possible, even though improvement always is. So don't look for utopia; you're not going to find it. Don't take land as a perfect model because it has its own internal difficulties and, in any event, is subject to evident grounds of distinction built into the nature of the resource itself. For today celebrate your successes; tomorrow you can again lament your failures.

Edward P. Lazear

Intellectual Property: A Discussion of Problems and Solutions

The major difficulty in dealing with intellectual property—the trade-off between static and dynamic efficiency—has been discussed for years. Static efficiency requires that once a technology exists, it should be sold at its marginal cost. Since the marginal cost of providing information to others is small, technology should be widespread so that its products can be sold in a competitive environment. The problem, of course, is that inventors whose products are going to be sold at marginal cost know that they will not earn a profit on the innovative activity. As a result, dynamic efficiency suffers. Innovative activity is stifled by the inability to capture the returns to the inventor's efforts.

This trade-off between static and dynamic efficiency was dis-

This research was supported in part by the National Science Foundation.

cussed early by Stigler,[1] who argued that patents are a compromise solution. Since a large fraction of the value of the invention is already captured by seventeen years of monopoly sales, the patent comes close to giving its innovators their full return. This is a compromise because, in the case where an invention is extremely important and has truly long-lasting effects, competition is restored after seventeen years, preventing the monopoly distortion from becoming enormous. For example, had Sir Isaac Newton patented calculus and had he and his heirs been able to sell the rights to its usage into the indefinite future, far too little calculus would be available and the social distortions would be enormous. Yet giving Newton rights into perpetuity for the invention of calculus is unlikely to have had much of an effect on his supply of effort. This is the logic that motivates the time limitation on patents.

Indeed, as a general matter, the seventeen-year limitation on patents is almost never binding. Most patents are not renewed even when firms have the ability to renew them.[2] Of course, those that are renewed have the largest value to the inventor, but their effect on the expected returns from innovative activity is probably minor, which again supports the argument for limiting patent duration.

Along with the discussion of the duration of the patent goes the issue of how broadly a patent should be defined. Obviously, the broader the definition of the patent, the more incentive for the original inventor to innovate. But also true is that the broader the patent, the less incentive for other inventors to innovate because their inventions may infringe on the original patent. The total

1. George J. Stigler, "A Note on Patents," in Stigler, *The Organization of Industry*, (Homewood, Ill.: Richard D. Irwin, 1968), pp. 123–25.

2. Ariel S. Pakes, "Patents as Options: Some Estimates of the Value of Holding European Patent Stocks," *Econometrica* 54 (July 1986): 755–84.

effect on innovative activity is, therefore, ambiguous. This point, coupled with the fact that patents produce static inefficiency, suggests that patents should be defined narrowly.

Other Solutions

The discussion of intellectual property, in general, has been too narrowly focused on patents. Patents are not the only way to protect intellectual property. Nor are they the only or the best way to provide incentives to innovate. The focus has been on patents in part because, in a business environment, it is self-serving for firms to argue in favor of lenient patenting of their own products. At our Hoover conference, George Johnston was quite honest in his appeal for lengthening the effect of patent life of pharmaceuticals. Other business panelists were somewhat less straightforward, but the point was clear. A particular business views patents that protect its innovations as beneficial and those that protect those of its rivals or suppliers as harmful.

Other countries and scholars have considered alternatives to patenting as a way to promote the formation of intellectual capital. In the next few paragraphs some of those alternatives are discussed.

Licensing

Any inventor who owns a patent has the option to license it. Some have argued that licensing reduces the static inefficiency associated with ownership of a patent. For example, if GE holds a patent on the light bulb but licenses Westinghouse to produce bulbs, then Westinghouse can compete with GE, driving the price of the bulbs down. Still, it is argued that GE captures the return on its invention from the license fee that it receives from Westinghouse.

Unfortunately, that argument is fallacious. The price that a licensee will pay for the license depends on the price at which the licensee can sell the product. If the price is not sufficiently high to produce a monopoly profit on the sale of the light bulb, then Westinghouse will be unwilling to pay GE much for the license. The only way that GE can collect the monopoly rents on the invention is to provide a complete monopoly to the licensee. Of course, doing so puts us right back into the same predicament: Westinghouse, rather than GE, restricts the supply of light bulbs, and static inefficiency results because Westinghouse, not GE, fails to produce the appropriate number of bulbs. If GE were to license enough firms so that competition would prevail, then no licensee would be willing to pay any amount for the license since they would sell the bulbs at or near marginal cost, thereby eliminating any profit from the license itself. Thus, voluntary licensing of in-novations does not solve the problem of static inefficiency. Indeed, the primary reason to license others to produce the product is that other firms have a comparative advantage in producing the prod-uct. In the Westinghouse/GE example, it would pay for GE to license Westinghouse if GE does not have the capacity to produce enough bulbs to capture the return to the monopoly invention.[3]

Consortia

Some have argued[4] that a consortium of businesses could agree to invest in a particular technology. Membership in the club would

3. An alternative explanation is provided by Andrea Shepard, "Licensing to Enhance Demand for New Technologies," *RAND Journal of Economics* 18 (1987): 360–68 and by Joseph Farrell and Nancy Gallini, "Second Sourcing as a Commitment: Monopoly Incentives to Attract Competition," *Quarterly Journal of Economics* 103 (November 1988): 673–94, who argue that licensing is a way to guarantee to customers that they will not be exploited after making a fixed investment in a particular technology.

4. Paul M. Romer, "Implementing a National Technology Strategy with Self-Organizing Industry Investment Boards," *Microeconomics 2*, Brookings Papers on Eco-nomic Activity, ed. Martin Neil Baily, Peter C. Reiss, and Clifford Winston (Washing-ton, D.C.: Brookings Institution, 1993).

be restricted to those who were willing to invest, and failure of any member to carry his fair share would result in exclusion from the club. Although such an idea seems promising, it suffers from the same problem as the licensing scheme. A person will not join the consortium or put resources into innovation unless she believes that there will be a payoff in terms of profits on the product of the inventive activity. For there to be profit on the product, the number of units sold must be restricted below the efficient level. Unless a higher-than-competitive price is charged on the product, the investment is not worthwhile. If a higher-than-competitive price is charged on the product, however, then we have created a static inefficiency. The problem that plagued us at the beginning is not solved by the consortium because too few units are sold at too high a price. In fact, this is simply a situation where a cartel, which may or may not be better than a monopoly, replaces a monopoly. Although the cartel may produce a number of units that are closer to the competitive amount, it will err on the side of dynamic inefficiency, producing too little innovative activity.[5] Thus, in the end a consortium is a form of horizontal integration that may or may not be better for economic efficiency and does not solve the problem of the tension between static and dynamic efficiency.

Government Purchase of Intellectual Property

Some have suggested that the government be granted eminent domain over particularly important innovations, arguing, for example, that neither Crick nor Watson should receive a monopoly profit on their breakthrough DNA discovery. Instead, it is argued, the innovation should be purchased at some fixed price by the government and then put into the public domain. (Like all eminent

---

5. Of course, there may be some gains from having people work together in teams produced by the consortium, but that could be accomplished by a reorganization of the firm that brings outside researchers into the organization.

domain arguments, this is essentially an infringement on individual rights in order to promote the common good.)

The eminent domain argument seems to make sense if used sparingly; but it is not without its problems, and the way in which it is implemented is particularly important. For example, were the government given right of first refusal, then the expected price that an inventor receives for his invention would be too low. The government could exercise its option when it pays to do so, forcing an inventor to sell at bargain basement prices. The government's failure to exercise its right would allow the inventor to sell it on the open market. But this could never offset the government's ability to pay below market price on some inventions, again giving rise to too little innovation activity. Of course, the government might actually pay too high a price. Because a government agency is in charge of selecting the price, too much rent-seeking activity by inventors takes place. Individuals try, and sometimes succeed, in convincing the government that the patent is more valuable than it is. Because there is no direct market test for the invention, the government is unable to determine the price in advance.

One variation on the scheme is to have the government pay royalties on every unit sold to the inventing firm but to make the information available to all other producers. In this way the good is sold at marginal costs, but the inventing firm collects an above marginal cost premium on each unit. Although somewhat better in gearing the value to the market, the subsidy per unit must still be chosen by the government. Too high a subsidy results in too much production by the original firm. Thus, the solution remains far from perfect.

One twist on the eminent domain scheme is provided by Kremer[6] through a second-price auction.[7] Firms would be allowed

---

6. Michael Kremer, "Patent Buy-Outs: A Mechanism for Encouraging Innovation," NBER Working Paper 634, December 1997.

to bid for the patent rights to any invention. Ninety percent of the time the government would buy the invention at the highest price bid and make it available to everyone in the market. Ten percent of the time, however, the highest bidder would be given the patent and be required to pay the second-highest bidder's price. This would ensure that bidders behave appropriately and provide the government with information on the market.

The scheme is not perfect. First, it invites collusion by bidders. Since 90 percent of the time the government is going to pay the highest price, it pays inventors to collude and bid prices that exceed the social value. Second, in those cases where the government does not buy the patent, and it is given to an individual firm, the monopoly distortion remains. (Since this only occurs 10 percent of the time, it is unlikely to be a major problem.) Third, because any bidder obtains the patent only in some fraction of 10 percent of the time, it may be difficult to induce many firms to participate in the auction scheme in the first place. Again, the Kremer scheme is a clever one but does not solve all the problems.

Pay for Input Rather Than Output

Some countries have used more radical solutions to deal with intellectual property, including some that have simply nationalized the entire research industry. In the former Soviet Union, research scientists were hired by the government and their output was owned by the government, so that all goods and services invented were immediately in the public domain. In the United States less of this is done, but academic research is funded, in part, by this approach. The National Science Foundation (NSF), for example, hires me by supporting my work through its research grants. The

---

7. A second-price auction is an auction where the highest bidder obtains the good but at the second bidder's price. This scheme ensures that everyone bids his true value on the good.

NSF selects inputs—in this case, researchers—to fund and owns the output, thus paying for input rather than output. Anything that I invent as part of my NSF grant is owned by the government and is in the public domain. If the government pays the appropriate amount for inputs and selects the right ones, it can provide exactly the right incentives for research and innovation. Rather than allowing a researcher to capture the returns to the invention, the government simply pays for her time, most of the time resulting in no output at all but once in a while resulting in a large technical innovation.

The primary problem of having the government pay for inputs rather than outputs is that it assumes a tremendous amount of knowledge on the part of government bureaucrats. Even the most motivated and diligent official cannot possibly be aware of all innovation activity in every field. Thus centralized funding of research is unlikely to produce all the appropriate innovations. For example, had Steve Wozniak applied to the National Science Foundation for a grant to invent the Apple Computer, he would most likely have been rejected. Despite this, individuals engage in rent seeking because a government agency is involved. Thus the existence of the National Science Foundation program in economics induces economists like myself to write grant proposals attempting to persuade the foundation to fund a particular line of research. Some of this work is socially valuable, but some proposal writing is simply rent seeking that has little social value.

The conclusion, then, is that government funding of inputs rather than outputs is probably warranted on a limited scale for basic research that would not be funded through alternative measures. It is difficult to extend the argument to funding applied research that leads to tangible, quick-paying innovations.

Hiding the Invention

The primary way an inventor captures return is by getting a head start on the competition. Sometimes refusing to patent an invention gives more protection than the patent itself, as witness Coca-Cola, the formula for which is not patented but is known by only a small number of people in the Coca-Cola Company. Since most inventions are valuable only to the extent that there are no good substitutes, the returns to innovation are generally captured within the first few years. Thus hiding the invention may go most of the way to providing incentives for innovation.

Indeed, when one thinks of high-tech industries, it is clear that neither patents nor copyrights are important in motivating innovation. Because software is improved so rapidly and because others can invent substitute software that renders the initial innovation obsolete, even a seventeen-year patent would be of little value. By the time the patent had run its course, far superior versions or products would have come along. Thus patent protection is unlikely to further significantly the amount of innovative activity in an economy.

Capturing the Returns to Innovation in a Wild West Environment

Suppose that an inventor had no protection at all. Suppose further that, the moment a new technology came into being, others immediately took advantage of it and incorporated it into their new or existing products. Would this mean that an inventor had no reason to innovate? The answer surprisingly is no. In fact, an important argument[8] suggests that one need not own the rights to an innovation in order to capture the returns to it. Information is itself valuable, and knowing that an innovation is about to be re-

---

8. Jack Hirshleifer, "The Private and Social Value of Information and the Reward to Inventive Activity," *American Economic Review* 51 (September 1961): 561–74.

leased can provide an opportunity for significant gains to the inventor.

Consider, for example, the invention of the automobile, specifically, Henry Ford's Model T, which lowered the cost of production dramatically and made automobiles available to a significant fraction of the market. But even if Ford had not owned the patent or had other protection on the Model T, he still could have made money, for the growth of automobiles also implied the growth in the value of oil and a decrease in the value of horse-drawn carriages. By selling carriage stock short and going long on oil stock, Ford could have made a fortune, independent of any property rights on the automobile itself.

The point is that the information, rather than the actual invention, has value in and of itself. Further, that information can be marketed to capture perhaps even more than the total value of the invention. This is most easily seen in the case of substitutes. When Microsoft Windows replaces the old IBM DOS, IBM stock falls. Bill Gates could have sold IBM short and invested in personal computer companies that would use the Windows product. Gates's ability to make money depends only on the suppliers of stock to him, which may be large if others do not have his information.

Such schemes, while clever, do not appear to be major motivators of investment in the real world, except venture capitalists, who are not inventors but instead obtain information on innovations and trade on the value of those innovations. But since inventors generally do not have the personal capital to take large trading positions, they must convince an investor to go along with the project by perhaps getting involved in the actual project.

Intellectual Capital Embodied in the Worker

One major issue that frequently arises involves the departure of a highly valued worker in whom is embedded a large amount of firm-specific intellectual capital. This important topic requires discussion.

Although the solution to this problem has been understood in academia[9] in the employment of summer workers, and in football for many years, a great deal of confusion remains in high-tech industries that employ research engineers in a market where wages are high and unemployment is low. The solution is deferred compensation. Consider the problem of employing a student who has left school for the summer. The student, who would like the job, claims that he is planning to stay with the firm for the next couple of years. He alleges that he wants to earn money and then to return to school after having accumulated assets, which he can live off of during his college years. The problem, of course, is that many college students say that, and then return to school in the fall. Firms solve this problem by paying relatively low salaries during the summer but offering a more-than-generous Christmas bonus. The worker who intends to stay prefers the higher pay, even if it comes at Christmastime. The worker who intends to leave before Christmas places, of course, no value on the Christmas bonus. Thus, a natural sorting takes place among applicants. Those who intend to remain with a firm are attracted to high-paying, albeit somewhat delayed, compensation; those who intend to leave early are deterred by such a compensation scheme.

Some object that it is difficult to get away with such a scheme in a tight market. Indeed, Philip White of Informix made an explicit statement at our conference exactly along these lines. But

9. Joanne Salop and Steven Salop, "Self-Selection and Turnover in the Labor Market," *Quarterly Journal of Economics* 90 (November 1976): 619–27. Gary Becker, *Human Capital* (New York: Columbia Press, 1964). Edward P. Lazear, "Why Is There Mandatory Retirement?" *Journal of Political Economy* 87 (December 1979): 1261–84. Shmuel Nitzan and Ariel Pakes, "Optimum Contracts for Research Personnel, Research Employment and the Establishment of Rival Enterprises," *Journal of Labor Economics* 1 (October 1983): 345–65.

White was confused. Competition affects the level of overall compensation, not the timing of it. This is a point that football players have understood for many years. To illustrate, consider the example of Steve Young, quarterback for the 49ers. The market for Young is "tight" in that many teams would like his services during his free-agency year. Thus Young has no concerns about being unemployed. Yet Young agreed to take a low salary during his initial contract year so that the 49ers could work within their cap structure (see table 1). Young, despite his altruistic tendencies, was not in reality taking a salary cut. He was simply deferring his compensation. He took less in 1997 but more in subsequent years and was willing to do so because the total amount of his compensation in present value was higher with the deferred plan than it was with the plan that paid high initial salaries.

Silicon Valley is full of examples of this sort. Workers accept options or promises for higher pay at start-ups instead of taking initially high-paying jobs at well-established firms. And they do so specifically because they are willing to take the bet. As with Steve Young, when the market is tight, the overall level of compensation is higher than when the market for engineers is soft. But the shape of the earnings over the career need not vary (see figure 1).

In figure 1, the tight market profile starts below the flat profile, but rises above it. Both correspond to tight markets, wherein competition for engineers is fierce and average salaries are high. This does not mean, however, that an engineer would never accept the stepped tight market profile over the flat profile, for the tight market profile has associated with it a 20 percent raise each year. The flat profile has no raise over time but a higher initial salary. Which profile is preferred? The tight market profile offers total compensation of $364,000 over a three-year period, whereas the flat profile offers total compensation of $330,000 over the same

TABLE I

Big Money (the top salary packages in the NFL,
according to announcements from agents and teams)

Player, Team	Package	Average
Steve Young, 49ers	$45,000,000/6 years	$7,500,000
Brett Favre, Packers	47,250,000/7 years	6,750,000
Troy Aikman, Cowboys	50,000,000/8 years	6,250,000
Mark Brunell, Jaguars	30,500,000/5 years	6,100,000
Drew Bledsoe, Patriots	42,000,000/7 years	6,000,000
Barry Sanders, Lions	34,560,000/6 years	5,760,000

Steve Young's new contract:

1997	$3,000,000	2000	6,550,000
1998	10,000,000	2001	7,825,000
1999	8,275,000	2002	9,350,000

In addition, Young will receive a one-time bonus of $1 million if the 49ers win the Super Bowl, provided he plays at least 75 percent of the offensive plays during the season and plays in the Super Bowl.

SOURCE: *San Francisco Chronicle* Sporting Green, July 31, 1997. © The San Francisco Chronicle. Reprinted with permission.

three-year period.[10] An engineer confident that he would remain with the firm throughout the three-year period would prefer the tight market profile to the flat profile. An engineer knowing he was going to leave after a year would prefer the flat profile. Thus a firm that placed high value on retaining high-quality engineers, particularly engineers with knowledge of trade secrets, in most circumstances would be willing to pay the extra $34,000 over a three-year period. Both firm and engineer are made better off by this steep profile, and it operates effectively, even in a tight market.

Notice that the soft market profile lies below the tight market

10. The numbers used in this example are assumed to be converted to present value.

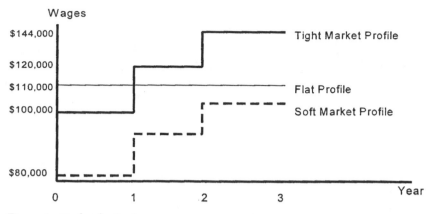

Figure 1. Market for Engineers

profile but is also steep. Although in a soft market, firms may pay engineers lower average salaries, this does not mean that they are not equally concerned about retention. Analogously, in a soft market engineers are also willing to make trade-offs, accepting a steeper profile to a flatter one as long as the steeper profile offers higher general earnings.

This point is not purely academic. The typical worker in the real world receives an upward-sloping earnings profile, a consequence of which is firm loyalty. This happens in retailing, in production, in education, in medicine, in accounting, in law, in finance, and in high tech as well. The state of the market alters the level of the profile but not necessarily its slope. Silicon Valley firms that have been most effective in retaining workers are those who tend to use steep profiles. Indeed, most of the successful CEOs have themselves received significant earnings increases over the years, which has the effect of tying them to their current firms. Although CEOs do move from firm to firm on occasion, turnover is relatively rare, mainly because of the higher earnings that they receive at their current firm relative to alternatives.

A firm that is losing its engineers, particularly to its competition, should reexamine the shape of its earnings profile. If it finds that it is easy to hire but difficult to retain quality engineers, then chances are that the initial salary is too high and the wage growth is too low.[11]

Conclusion

Things might be better for industry if government regulation changed, but they could also be much worse. In this chapter I have outlined a number of possible solutions to the intellectual property problem. Most carry more difficulties than solutions. Indeed, there is little evidence that technological progress has been slow or that the failure to provide protection for intellectual property has impeded growth. In those fields that have seen the most growth, the seventeen-year patent protection is highly redundant and almost irrelevant. When technology changes rapidly, the main protector of intellectual property is the time that it takes to reverse-engineer a product or a process. Despite the whining or self-serving statements of several CEOs and others, there is no strong case to be made for increased government protection of intellectual property.

Because patents have a tournament or racing element to them,[12] it can be argued that there is too much rather than too

11. Edward P. Lazear, *Personnel Economics for Managers* (New York: John Wiley & Sons, 1998), p. 358–59, discusses this point.

12. Jennifer Reinganum, et al., "On the Diffusion of New Technology: A Game Theoretic Approach," in Reinganum et al., *The Economics of Technical Change* (Aldershot, U.K.: Edward Elger Reference Collection, 1993). Edward P. Lazear and Sherwin Rosen, "Rank-Order Tournaments as Optimum Labor Contracts," *Journal of Political Economy* 89 (October 1981): 841–64; reprinted in *Labor Economics/The International Library of Critical Writings in Economics* 47, ed. Orley C. Ashenfelter and Kevin F. Hallock (Aldershot, U.K.: Edward Elgar Publishing Ltd., 1995), pp. 422–45. Dale Mortensen et al. "Matching: Finding a Partner for Life or Otherwise," in Sherwin Rosen and Christopher Winship, eds., "Organizations' and Institutions' Sociological and Economic

little attention paid to innovation and intellectual property. Being first by a minute has little social value but may have enormous private value to a particular investor who captures the patent. As a result, a narrowly defined patent, of relatively short duration, probably serves society reasonably well. Eminent domain and compulsory licensing should be used only in extreme circumstances, if at all, and government funding of research is unlikely to be warranted for applied technology.

Approaches to Analysis of Social Structures," *American Journal of Sociology* 94 Supplement: 215–40.

John H. Barton

Intellectual Property Rights and Innovation

Intellectual property rights are currently viewed as a way to encourage innovation and the development of new technologies. The compelling force of the theories supporting intellectual property rights might suggest that the effectiveness of intellectual property systems is so great as to be beyond question—but the results of empirical economic analysis are frequently agnostic and certainly suggest significant industry-to-industry differences.[1]

1. See R. Levin, A. Klevorick, R. Nelson, and S. Winter, "Appropriating the Returns from Industrial Research and Development, *Brookings Papers on Economic Activity* 3, no. 783 (1987).

The Intended Mechanism

The basic intended operation of intellectual property rights can be readily stated: Information and technological innovation are goods that can often be developed only at significant expense; they may be of enormous value to the society but can be readily copied. Hence, in the absence of intellectual property rights, an innovator may be unable to recoup an adequate portion of the benefits provided by the innovation and will therefore underinvest in it. By creating a monopoly for a period, as through a patent or a copyright, the innovator is enabled to exclude competitors, will therefore be able to appropriate a greater portion of the value created by the innovation, and to invest at a higher level in innovation.[2]

This logic especially applies to those situations in which developing a product is expensive, but copying is cheap. The classic examples are pharmaceutical products and computer software, and the benefits of an intellectual property system in those areas are clear. A firm would not invest hundreds of millions of dollars to bring a pharmaceutical product through clinical trials unless it had a number of years of opportunity to recoup these costs in a protected market. And a firm would be unable to invest in writing computer software unless it were able to keep others from selling direct copies of that software.

One reason an economic analysis of the intellectual property system often reveals disappointing performance is that in some circumstances the system provides too small a return. Even with intellectual property, the effective return to the innovator may often be far less than the actual economic value of the innovation.

---

2. See J. Schlicher, *Patent Law: Legal and Economic Principles* (Deerfield, Ill.: Clark, Boardman, Callaghan, 1992), 2-1 through 2-61.

The innovator must share that value with its customers to induce them to purchase the innovative product; a royalty designed to obtain the entire benefit will leave the customer no incentive to use the product. Market structures and competition may force prices down even further. And the product cycle may be significantly shorter than the time needed to obtain some forms of intellectual property protection, particularly patent protection. The result is that royalties typically run at only 25–30 percent of an invention's economic value.[3]

At the same time, some incentives for innovation do not depend on the intellectual property system. Public funds support innovative efforts, whether or not these efforts yield marketable products. In the academic context, the Nobel Prize is a more important incentive than intellectual property rights. And, in many commercial contexts, competitive pressures lead to constantly improving quality; innovations are replaced before they can be copied; and the ability to have the first product on the market with a particular feature may enable a firm to dominate that market. The time delay involved in copying a product thus provides an exclusivity analogous to that of intellectual property.

It is difficult to estimate the actual economic benefit from new innovations; but one can readily estimate the amount of research that is associated with, and therefore may be encouraged by, a patent. This amount ranges from about $0.5 to about $5 million per patent, depending on the industry (see table 1).

3. See J. Barton, R. Dellenbach, and P. Kuruk, "Toward a Theory of Technology Licensing," *Stanford Journal of International Law* 25, no. 195 (1989). For insight into the complexity of the task of allocating profits between licensor and licensee, see Internal Revenue Code Regulation 1.482-4, "Methods to determine taxable income in connection with a transfer of intangible property," reflecting significant revisions in T.D. 8552, 59 Fed. Reg. 35016 (July 8, 1994).

TABLE I

Research Expenditures per Patent Application

Research Area	Total Research [a] (in billions of $)	Number of Patent Applications [b]	Ratio (millions of $ per application)
Total industrially funded	$97.1	109,981	$0.9
Biotech	9.6	15,562	0.6
Large computer and semiconductor	13.7	3,120	4.4
Small computer and semiconductor	3.4	1,010	3.4

[a] Industrial research expenditures and biotech expenditures from National Science Foundation, *Survey of Industrial Research & Development 1994*, table A-7 (1994 numbers), using "drugs and medicines" as equivalent to biotechnology. Computer and semiconductor numbers from published company data assembled in M. Farn, "A Quasi-Statistical Analysis of the Acquisition and Enforcement of Patent Rights in the Computer and Semiconductor Industries for the Period 1986–1995" (Stanford Law School directed research, fall 1996).

[b] Overall numbers from World Intellectual Property Organization, IP/STAT/1994/A, Patents (1994 resident numbers); biotechnology estimates from U.S. Patent and Trademark Office, Group 1800 Workload Statistics (FY 1995 numbers); computer and semiconductor numbers from Farn, "Quasi-Statistical Analysis," based on Lexis search of issued patents. To compensate for the fact that these numbers do not reflect ungranted applications, they were multiplied by 2.06, the current U.S. ratio (derived from World Intellectual Property Organization) between applications and patents.

Administrative Costs

One important question about the intellectual property system is whether its administrative costs are large compared to the research that it gives rise to. The domestic answer here is favorable to the system; the global answer is not. (The implications of costs for the relative competitive positions of large and small firms—a serious issue—is dealt with in a later part of this chapter.)

Patents are the most expensive of all forms of intellectual property protection. The cost of preparing and prosecuting a patent application in the United States is approximately $20,000, covering both legal fees and filing fees. The administrative costs in the U.S. patent office are about $3,000 per application and $6,000 per patent.[4] A patent is likely to be meaningless unless one is prepared to litigate it, and patent litigation is enormously expensive in the United States. Industry folklore is that the costs are typically $0.5 million per side per claim litigated, but the costs of a suit can easily reach $2.5 million, and the numbers in Europe are somewhat smaller, but still significant.[5] Yet, these amounts are still relatively low on a per-patent basis. The number of patent suits filed per year in the United States is on the order of seventeen hundred[6]; if all were brought to trial, the costs would total about $1.7 billion, taking into account both sides to the suits. This is approximately $17 thousand per patent, or, on average, comparable to the amount spent obtaining the patent. The sum of these costs is significant, perhaps averaging $35,000–40,000 per patent but still small compared with amounts of research incented. The costs of the copyright system (for computer programs) and the various

4. The numbers of $585 million in expenses for 191 K applications and 105 K patents are taken from United States Patent and Trademark Office, *Annual Report for FY 1996*, available at www.uspto.gov.

5. A. Bouju, *Patent Infringement Litigation Costs* (prepared for the Commission of the European Communities, 1988), as cited in W. Kingston, "Reducing the Cost of Resolving Intellectual Property Disputes," *European Journal of Law and Economics* 2, no. 85 (1995). A U.S. commentator estimated an average cost of $350,000 in 1991; see Vandenburg, *Journal of the Patent and Trademark Office Society* 73, no. 301 (1991).

6. Administrative Office of the United States Courts, *Statistical Tables for the Federal Judiciary*, tables C-2 and C-4 (June 30, 1996), lists 1,682 patent cases filed annually (in addition to 2,598 copyright cases and 2,710 trademark cases), with 6.3 percent of cases reaching trial (a high percentage compared to other forms of litigation), fifty-one without a jury and fifty with a jury. J. Lerner, in "Patenting in the Shadow of Competitors," Harvard Business School Working Paper no. 94-069, states that 1,318 patent suits were filed in the July 1989–June 1990 year and estimates a total cost of about $1 billion.

special forms of intellectual property protection, such as for computer chips or plant varieties, are much lower.

Even though these administrative costs may be small in the overall context, they are not small in some industries and definitely not small internationally. Stories—which one hopes are generally apocryphal—are told of small firms spending more on litigation than on research. And because the patent system involves parallel coverages in different nations, the average is at least eight filings per invention.[7] Although the basic legal fees of drafting may not be duplicated, there will be additional filing fees, translation fees, and administrative costs. Some efforts are made to do searches in one office on behalf of another on a contract basis, and the decisions of one jurisdiction may be relied on in other jurisdictions.[8] Nevertheless, the totals mount up, and the European costs, in particular, are significantly greater than U.S. costs. A recent survey indicates that European industry spent about 3.3 billion deutsche marks *obtaining* and *maintaining* patents in Europe in 1993 and estimated that this number should be increased to about 9 billion deutsche marks if litigation costs are included.[9] This works out to about $59

7. Based on World Intellectual Property Organization, *Industrial Property Statistics* (1994), there are about 2.4 million filings per year, globally. It is unlikely that these reflect more than 300,000 separate inventions—the U.S. filing totals are about 210, 000 and the European Patent Convention filings about 74,000. Hence, on average, each invention is filed for at least eight times.

8. "The Costs of European Patent Protection," *Managing Intellectual Property* 19, no. 57 (March 1996).

9. European Patent Office, "Cost of Patenting in Europe," *International Review of Industrial Property & Copyright Law* 26, no. 650 (1995). This reflects about 89,000 first filings, or perhaps 50,000 patents, using ratios derived from *Industrial Property Statistics*. These costs may have increased since 1993. M. Kirk, Executive Director of the American Intellectual Property Law Association, testified in 1997 that the costs of simply obtaining and maintaining a patent in all the European nations are more than $100,000; see Prepared Statement for Hearings before the Senate Committee on the Judiciary on S. 507, the Omnibus Patent Act of 1997, May 7, 1997.

thousand per European application or slightly over $100 thousand per patent. It seems likely, therefore, that the overall costs of global patent coverage are in the low hundreds of thousands of dollars per patent (i.e., on the order of 10 to 20 percent of the research incented). This is not negligible.

The implications of the Uruguay Round Agreement on the Trade-Related Aspects of Intellectual Property Protection are that practically every developing nation is staffing up its own patent office—the total annual number of patent applications in developing nations and former Soviet-bloc nations is more than 560,000, filed in large part by nonresidents.[10] The review of these applications is a tragic waste and misallocation of important human resources.

Follow-On Innovation

In most industries, innovation is incremental. In science and technology one person's inventions build on the inventions made by others and serve as a platform for further inventions. It is difficult, however, for an intellectual property system to deal effectively with such sequential innovation; strengthening incentives for an initial innovator may weaken incentives for the follow-on innovator and vice versa.[11]

10. Calculated from *Industrial Property Statistics*.

11. See J. Barton, "Patents and Antitrust: A Rethinking in Light of Patent Breadth and Sequential Innovation," *Antitrust Law Journal* 65, no. 449 (1997); J. Barton; "Patent Scope in Biotechnology," *International Review of Industrial Property & Copyright Law* 26, no. 607 (1995); R. Merges, "Intellectual Property Rights and Bargaining Breakdown: The Case of Blocking Patents," *Tennessee Law Review* 62, no. 75 (1994); R. Merges & R. Nelson, "On the Complex Economics of Patent Scope," *Columbia Law Review* 90, no. 839 (1990); S. Scotchmer, "Standing on the Shoulders of Giants: Cumulative Research and the Patent Law," *Journal of Economic Perspectives* 5, no. 29 (1991).

In some situations, the initial inventor may not have enough incentives. The classic example is "patent flooding," a possible problem of the Japanese patent system,[12] whereby patenting in Japan requires a relatively small innovative step. Someone licensing technology in Japan (or even marketing in Japan) therefore faces the risk that a licensee or potential competitor will file a large number of patents for minor improvements to an existing product. Ultimately, it becomes impossible to market the product without infringing one of these subsequent patents; the subsequent minor innovator has, in effect, appropriated the invention.

The more common pattern, however, is that the follow-on innovator has too little incentive. An example is "research tool patents," a significant concern at the National Institutes of Health.[13] Suppose, for example, that a firm obtains a patent on a receptor, which is a biological molecule important in information transfer into a cell. In general, this receptor is not likely to be an important pharmaceutical; it is important, however, in screening possible pharmaceuticals, for molecules that interact with the receptor may be useful pharmacologically. The typical patent for such a receptor seeks exclusive control over techniques of using the purified receptor for screening purposes. A firm with such a patent can thus block off a significant area of research. As a number of firms obtain such patents, we may be moving to a mesh of blocking rights.

Other forms of intellectual property are being used in ways that seek to restrict subsequent innovation. Thus, to obtain copyright protection for a computer program, one need not disclose the program,[14] and the contract distributed with the program typ-

12. See M. Helfand, "How Valid Are U.S. Criticisms of the Japanese Patent System?" *Hastings Communications and Entertainment Law Journal* 15, no. 123 (1992).

13. See, for example, E. Marshall, "The Mouse That Prompted a Roar," *Science* 277, no. 24 (4 July 1997).

14. 37 C.F.R. § 202.20 (vii).

ically includes provisions designed to prevent users from decompiling the program to find out how it works. Similarly, seed is often marketed today with a label that is designed to prevent its use for any purposes other than growing a crop. If these contractual provisions are enforceable (or if the law of copyright or patent is read to create similar restrictions),[15] then the ideas contained in the program and the gene combinations contained in the seed are unavailable for further research. In another example (which resulted in an important antitrust consent decree, the Pilkington case)[16] the industry leader licensed patents for float glass manufacture with contractual requirements containing such substantial grant-backs of rights to improvement inventions that there was no incentive to make such inventions, and the industry stagnated for several decades.

Tying is a final example of using intellectual property rights in a way that can weaken incentives for later innovation. Particularly in the computer software context, it is possible to design software—properly protected against copying through copyright—in a way that affects competitive possibilities in follow-on markets. The obvious example is Microsoft's power in the operating-system market, which is protected by copyright. Is it being properly or improperly extended into other areas when the software is designed in a way that makes it easier to use Microsoft application systems or Internet connection systems than competitive systems?

---

15. An important recent case did hold such contract provisions enforceable, *ProCD, Inc. v. Zeidenberg*, 86 F.3d 1447 (7th Cir. 1996), but earlier cases in other circuits took the opposite position, *Step-Saver Data Systems, Inc. v. Wyse Technology, Inc.*, 939 F.2d 91 (3d Cir. 1991); *Vault Corp. v. Quaid Software, Ltd.*, 847 F.2d 255 (5th Cir. 1988). Proposed revisions of the Uniform Commercial Code would also make such agreements enforceable in the software context, May 5, 1997, Draft Uniform Commercial Code Article 2B, Licenses, § 2B-307.

16. *United States v. Pilkington*, Civ. Action No. 94-345, Competitive Impact Statement (D. Ariz. filed May 25, 1994), 59 Fed. Reg. 30,604 (June 14, 1994).

Almost all these cases present problems of balancing incentive structures between initial and follow-on innovation. And a follow-on innovator with a good concept protected by a patent is in a strong position to negotiate a cross-license with the initial innovator. Yet, in general, the intellectual property system is probably weighted too heavily toward the initial innovator. The law leaves a subsequent innovator little opportunity to obtain a court ruling that an earlier patent is invalid or not infringed, thus making it difficult for such an innovator to obtain capital or to enter negotiations for a license with a strong hand.[17] Most important, control of broad areas of technology in one group of hands is probably a recipe for stagnation rather than for innovation—technology did not move as quickly in the old days, when AT&T could control all attachments to the phone system or when IBM could effectively control all attachments to computers.[18] It is impossible to estimate the total amount of research forgone, but it must be substantial.

Industry Structure Issues

Probably the most important limitations of the intellectual property system derive from the system's relationship to industry structure, sometimes favoring inefficient industry structures and slowing change in them. If this is the case, it both slows innovation and harms those who benefit from industry flexibility—especially in developing nations.

The intellectual property system almost certainly favors large firms over small ones. Partly, this is a result of the ability to finance filing of patents—IBM files six hundred software patents a year, compared with one hundred "for a well-known West Coast com-

---

17. *Cygnus Therapeutic Systems v. ALZA Corp.*, 92 F.3d 1153 (Fed. Cir. 1996).
18. See Barton, "Patents and Antitrust," p. 455.

petitor."[19] More important is the cost of litigation. Although the $0.5 million required for patent litigation is not that large when compared with the amount of research involved, it is a lot for a small firm. A recent study of patent litigation in the computer and semiconductor industries found that large companies were responsible for most of the litigation and that they typically sued smaller or similar-sized companies and only rarely larger companies.[20] Hence, a patent in the hands of a small firm is significantly less valuable than one in the hands of a large firm—and the threat of patent litigation can become a tool against a possible new entrant into a market.[21] The Advisory Commission on Patent Law Reform stated in 1992: "If the patent owner does not have a strong financial posture, threatened litigation can be used as a bargaining tool to decrease or even eliminate the potential value of a patented invention to the patent owner."[22] These imbalances are even greater for an innovator in the developing world, who may well be unable to find the funds to file a patent application, let alone litigate it.

Obviously, there is a question as to whether this probable favoritism of large firms against small firms is harmful to innovation—but the Silicon Valley working assumption has certainly been that new small firms are more efficient and aggressive innovators than are large firms. If this assumption is correct (and it almost certainly is), then intellectual property systems are harmful to the extent that they favor large firms.

Intellectual property systems are also frequently associated

19. "Two Years On, the IBM Gospel according to Louis V. Gerstner," *Computergram International*, August 22, 1995.

20. Farn, *supra*. A very brief statistical analysis conducted by F. Scherer suggests, however, that small firms do not disproportionately lose at the appellate level; see A. Silverman, "Symposium Report; Intellectual Property Law and the Venture Capital Process," *High Technology Law Journal* 5, no. 157 (1990).

21. Silverman, "Symposium Report."

22. Advisory Commission, *supra*, at 76.

with oligopolistic competition structures, marked by litigation or formal or informal cross licenses. Typically, the various firms in the industry have each developed or acquired a substantial number of broad patents that (if valid) are being infringed by others in the industry. Sometimes suits are brought. Sometimes the patent disputes are resolved by cross licenses or mergers. Sometimes threats of infringement suits are met by threats of countersuits based on patents that the putative plaintiff may be infringing, which amounts to a tacit cross license. In the paradigm case, every member of the oligopoly is infringing possibly valid patents held by every other member of the oligopoly, but no one wants to drop the litigation bomb out of fear of retaliation. This pattern is exemplified in the semiconductor industry by elaborate cross licenses and in the agricultural biotechnology industry by substantial litigation but also substantial merger activity.[23] And the pattern seems likely to arise in other industries in which there are a number of competitors and in which relatively broad patents are possible.[24]

Although it would be hard to say that innovation is—at least at this point—slow in either semiconductors or agricultural biotechnology, the patents may not be helping to encourage innovation, at least in the semiconductor case. On the positive side, the oligopolistic structure does permit the participants to obtain a partial monopoly rent because of the possibility of charging a higher price than would emerge under competition. This is a form of return for the various innovations produced by the different members of the industry. And, when a major player purchases a small firm for the

23. See Barton, "Patents and Antitrust," 462–465; J. Barton, "The Impact of Contemporary Patent Law on Plant Biotechnology Research," delivered at Crop Science Society of America Symposium, Washington, D.C., June 4, 1997; J. Ordover, "A Patent System for Both Diffusion and Exclusion," *Journal of Economic Perspectives* 5, no. 43, 51-54 (1991).

24. Merges and Nelson, "Complex Economics of Patent Scope," present a number of examples, including the aviation industry (before World War I).

sake of that firm's technology, the venture investors who helped support that firm receive a return and thus innovation is stimulated.

On the negative side, however, the tie between innovation and return is attenuated in a way that may not encourage innovation. In the semiconductor industry, the high rate of innovation is probably tied more to product quality competition among the industry leaders than to intellectual property regimes. Indeed, the possibility of intellectual property litigation provides an additional tool (beyond price undercutting) to discipline a price-reducing firm. And the intellectual property incentives are perverse. It is more important to obtain patents that other members of the industry will infringe (to maintain bargaining chips to protect freedom of action) than to obtain patents that one will utilize. And litigation is unappealing, except when one is doing badly in the market and therefore has little to lose from the countersuits; the result is that litigation becomes a kind of spoiler initiated by firms who are otherwise failing. Litigation can also be used to keep firms from entering the market. Certainly a new firm with an important innovation has a bargaining chip that may facilitate entrance into the oligopolistic community; but any member of the oligopoly that feels threatened by the new technology can bring a suit that bars entry, and the new firm may also find that its only future is acquisition by an oligopoly member.

Although more careful analysis of this and other examples is needed, it appears plausible that, in the pattern just described, the intellectual property system is unhelpful to innovation and contributes to an unnecessarily concentrated industrial structure. This pattern is likely to occur in any situation in which there are several centers of innovation, in which patents are broad, and in which commercialization of the innovation requires several patents. This may come to include the pharmaceutical sector as the number of broad and basic research tool patents grows, creating an important tension. In semiconductors, it is possible for the intellectual property issues to be a kind of legal game played alongside the technological competition; in biotechnology, however, the role of patents on products is crucial, and it may be difficult to live with the need to maintain full exclusivity for some technologies while relatively freely cross licensing others.

Implications

In some industries, the intellectual property system is essential to encourage innovation; in others it may make relatively little difference. And in some of those industries, it imposes a significant cost on the industry and may slow innovation. Those costs take the form of legal and intellectual property costs, barriers to subsequent innovation and entry, and possibly a conservatism of industrial structure. Because of the benefits of the sytem in some contexts, it is foolish to argue that the intellectual property system should be abandoned.[25] Nevertheless, the problems indicate that substantial tuning and adjustment are needed.

First is the need to reduce administrative costs. The analysis shows that these are minor within the United States, but that they become major as one goes global. We would be wise to move as quickly as possible to a globally integrated patent system in which there are uniform standards, one careful search in one patent of-

---

25. One might consider the wisdom of replacing the patent system by an expanded orphan drug system, under which market exclusivity would be created through administrative action in the product approval process. The Orphan Drug Law was initially enacted as Pub. L. 97-414, Jan. 4, 1983, 96 Stat. 2049, and has been amended since. The exclusivity provision is codified at 21 U.S.C. § 360bb. The logic would be that some form of market protection is essential in industries such as pharmaceuticals, which face high regulatory costs, and that the performance of the patent system has been relatively lackluster in other industries. The difficulty is that there may be few regulatory needs associated with future technologies that need protection because of a combination of large research costs, low copying costs, and long product lifetimes.

fice, and automatic global extension of rights. Such reform poses difficult global harmonization issues, particularly with respect to the scope of intellectual property rights in biotechnology and computer software. Moreover, it may be difficult to persuade patent offices and patent bars of the wisdom of such reform. Nevertheless, industry would strongly support the result. It would be ideal to balance such an arrangement with global arrangements to make the system available to the impecunious innovator, whether in the developing or developed world.

Second, the standards for intellectual property should be modified. For patents, there should be a strengthening of the "nonobviousness," or "inventive step" requirement, so that patents are issued only for inventions that are likely to be important. This would decrease administrative and legal costs and the possibility of misuse of patents because there would be fewer patents, but it would leave the system in place to promote important innovations.[26]

The scope of the monopoly conferred by a typical basic invention should also be narrowed, for broad-scope inventions are most likely to lead to the oligopolistic cross licenses described above or to the possibility that one firm can block progress in an entire industry. This can be done by genuinely enforcing the enablement requirement (i.e., the requirement that the scope of the patent conform to the new approaches disclosed in the patent application).

Third, the position of the subsequent innovator should be strengthened. On the patent side, one could use the utility requirement, which is among the statutory requirements for the issuance of a patent, to avoid subjecting basic scientific principles to the patent system. One could also make clear that both academic and

---

26. See C. Quillen Jr., "Proposal for the Simplification and Reform of the United States Patent System," *AIPLA Quarterly Journal* 21, no. 189 (1993): 192–95.

commercial researchers can freely use an invention for certain experimental purposes. (Such an arrangement must, of course, be devised in a way that protects the incentives for a firm to invent and market such an invention.) In other contexts, copyright law could be reasonably interpreted to permit decompilation of computer programs, and trade secret or contract law could prohibit or treat as unenforceable contract provisions designed to restrict reverse engineering. The House of Lords recently took a position in accord with these recommendations, stating that "care is needed not to stifle further research and healthy competition by allowing the first person who has found a way of achieving an obviously desirable goal to monopolize every other way of doing so."[27]

Finally, the competition law issues associated with intellectual property should be rethought. Again, the issues are difficult, and it is important not to undercut the genuine incentives intended by the intellectual property system. Nevertheless, there are several practices that raise significant questions. One is the use of intellectual property–based market power in one market to extend power into other markets. It is the nature of technological innovation to move from market to market as one market disappears and another arises, and firms must be able to compete by moving from old areas of expertise to new ones. Yet certain practices extending power from one market to another clearly perpetuate monopoly. Similarly, there is concern about the use of intellectual property rights to restrict entry of new firms into a tacitly or explicitly cross-licensed industry. When is such an effort a reasonable result of the exchange of rights under broad blocking patents, and when is it more a concerted effort to prevent entry of new competitors into the industry? Further, when should we be concerned about a merger or acquisition that brings together important patent rights,

---

27. *Biogen Inc. v. Medeva PLC*, [1997] RPC 1, 52 (House of Lords, 1996).

even though the parties to the merger may not be competing in a particular current market?

In short, when one examines the intellectual property system in action, one finds a situation frequently—but not always—very different from the ideal of a low transaction cost way to encourage innovation by preventing copying. Transaction costs and the breadth of intellectual property rights can shape incentives and industrial structure in ways that may not encourage innovation. Reform is essential.

David Henry Dolkas

9

The Inevitable Collision of Rights: What Happens When Rights of Trademark Owners and Domain Name Owners Collide

A few short years ago, few companies, if any, advertised or promoted the company's goods or services through the use of the company's domain name (assuming the company even had one). Web sites began to flourish about 1995 and exploded in 1996.[1] Today, most businesses have web sites and e-mail addresses for employees using the company's domain names. In fact, some companies obtained domain names just for the purpose of stockpiling them.[2]

Many traditional storefront businesses with strong brand-name-type trademarks, recognizing the vast potential of using

1. See D. Krovoshik, "Paying Ransom on the Internet," *N.J.L.J.*, October 23, 1995, p. 10.
2. Ibid.

those trademarks on the Internet, rushed and continue to rush to the Internet, only to discover that someone else had taken "their name" on the Internet.[3]

In some instances their name had been registered as a domain name by a "cyber squatter," or pirate—an enterprising individual with the foresight to see the value of a domain name to the storefront business—who would offer to sell the name to the company for a bounty. The courts' had little trouble addressing these situations.[4] In other instances, the name was acquired innocently by a small business with no intention whatsoever of trading on it.[5] These types of disputes are more troublesome and not as easy to decide. This chapter discusses the inevitable collision of rights leading to the growing numbers of disputes and the current state of the law.

3. The words *their name* are meant pejoratively because no one actually legally owns an Internet domain name, at least not in the sense of owning an item of property, like a trademark. Some of the early cases proved amusing. For example, in *MTV Networks v. Curry*, 867 F.Supp. 202 (S.D.N.Y. 1994), a former MTV video jockey obtained the domain name *mtv.com*. MTV sued the video jockey to obtain "their name." The case was ultimately settled, with the video jockey agreeing to relinquish the domain name.

4. See, for example, *Panavision Int'l, L.P. v. Toeppen*, 945 F.Supp. 1296 (C.D. Cal. 1996), in which the district court characterized the individual, Dennis Toeppen, who had obtained the domain name *panavision.com*: "Toeppen's 'business' is to register trademarks as domain names and then to sell the domain names to the trademarks' owners. Toeppen's business is evident from his conduct with regard to Panavision and his conduct in registering his domain name of many other companies. His 'business' is premised on the desire of the companies to use their trademarks as domain names and the calculation that it will be cheaper to pay him than to sue him." 945 F.Supp. 1303.

5. See, for example, *Gateway 2000, Inc. v. Gateway.com, Inc.*, No. 96-1021, 1997 U.S. Dist. LEXIS 2144 (E.D.N.C. Feb. 6, 1997). The district court denied Gateway 2000's motion for a preliminary injunction based, in part, on the finding that *Gateway.com* had legitimately used the domain name for several years.

Trademarks versus Domain Names

In 1997 there were more than 750,000 registered U.S. trade-marks.[6] Trademarks in the United States are issued by the U.S. Patent and Trademark Office (USPTO) following a rigorous screening process, including determining whether the proposed registration interferes with or infringes on any existing registra-tions for goods or services in the same or related uses.[7] Trademarks exist in physical space and identify and distinguish goods and indi-cate the source of those goods.[8] Traditionally and historically, trademarks are confined by the particular nature of the use and are regionally based—meaning there can be multiple owners of an identical trademark for different uses or in different geographic markets.[9] Existing trademark laws allow the owner of a trademark to apply for registration on the basis of actual use or *intent* to use the trademark,[10] causing some commentators to declare that a trademark naming crisis exists because all the good names have been taken.[11]

More than one million Internet domain names use the top-level domain: *.com*. Domain names are registered by Network Solutions, which does not and is not required to conduct any form of screening process. Clearly, the same crisis that affects trade-marks affects domain names—most of the good names are gone. Domain names exist in cyberspace and are used globally. In their truest form, domain names are intended to serve as addresses on the Internet, not as trademarks (i.e., to designate the origin, affili-

---

6. Alex Frankel, "Name-o-rama,™" *Wired Magazine*, June 1997, p. 97.
7. Lanham Act § 2(d), 15 U.S.C.
8. Lanham Act § 45, 15 U.S.C. § 1127.
9. "Net Interest," *Wall Street Journal*, June 5, 1997.
10. Lanham Act § 1(a)–(b), 15 U.S.C.
11. Frankel, "Name-o-rama,™" pp. 97–98.§ 2(d), 15 U.S.C.

ation, or sponsorship of any goods or services). Because each domain name constitutes a unique address on the Internet, there cannot be more than one domain name.

A Hypothetical Domain Name Dispute

The following hypothetical domain name dispute addresses the above points. Assume that Acme Corporation manufactures and sells shotgun shells under its federally registered trademark EMMA and EMMA's, the Original Shotgun Shells. Acme Corporation, based in Billings, Montana, is one of the oldest and largest employers in the state, where the corporation and its shotgun shells are well known. Acme Corporation is a good corporate citizen of Montana, a contributor to various Montana-based charities, and a strong proponent of firearm rights for responsible individuals.

Then assume that Emma Smith owns and operates a small (ten employees) company, Emma Dot Com, a California corporation based in San Francisco. The company publishes an Internet magazine known as *EMMA'S*, accessible only on the Internet using the domain name *emma.com*. The company has no offices outside San Francisco, but the on-line magazine can be accessed anywhere in the world using the Internet, including Montana. It does not charge a fee to persons who access it; the company makes its money exclusively through advertising on its web site.

The on-line magazine features guides to and critiques of upscale restaurants located in cities around the world, as well as gourmet recipes from top chefs. The highly acclaimed on-line magazine has received numerous awards for excellence from various on-line groups. Emma Dot Com's web site is linked with thousands of other web sites on the Internet. The small company applied for various trademark registrations employing the word EMMA, including Emma Dot Com, EMMA'S, and EMMA's Original Restaurant and Food Guide, but no registrations have been issued. Before the ensuing litigation, Emma Smith had never heard of the Montana-based shotgun shell manufacturer or any of its products. Emma Smith acquired the domain name *emma.com* in 1995. (Acme Corporation acquired its domain name, *emmashells.com*, in September 1996.)

On July 1, 1997, Acme Corporation filed suit against Emma Dot Com in federal district court in Montana for, among other claims, trademark infringement and trademark dilution (under the new federal statute). A few days later, Emma Dot Com filed suit for declaratory relief and trademark misuse against Acme Corporation in federal court in California (San Francisco). Soon after filing suit, Acme Corporation made a formal challenge to the domain name registrar, Network Solutions, requesting that it place the domain name *emma.com* on hold. In response, Network Solutions deposited the domain name in the registry of the federal court in Montana. Thus, the federal court in Montana now exclusively controlled which party had the right to use *emma.com* on the Internet.

After filing suit, Acme Corporation also filed a motion for a preliminary injunction under the new federal antidilution law seeking an injunction from the Montana federal court prohibiting further use by Emma Dot Com of the domain name *emma.com*. Emma Smith believes that, if Emma Dot Com is enjoined from using the domain name *emma.com*, her company will go out of business. The business, which has no storefront in the traditional sense, is only accessible on the Internet.

The following questions arise from this hypothetical scenario:

- Where will this dispute be decided—in Montana or California? Does it matter?

- Can the use of an Internet domain name, intended to serve as a unique Internet protocol address on the Internet, support and serve as the basis for claims of trademark infringement and trademark dilution?

- Can Acme Corporation prove trademark infringement against Emma Dot Com?

- Can Acme Corporation prove trademark dilution against Emma Dot Com?

To address these questions adequately we must first determine why domain names are important and the context of the legal dispute.

Importance of Domain Names

Every computer on the Internet must have an address in order to send and receive data under the transfer control protocol (TCP). The address has a numeric address, sometimes called the dotted quad. Because these dotted quad numbers are difficult to remember, the Internet authorities permit the use of names or prosaic words to serve as substitutes for the dotted quad.[12] For example, the numbers 1978.137.240.291 are the numeric Internet protocol (IP) or address, for the dotted quad for the domain name *whitehouse.gov*.[13]

The Domain Name System (DNS) functions as a large database in which the upper or top-level domains branch out. Several large branches emanate from the trunk of the DNS consisting of the top-level domains (TLD). Obviously, the most popular branch, or

12. Ibid.
13. Rodrich Simpson, "Critical Mess—Sorting Out the Domain Name System," *Wired Magazine*, June 1997, p. 92.

TLD, is the *.com*, which is used to designate businesses or commercial users.[14]

Domain names are used in virtually all aspects of electronic data transfer sent over the Internet using a uniform resource locater (URL) for an e-mail address (e.g., ddolkas@gcwf.com) or a web site address (e.g., http://www.gcwf.com). The U.S. Patent and Trademark Office also permits the registration of a trademark using the *.com*; however, the *.com* must be disclaimed by the registrant.

Domain Name Registration

In January 1993, the National Science Foundation, under the terms of a cooperative agreement, assigned responsibility for the registration of top-level domain names to Network Solutions, a private company based in Herndon, Virginia. (That agreement expires in September 1998.) Domain names are registered with Network Solutions on a "first come, first served" basis. Network Solutions provides no screening or review process of a registration application for a domain name, and there is no requirement that such a review process occur. The registration of domain names takes little time and can be entirely accomplished over the Internet, as opposed to the lengthy processes involved in obtaining trademarks. The quick registration of domain names has expanded the use of the Internet because companies and individuals can obtain critical IP addresses in a short time and without much expense.

The Domain Name Dispute Policy

With the permission of the National Science Foundation, Network Solutions created the Domain Name Dispute Policy in July

---

14. The other top level domain names include: *.edu* for education (e.g., *stanford.edu*), *.net* for network (e.g., *sprintlink.net*), *.org* for a charitable organization (i.e., nonacademic, nongovernmental, and noncommercial organizations), *.gov* for a government (e.g., *nasa.gov*), and *.mil* for military uses (e.g., *usmc.mil*).

1995 (amended in November 1995 and again in September 1996) to deal with the growing number of disputes between trademark owners and domain name holders. Under the current policy, three important provisions set forth the position of Network Solutions as the neutral registrar of domain names.

First, the policy states that "by registering a domain name, Network Solutions does not determine the legality of the domain name registration, or otherwise evaluate whether that registration or use may infringe upon the rights of a third party,"[15] meaning that Network Solutions does not act as the USPTO (i.e., as a reviewing entity passing on or assessing a particular domain name to ensure that no third party's rights are violated). Under the policy, the *registrant* must warrant that the particular domain name registered does not "interfere with or infringe upon the rights of any third party."[16] In December 1996, the United States District Court for the Central District of California held that Network Solutions had no general duty (or obligation) to investigate whether a particular domain name selected by a registrant violated the rights of a trademark owner.[17]

Second, the policy sets forth what actions Network Solutions may take when presented with a challenge to the use of a domain name but does not define the rights of either the trademark owner or the domain name holder as against each other.[18] In the event a challenge is made by a trademark owner, she or he must serve an unequivocal notice on the domain name owner that its use of the domain name violates the legal rights of the trademark owner.[19] Unless the domain name holder can present proof of an existing

---

15. Policy Introduction, as amended in September 1996.
16. Ibid.
17. *Panavision Int'l, L.P. v. Toeppen, et al.* (C.D.Cal. 1996).
18. The policy states that a complainant is *not* required to use the policy.
19. Ibid.

trademark, the subject domain name can be placed on hold by Network Solutions and not returned to active status until the dispute is resolved.[20] If either the trademark owner or the domain name holder initiates litigation, the policy provides that Network Solutions shall deposit control of the domain name into the registry of the court.[21]

Third, the policy specifically provides that it does not confer "any rights, procedural or substantive, upon third-party complainants" (e.g., trademark owners). In May 1997, the United States District Court for the Middle District of Tennessee (Nashville Division) granted a summary judgment in favor of Network Solutions, finding that a trademark owner/challenging party was not a third-party beneficiary of the policy.[22]

Legal Disputes Involving Domain Names

Lawyers and the courts struggle to apply existing laws to disputes involving domain names. Most claims asserted by trademark owners against domain name holders are based on claims of federal or state trademark infringement or trademark dilution laws and, occasionally, claims of unfair competition. For the reasons discussed below, applying traditional trademark infringement laws does not usually work well in these disputes. In contrast, applying trademark dilution laws has had much more success and will continue to be successful, largely because of a federal antidilution law which went into effect in January 1996.

Traditional Trademark Infringement Claims

The purpose of the trademark laws, which are set forth in a statutory body known as the Lanham Act, is to protect the con-

---

20. Ibid.
21. Ibid.
22. *Data Concepts, Inc. v. Digital Consulting, Inc. v. Network Solutions, Inc.* (1997).

sumer from confusion or deception. Trademark infringement claims are premised on two fundamental requirements that a trademark owner must prove to stop another from using a deceptive or confusingly similar trademark. First, the trademark owner must establish that the trademark is inherently distinctive,[23] and, second, that use of the allegedly infringing trademark will likely cause confusion in the mind of the relevant buyer.[24] All the federal courts apply some variation of a multifactor test to determine whether there exists a "likelihood of confusion" caused by two competing marks by assessing the competitive proximity of the two marks, that is, whether the parties are competitors with similar goods or services offered in similar channels of trade to the same customer base. The closer the circles of competitive proximity, the greater the probability of a court's finding a likelihood of confusion. If so, a variety of remedies can be awarded by a court, including prohibiting the use of the trademark that has been found to likely cause confusion with the plaintiff's trademark.

Traditional trademark laws work well when the disputes involve two competitors operating in closely similar markets or channels of trade with closely similar goods or services. Most domain name disputes, however, do *not* involve competitors or businesses operating in markets or channels that are competitively proximate. A good example is the case of *Giacalone v. Network Solutions, Inc.*, which was filed in the United States District Court for the Northern District of California in May 1996.[25] Philip Giacalone registered the domain name *ty.com* (his son's name was Ty). Thereafter, Mr. Giacalone used the domain name in connection with his business as a software consultant. The defendant, Ty, Inc.,

---

23. See *Two Pesus, Inc. v. Taco Caban, Inc.*, 505 U.S. 763 (1992).

24. See *AMF, Inc. v. Sleekcraft Boats*, 599 F.2d 342 (9th Cir. 1979).

25. *Giacalone v. Network Solutions, Inc., Ty, Inc.*, United States District Court for the Northern District of California, Case No. 96-20434 (N.D.Cal. 1996).

an Illinois-based toy company and doll maker, owned the U.S. trademark registration TY for dolls. After Ty, Inc., sent a cease and desist letter to Mr. Giacalone and instituted a challenge with Network Solutions, Mr. Giacalone filed suit in federal court saying that his use of the domain name did not interfere with or infringe the rights of Ty, Inc. Mr. Giacalone contended that Ty, Inc., was attempting a "reverse domain name hijack" (i.e., Ty, Inc., a wealthy trademark owner, was attempting to hijack a domain name from an innocent and legitimate domain name holder). On June 14, 1996, the federal court entered a preliminary injunction against Ty, Inc. prohibiting it from taking any further action to stop Mr. Giacalone's use of the domain name.

The *Giacalone* case exemplifies the difficulty of applying traditional trademark infringement laws and analysis to domain name disputes. Ty, Inc., would have had a difficult time proving trademark infringement by Mr. Giacalone given the disparity in the goods offered by Ty, Inc. (toys and dolls) and the services offered by Mr. Giacalone (software consulting). In other words, because of the lack of competitive proximity, proving trademark infringement was difficult.

The New Federal Antidilution Law

Trademark owners were given a significant boost when Congress passed the Federal Trademark Dilution Act in December 1995. The act, which took effect in January 1996, gives significant rights to owners of "famous" trademarks, providing that the owner of a famous, nationally known trademark may exclude the use of similar trademarks even if there is *no* competitive proximity or likelihood of confusion. Dilution under the act is broadly defined as the "lessening of the capacity of a famous mark to identify and distinguish goods or services."[26]

26. Lanham Act § 45, 15 U.S.C. § 1127.

Before the passage of the act, no federal statute gave specific rights and remedies to trademark owners on the basis of a claim of trademark dilution. Trademark owners typically joined claims of trademark infringement with claims of dilution based on state law. The antidilution statutes in the various states, however, were not uniform and varied considerably. The new act gives the trademark owner specific and uniform rights. Thus, a federal court may consider whether a mark is distinctive and famous based on its

- Degree of inherent or acquired distinctiveness
- Duration and extent of use in connection with the goods or services with which it is used
- Duration and extent of advertising and publicity
- Geographic extent of the trading area in which it is used
- Channels of trade for the goods or services with which it is used
- Degree of recognition in the trade areas and channels of trade used by the mark's owner and the entity against whom the injunction is sought
- Nature and extent of use of the same or similar marks by third parties
- Registration on the principal register or under the 1881 or 1905 Trademark Acts[27]

In the event dilution is found by the court, a nationwide injunction can be granted.[28] Damages, attorneys' fees, and destruction of the goods bearing the offending mark can be awarded if the

27. Lanham Act § 43, 15 U.S.C. § 1125(c)(1).
28. Lanham Act § 43, 15 U.S.C. § 1125(c)(2).

court concludes the defendant intended to trade on the owner's reputation or cause dilution of the mark.[29]

The act's legislative history is relatively scant. There is, however, support for the assertion that Congress intended the new statute to apply to the use of domain names on the Internet.[30] Several courts have applied the act to domain name disputes without much hesitation, especially in those cases in which the domain name owner could not articulate a valid reason for registering a domain name using a well-recognized trademark other than to trade on the name. In such cases, the domain name holder was typically labeled by the court to be a "squatter" or "domain name pirate."[31] Relief was also granted against defendants using well-recognized trademarks to promote sexually explicit Internet sites.[32]

The statute provides that the following are defenses to a claim of dilution:

- Defendant's ownership of a valid registration under the 1881 or 1905 Trademark Acts or on the principal register

29. Ibid.

30. The Federal Trademark Dilution Act of 1995 passed the House of Representatives under suspension of rules on December 16, 1995, and was passed by the Senate on December 29, 1995. The floor remarks indicate that the act was a means to secure better protection for U.S. companies *and* to address deceptive Internet domain names. Senator Patrick J. Leahy (D-Vt.) noted that the dilution bill would prove useful in preventing the use of deceptive Internet domain names.

31. See, e.g., *Intermatic, Inc. v. Toeppen*, 947 F.Supp. 1227 (N.D. Ill. 1996) (injunction addressing the registration and use of *intermatic.com*); *American Standard, Inc. v. Toeppen*, No. 96-2147, 1996 U.S.Dist. LEXIS 14451 (E.D. Ill. Sept. 3, 1996) (injunction addressing the registration and use of *americanstandard.com*); and *Panavision Int'l, L.P. v. Toeppen*, 945 F.Supp. 1296 (C.D. Cal. 1996) (injunction addressing the registration and use of *panavision.com*).

32. See, for example, *Hasbro, Inc. v. Internet Ent. Group, Ltd.*, 40 U.S.P.Q. (BNA) 1479) (W.D. Wash. Feb. 9, 1996) and *Toys "R" Us, Inc. v. Akkaoui*, 40 U.S.P.Q. (BNA) 1836 (N.D.Cal. Oct. 29, 1996).

- Fair use of a famous mark in a corporate commercial adver-
  tisement or promotion to identify competing goods or services

- No commercial use of the mark

- All forms of news reporting and news[33]

Resolving the Questions

Returning to the hypothetical case set forth above and in light
of the previous discussion, we can now turn to the questions previously raised.

Where will the dispute be decided and does it matter? The fact that
Acme Corporation filed first in Montana and before Emma Dot
Com filed suit in California will significantly assist Acme Corporation in convincing the California court that it should stay its proceedings pending the outcome of the case in Montana. Many federal courts follow a "first to file" rule, which generally holds that
the court that first received a complaint is given preference and is
typically held to be the court that should decide the dispute.

Acme Corporation will still need to establish to the satisfaction
of the federal court in Montana that it has proper jurisdiction and
venue to hear the matter. If those issues are raised by Emma Dot
Com, Acme Corporation must establish that Emma Dot Com's
contacts with the state of Montana, which are exclusively by virtue
of the Internet, are sufficient "minimum contacts" to support jurisdiction over Emma Dot Com in Montana. This issue (i.e., jurisdiction based on Internet presence) is being hotly contested in several
courts around the country. To date, no federal appellate court or
the Supreme Court has issued a decision setting forth the guidelines
for the lower courts to follow in cases involving minimum contacts

33. Lanham Act § 43, 15 U.S.C. § 1125(c)(4).

by a defendant within the forum state based solely on the defendant's presence.

The issue of where the case will be decided could be outcome determinative, especially if the case is ultimately presented to a panel of jurors. A federal jury in Montana may be predisposed to aid a well-known corporate citizen as against an out-of-state company that is operating a web site using a trademark well known in Montana. In contrast, a jury in San Francisco may be significantly less tolerant of a firearms manufacturer and may favor a small, local start-up company.

Can the use of an Internet domain name support claims for trademark infringement and trademark dilution? Clearly the use of a domain name can support and serve as the basis for claims of trademark infringement and trademark dilution, as well as other claims. The fact that the domain name *emma.com* was innocently selected—not for the purpose of trading on the goodwill or recognition of the trademark for the shotgun shells—may serve as an argument in defense of these claims but does not provide immunity.

Can Acme Corporation prove trademark infringement against Emma Dot Com? Proving trademark infringement by Emma Dot Com will prove difficult for Acme Corporation because of the decided lack of competitive proximity between the goods offered by Acme Corporation (i.e., shotgun shells) and the service offered by Emma Dot Com (i.e., an on-line magazine). Hence, Acme Corporation is likely to focus its efforts on the claim of trademark dilution.

Can Acme Corporation prove trademark dilution against Emma Dot Com? If so, will Acme Corporation be successful in obtaining a preliminary injunction against Emma Dot Com? To prove trademark dilution, Acme Corporation will need to establish that its mark is famous under the act and that Emma Dot Com's use of *emma.com* causes dilution. Proving dilution is by no means a "slam dunk," and Emma Dot Com has numerous equitable defenses that the court may consider. Emma Dot Com should focus on the equitable factors that make denial of an injunction a reasonable finding under the act. The act states that the court may base its decision to grant or deny injunctive relief on the basis of "principles of equity and on such terms as the court deems reasonable."[34]

Conclusion

As potential names to be used as trademarks and domain names become evermore scarce, and as the Internet continues to globalize both trademarks and domain names, more disputes will emerge between trademark owners and domain name holders. Several factors account for this growing number of disputes. Clearly a wise domain name holder should register his or her trademark and domain name as a trademark or service mark as soon as possible. Registrations will serve as complete defenses to challenge proceedings made with the registrar, Network Solutions, and in actions brought by trademark owners for trademark dilution. Domain name holders should also be aware that Internet presence (i.e., digital contact through the Internet with a particular state) may support jurisdiction under traditional and long-standing judicial precedence. A company engaged in Internet commerce could easily find itself in a lawsuit in a far-off locale solely by virtue of its Internet presence. Consequently, when faced with a dispute or a possible dispute, both the trademark owner and the domain name holder should consider immediately filing suit. By taking advantage of the first to file rule followed by many courts, the owner will be able to preserve a "home field" advantage.

34. Lanham Act § 43, 15 U.S.C. § 1125(c)(1).

Barbara Simons

Regulating Content
on the Internet

Before the widespread use of digital technologies and the Internet, nonlawyers such as myself seldom were involved with discussions relating to what intellectual property is and what the rights and responsibilities of owners of intellectual property ought to be. Now one cannot analyze intellectual property legislation without mentioning terms such as cryptography, bitmaps, and browsers. Contentious issues relating to intellectual property law involve computer scientists and engineers, as well as intellectual property lawyers. We can no longer deal with intellectual property without having some understanding of what the Net is and how it works. Ideally, once such an understanding is attained, it will be easier to reach consensus on ways in which the Net and related technologies can and should be regulated in regard to intellectual property issues.

One goal of this chapter is to present a computer scientist's view of how the Net, technology policy, and intellectual property interact. A second goal is to encourage lawmakers to consider how the same technology they see as creating difficulties might help solve some of the problems that concern them. To the extent that we need new legislation, it should be written with the technical characteristics and qualities of the technology in mind.

Why People Are Afraid of the Net

I recall watching with combined amusement and horror as industry and the government discovered the Net. It was seen as a tool for making lots of money, although there seemed to be some confusion as to just how all the money was going to be made. Remember the six hundred movie channels and the accompanying buying frenzy of movie studios a few years ago? After the initial excitement, people started to get serious about learning more about the digital world and the Net. The learning was accompanied by increased concerns reflecting the following:

- Unlike photocopy and audiotape machines, a copy of a digitized document is as good as the original. In fact, it is identical to the original.

- It is easy and cheap to make multiple copies of digital files, as long as the files are not too large.

- It is easy and cheap to distribute digital copies over the Internet, again as long as the files are not too large.

- It is easy to modify digital files that have not been encrypted, meaning that a modified file could be passed off as the original. Furthermore, it is essentially impossible to know that there are modifications unless one can compare the modified file with the original.

- The electronic infrastructure of our country is not secure against possible attacks by crackers, criminals, and terrorists.

- There is no central control of the Net.

- It is sometimes impossible to determine who sent what, especially as long as there are anonymous remailers. It is easy to impersonate someone else.

- The Net is an uncensored source of information, much of it junk and some of it valuable. Although there is offensive material on the Net, there is also political speech that needs to be protected.

Individuals make suggestions for dealing with the Net and intellectual property according to their backgrounds. Lawyers and policy makers tend to suggest new laws or modifications to old ones, whereas computer scientists, engineers, and other technologists tend to come up with new technologies as solutions. Meanwhile, the two communities view each other with skepticism and, occasionally, hostility.

Some media people, lobbyists, and policy makers have been behaving toward the Net in an irresponsible, almost demagogic, fashion. For instance, the word *hacker* was once a term of admiration and respect. But in the hands of the news media, hacker has become someone who behaves unlawfully on the Net. Using a loaded word like *piracy* when referring to misappropriation of intellectual property can also impede a rational discussion. Overuse of the words *smut* and *pedophile* has created the impression that evildoers can reach through the monitor screen and grab innocent children. People seem to forget that a child is more vulnerable to abuse by strangers when outside of the security of his or her home, say, in a shopping center. They may also forget that other communication media, such as the telephone, can be used to arrange illicit meetings.

"Indecent" Intellectual Property:
The Rimm Study and the Communications Decency Act

The July 3, 1995, issue of *Time* magazine featured a dramatic cover showing a young wide-eyed boy sitting in front of a computer monitor. The accompanying story on cyberporn was based on research by Marty Rimm, a Carnegie Mellon undergraduate. *Time* concluded that "there is an awful lot of porn online." Rimm's study had not been peer reviewed, but the publicity generated by *Time* caused many people to examine the report. It was subsequently discredited on the bases of misrepresentation of results, shoddy statistical methods, and possible plagiarism, among other accusations. (For references to the Rimm study, the *Time* magazine article, and critiques of both, see http://www2000.ogsm. vanderbilt.edu/cyberporn.debate.html.)

The sensationalism and prominence of the *Time* article and the lack of any kind of equivalent retraction appear to have had a pivotal role in the passage of the Communications Decency Act (CDA), which attempted to outlaw "indecent" material on the Net, despite the fact that obscenity and child pornography laws automatically apply to the Net. Since it is often impossible to verify the age of someone on the receiving end of a piece of e-mail, the CDA would have lowered the level of much of the discourse on the Net to that appropriate for a schoolchild. Partially for this reason, CDA was declared unconstitutional by the Supreme Court. Even though the Court upheld First Amendment rights on the Net, the Rimm/ *Time*/CDA spectacle is a case study in how *not* to formulate policy and legislation.

The Net and Its Challenges

One major problem confronting those who would like to pass regulations and legislation, such as CDA, relating to the Net, is the lack of precise definitions of many of the terms and technologies. The problem is exacerbated by the fact that many policy makers have little or no understanding of the basic mechanisms of the Net and frequently make little if any use of it. This lack of understanding will dissipate over time; however, major efforts are under way to pass laws now, before we have the required experience and insights to legislate judiciously and to understand how technology might solve some of the problems it appears to have created.

Basic questions concerning which laws and rights apply to the Net cannot be addressed until we have a clear picture of just what the Net is. Is it

- Publishing? In which case there are broad free speech rights.

- Broadcasting? In which case many of the current restrictions that apply to radio and TV would carry over.

- A communication channel similar to a telephone? In which case it would be treated as a common carrier.

- A mixture of all of the above? In which case different laws would apply according to the context.

- An entirely new medium? In which case entirely new laws may have to be developed.

In short, there is little consensus as to what the Net is. Additionally, the new technology raises questions about fundamental concepts we thought we had agreed on long ago. For example, when a document is transmitted across the Net, it is first divided into packets that are shipped separately, possibly along different paths, and reassembled by the receiver. Furthermore, each computer on the transmission path of a packet must make a copy of that packet in order to forward it. Packets are only one aspect of the Net's technology that has upset traditional definitions of a copy.

For example, is something a copy if it (1) has been encrypted or modified by a formatting program? or (2) has been transformed using data compression? or (3) is one of several packets?

A tendency to propose simplistic solutions accompanies a lack of understanding of the Net. The question is how to monitor the vast quantity of material on the Net when

- Material from Europe intended for Asia may be in transit through the United States.
- Information may be sent in hundreds of different languages.
- Information may be sent in an encrypted format.
- Information may be sent in a compressed format to make the sending more efficient.
- Information may be sent after having been preprocessed using some formatting program so that the initial version can be read only after another processing phase.
- Different packets from the same file might use different paths through the Net.
- Information and technologies that are legal in one country might be illegal in another.
- It is possible to conceal the name and location of the sender or even to make it appear to be someone else.

Because computers in one country can be accessed from another country, the Net does not adhere to state or national boundaries. As a result we are confronted with issues ranging from the lack of enforceability of U.S. laws outside the United States to the problem of determining community standards within our country.

Unanswered questions are legion. For example, should Saudi Arabia's views of women require that all pictures of women on the Net show them wearing veils? How do we deal with a country that has not signed an intellectual property treaty? Should the views of some rural residents of Tennessee as to what is pornographic apply to urban residents of California? Should fundamentalists be allowed to censor web pages that inform homosexuals of safe sex practices? Should homosexuals be allowed to censor web pages of fundamentalists that describe homosexuality as a perversion?

Further, who decides about a museum's on-line photograph of, say, Michelangelo's *David* or on-line news containing photographs of atrocities or of starving children? (See *http://www.sjmercury.com/business/Netrate110397.htm.*) What tools are appropriate? Should we support blocking web pages to protect our children from pornography, even if the blocking prevents a breast cancer victim from maintaining a web page on breast cancer? (For a discussion of America Online's blocking of a breast cancer site, see *http://www.epic.org/free_speech/censorship/aol_censorship.txt.*)

Should there be any restrictions on programs that filter web sites for undesirable content? Should parents have a say, and should filtering programs be required to reveal which sites are being filtered and why? Should sites be required to rate themselves, and, if so, who evaluates those ratings? (For information about a self-rating system called Platform for InterNet Content Selection, or PICS, see *http://www.w3.org/PICS/.* For critiques of PICS, see *http://www.epic.org/free_speech/censorware/.*)

Some of the complexities of filters and monitoring are illustrated by what happened to (then) eighteen-year-old Bennett Haselton, who reverse engineered the blocking software of Cybersitter, a product produced by Solid Oak Software. (This is a case in which reverse engineering is relatively easy to do, as one can see by trying to access a particular site using the blocking software.) Haselton published the list of blocked sites, which included the home pages of Greenpeace and the National Organizaton of Women. Cybersitter subsequently expanded its list of blocked sites to include any that criticized Cybersitter, including Haselton's. Additionally, Haselton was threatened with a lawsuit by the president of Solid Oak Software. (See *http://www.wired.com/news/poli-tics/story/901.html*.) Haselton later posted a program for decryp-ting the list of sites blocked by Cybersitter, which again generated the threat of a lawsuit. (See *http://www.wired.com/news/politics/story/3355.html*.)

Several interesting questions arise out of the Haselton/Cyber-sitter story. Given that the Clinton administration is promoting filters as an alternative to the Communications Decency Act, should the government regulate services that provide filters? Should there be a parents' right-to-know law, that is, should par-ents be able to obtain information on the sites that have been blocked and the criteria used in the blocking? Or is a list of blocked sites' intellectual property unavailable for disclosure? And if the list of sites is intellectual property, is reverse engineering a viola-tion of the intellectual property rights of the organization doing the filtering?

Technologies for Protecting Intellectual Property on the Net

Although monitoring the Net for pornography or intellectual property violations is not feasible, several promising technologies could protect intellectual property on the Net. These include the following:

Electronic payments

If a document can be obtained by clicking a button and paying for it electronically, the incentive to search for an illegal copy is reduced. Companies that provide electronic charging and elec-tronic cash already exist. (For an example, see *http://www.cybercash.com/cybercash/*.)

Watermarking

Digital watermarking involves modifying the digital version of a file or document so that each copy is slightly different, thereby making it possible to determine the person to whom a particular version was sent. Watermarks can be visible or invisible. Invisible watermarks work especially well for images but can also be applied to documents in some cases. (See *http://www.thomtech.com/mmedia/becker/wmark3.htm* and *http://www.software.ibm.com/is/dig-lib/v2factsheet/page2.htm.*)

Encryption

Encryption is critical for electronic funds transfers and payments, but is also needed to protect a digital work from being stolen as it is being transported over the Net. (A commercial example is cryptolopes, an IBM product that enables an entire transaction, from purchase to the shipping of a document—article, figure, or song—to take place securely on the Net. See *http://www.cryptolope.ibm.com/.*) Encryption also could be combined with special-purpose devices that print a decrypted file from an encrypted original without making a digital version of the decrypted file available. This technology could be used for any kind of device that produces a readable version, such as a monitor. Yet another approach is smart cards, which would be required to obtain a printed copy. These are current research topics in both academic and industrial settings.

Flickering

To make it impossible to copy a document by doing a screen dump, flickering produces alternating bitmaps that look like a normal screen to the viewer but that, if downloaded and printed, produce garbage. This technology is still in the research phase, with some of that work being done at Bellcore. (See *http://community.bellcore.com:80/lesk/flicker.html.*)

Electronic Publishing—
the Association for Computing Machinery Policy

Some of the technological approaches to securing intellectual content on the Net are problematic in that they imply a contractual relationship between the consumer and the provider. Contract law may be appropriate for, say, the sale of software, but does not provide the rights of first sale and fair use that are included in our current copyright law. Fair use is a defense against infringement of copyright when an insubstantial portion of the work has been copied for educational use, quotations in reviews or criticisms, and so on. If I were to purchase a book over the Net under a contractual arrangement using some of the techniques described above, I might be unable to give that book to a friend (first sale). I might also be unable to avail myself of fair use rights that would apply had I purchased the book from a bookstore.

Should readers forfeit rights simply because they purchased a book or article over the Net or in some other computer-related format? The Association for Computing Machinery (ACM), whose U.S. Technology Policy Committee I chair (*http://www.acm.org/usacm/*), has grappled with this issue in developing our Interim Copyright Policy. Since ACM is a publisher, as well as a professional society, the situation is especially instructive. (See *http://www.acm.org/pubs/copyright_policy/*.) Our researchers, who are also our authors, produce intellectual property. Our members, who read our various journals and who may also be authors, use intellectual property; ACM Press, the publisher of our scholarly journals and books, publishes intellectual property. The ACM represents the computing profession, and we are trying to establish a policy that is both is fair to our members and allows ACM to continue to provide publishing services. Although we are experts in the technology, we have difficulty predicting its future. Consequently, our policy is an interim one but one we feel might be considered by other organizations, and because the policy is interim, we can make adjustments as both the technology and our understanding of it mature. By contrast, once legislation is passed, it is often difficult to modify it.

The ACM interim policy deals with several issues:

Maintaining Integrity of Works

The ACM will warrant that the copies of works in its digital library are definitive and have not been modified or altered without author and editor permission. The ACM will be able to provide proof of these warrants. The ACM will store the definitive versions and give unlimited permission to copy links to those versions.

Transcopyright Permission

ACM incorporates a principle similar to "transcopyright," whereby ACM will hold its copyrighted works on its servers and give free and unlimited permission to create and copy links to those works or their components. The ACM will provide a way of linking a component to its parent work so that readers can locate the context from which an excerpt was drawn. Readers following links will gain access on payment of a fee or presentation of a valid authorization certificate to ACM or ACM's agent, who will issue a personalized certificate of ownership to that reader. A person owning a copy may not replicate that copy and give it to others unless the copy carries explicit permission for further replication.

Author-Friendliness

The ACM intends to be the author's agent in reaching the widest possible readership and protecting the author's interests against plagiarism and unauthorized copying or attribution. The ACM grants authors liberal retained rights including unlimited reuse of the work with citation of the ACM publication and the right to post preprints and revisions on a personal server. The ACM will take legal action against those who infringe its copyrights.

Value-Added Services

The ACM is a member organization chartered to disseminate information about computing to its members and the public. The ACM will assist readers in locating materials of value to them. The ACM treats copyright ownership as a means to provide a digital library to its members and the public and to act against anyone attempting to duplicate ACM's library; the ACM does not treat copyright permissions as a significant source of revenue.

Copyright Notice

The ACM's copyright notice specifically allows fair use as follows:

A Final Word

New technologies frequently require new approaches. Consider, for example, how the Indian cable company Star dealt with the issue of intellectual property. When people purchased satellite dishes to receive Star programming, some turned around and sold the programming to the apartment buildings in which they lived. Instead of prosecuting these small entrepreneurs, Star made its product free to everyone and exploited the large audience as a selling point for advertisers.

I am not suggesting that owners of intellectual property give up their rights in exchange for new business opportunities. But they might keep in mind that a web lifestyle is emerging. Over time we will communicate with friends and acquaintances, purchase goods and services, obtain news and entertainment, and run businesses on the Net. Just as this media creates new challenges, it also offers new opportunities for those who are willing to discard some of the old paradigms.

Good legislation will make the Net a friendly place for producers and consumers of intellectual property. Bad legislation can seriously harm the Net and ultimately create more problems than it solves. The U.S. Technology Policy Committee of the ACM has been working to educate policy makers and the public on the implications of various approaches. It is our hope that policy makers will consider all aspects of the technology and the possible unintended implications of proposed legislation.

Appendix: Current Legislation (1997)

Regulations concerning the export of cryptographic products have been in existence for some time. Legislation has been proposed to both decrease and increase restrictions on the use and export of cryptography on the Net. Legislation has also been proposed to control the wholesale mailing of unsolicited e-mail, otherwise known as "spamming." Rather than attempt a comprehensive survey of all legislation that has any relevance to content on the Net, the review below is limited to legislative proposals that focus on more narrow definitions of intellectual property.

In contrast to the ACM's interim approach, the Clinton administration called for new legislation relating to intellectual property on the Net. Bruce Lehman, the assistant secretary of commerce and commissioner of patents and trademarks, has been a leader in the development of the administration's intellectual property policy. Lehman also chaired the Intellectual Property Working Group of the administration's National Information Infrastructure (NII) task force, and was the driving force behind a white paper entitled "Intellectual Property and the National Information Infrastructure." Legislation to implement the white paper recommendations was introduced in the House (H.R. 2441) and Senate (S. 1284) in 1996. The legislation did not come to a vote in Congress, but most of the same recommendations were included in the draft treaties that the United States championed in the World Intellectual Property Organization (WIPO) meeting in December 1996.

H.R. 2281 and S. 1121

In July 1997 H.R. 2281, the WIPO Copyright Treaties Implementation Act (Coble) (*http://thomas.loc.gov/cgi-bin/query/z?c105: H.R.2281:*), and S. 1121, the WIPO Copyright and Performances and Phonograms Treaty Implementation Act of 1997 (Hatch), (*http://thomas.loc.gov/cgi-bin/query/z?c105:S.1121:*), were introduced. Sections 1201 and 1202 of the implementation legislation contain provisions from the 1996 legislation that were not covered in the WIPO treaties, including a ban on circumvention devices and making distributing material from which copyright management information has been removed illegal. The intent to infringe is not required.

Subsection (b)(2)(B), included below, is interesting because of its breadth. Note that a measure does not have to be effective in the technical sense (i.e., it need not be difficult to break).

(B): A technological protection measure effectively protects a right of a copyright owner under this title if the measure, in the ordinary course

> of its operation, prevents, restricts, or otherwise limits the exercise of
> a right of a copyright owner under this title.

By contrast, because copyright owners are not required to institute strong measures to protect their property, the criminal penalties can be draconian. The first offense of Section 1201 or 1202 can result in a fine of $500,000 and imprisonment for five years; the maximum fine and term of imprisonment is doubled for subsequent offenses.

The U.S. Technology Policy Committee of the ACM raised some issues in a 1996 letter to Commissioner Lehman about the proposed WIPO treaty (*http://www.acm.org/usacm/copyright/wipo_copyright_letter.html*), that apply to the 1997 (WIPO) implementation legislation.

Article 13

Devices to Circumvent Copyright Protection Systems, Article 13, would have the same undesirable effect on technological development as Section 1201 of the National Information Infrastructure Copyright legislation proposed in the 104th Congress. This legislation would bar the importation, manufacture, or distribution of any device or service whose "primary purpose" or "primary effect" is to defeat a copyright protection system. This statute could adversely affect a company that legitimately develops a product people use for purposes other than that for which it was developed. Since it is likely to be difficult for a developer to collect data about the product's primary use, it may be impossible to refute copyright holders' claims that the primary effect of a particular device is copyright infringement. As a result, the article could dissuade manufacturers or software producers from investing in a new technology with substantial noninfringing purposes for fear that an anxious copyright holder might pursue litigation using the "primary effect" standard. The article should address the intent of the individual or company, not the effect of its actions or product.

There could be other unintended side effects of Article 13, as well. For example, we need secure and unbreakable forms of encryption if the information infrastructure is to be secure from attack by terrorists and blackmailers. Since it is impossible to prove mathematically that any form of encryption is absolutely secure, we depend on the fact that many smart people have tried to break the encryption system and failed. But since encryption is frequently used in copyright protection systems, third-party testing of encryption systems is likely to be criminalized under Article 13, thereby potentially exposing the nation to significant harm.

S. 1146

The Digital Copyright Clarification and Technology Education Act of 1997, S. 1146 (Ashcroft), is an alternative to H.R 2281 and S. 1121. In contrast to the language contained in the other legislation, the circumvention language of S. 1146 requires facilitating or engaging in an act of infringement, using the word *infringement* to describe various actions.

The definitions contained in Section 1201 of S. 1146 are more specific and precisely defined than those of H.R. 2281 and S. 1121, as we see in the following:

> (c): The Definition of Effective Technological Measure. As used in this section, the term "effective technological measure" means information included with or an attribute applied to a transmission or a copy of a work in a digital format, or a portion thereof, so as to protect the rights of a copyright owner of such work or portion thereof under chapter one of this title, and which—
>
> > (1) Encrypts or scrambles the work or a portion thereof in the absence of access information supplied by the copyright owner; or (2) Includes attributes regarding access to or recording of the

work that cannot be removed without degrading the work or a portion thereof.

Section 1202 of S. 1146 also discusses copyright management information but, unlike the other legislative proposals, requires intent.

All the proposed legislation contains provisions for civil penalties in Section 1203, but S. 1146 has no provisions for criminal penalties (i.e., there is no Section 1204). In addition, S. 1146 contains a Section 202, which addresses fair use, whereas the proposed implementation legislation does not. Finally, S. 1146 addresses the manner in which files are shipped around the Net so as to guarantee that aspects of the technology are not inadvertently made illegal.

H.R. 2180

H.R. 2180, the On-Line Copyright Liability Limitation Act (Coble), also addresses transmission on the Net. (See *http://thomas.loc.gov/cgi-bin/query/z?c105:H.R.2180.*) As stated in the bill summary, the purpose of the bill is "to amend Title 17, United States Code, to provide limitations on copyright liability relating to material on-line, and for other purposes." The liability exemptions included in the bill reflect the transmission technology of the Net.

Section 512

This section covers limitations on liability relating to material on-line:

(a) Exemptions—A person shall not be liable—
    (1) For direct infringement, or vicariously liable for the infringing

acts of another, based solely on transmitting or otherwise providing access to material on-line, if the person—

(A) Does not initially place the material on-line;

(B) Does not generate, select, or alter the content of the material;

(C) Does not determine the recipients of the material;

(D) Does not receive a financial benefit directly attributable to a particular act of infringement;

(E) Does not sponsor, endorse, or advertise the material; and

(F) (i) Does not know, and is not aware by notice or other information indicating, that the material is infringing; or

(ii) Is prohibited by law from accessing the material.

H.R. 2652

The Draft Treaty on Intellectual Property in Respect to Databases was introduced at the WIPO meeting by the United States. The treaty was based on the Database Investment and Intellectual Property Antipiracy Act of 1996, H.R. 3531. There were no hearings, debates, or votes on H.R. 3531. The treaty would have created a new sui generis property right for databases. The proposed new property right generated widespread opposition from the academic community. Probably for the first time, the presidents of the National Academy of Sciences, the National Academy of Engineering, and the Institute of Medicine signed a joint letter in opposition to the database treaty. (See *http://www.arl.org/info/ frn/copy/data.html.*) USACM also opposed the treaty. (See *http:// www.acm.org/usacm/copyright/wipo_database_letter.html.*)

The treaty was not passed during the WIPO meeting. (See *http://www.wipo.org/eng/diplconf/distrib/94dc.htm* and *http:// www.wipo.org/eng/diplconf/distrib/95dc.htm* for the text of the passed treaties.) H.R. 2652, the Collections of Information Antipiracy Act (Coble), was introduced in the House on October 9, 1997. (See *http://thomas.loc.gov/cgi-bin/query/z?c105:H.R.2652.*)

H.R. 2652, like H.R. 3531, would create a new sui generis property right for databases. It also contains draconian criminal provisions, namely, a maximum of five years imprisonment and a $250,000 fine for the first offense and ten years imprisonment and a $500,000 fine for all subsequent offenses.

Abraham D. Sofaer

Comment:
Issues in Law, Regulation,
and Property Rights

Lawyers always have the edge when it comes to discussing themselves because we have the benefit of being largely in control of the system. If businesspeople say we lawyers should replace ourselves, all we have to do is say "no." We will also remind businesspeople how badly off they would be without us, since they don't know exactly who or what would take our place. And we have a point. Things could be worse. The often-heard quotation "let's kill the lawyers" comes from *Henry VI*; it is, to be precise, the first thing that the tyrants decide to do when they take over because lawyers are good at stopping government from doing things, including evil ones. So getting rid of the law or lawyers seems both unlikely and undesirable.

Of course, my Hoover colleague Bob Hall is right when he says that we're a very wealthy nation and can afford some waste. I think, though, that we could be an even wealthier nation if we had a somewhat less costly and litigious system. The current system has grave deficiencies. Companies in America have far too much difficulty and face too much uncertainty in protecting and exploiting their intellectual property. When I was a practicing lawyer, I had less empathy with those companies, but now I serve as a member of some company boards and as an investor in some venture capital operations and have learned more about our legal system's inadequacies in the area of intellectual property.

The deficiencies of our litigation system are, I think, exacerbated by the complexity of intellectual property. The cases take longer. They are costlier to resolve, and because they involve both the federal and state legal systems, their resolution is particularly unpredictable. Unpredictability may, ironically, be a mixed blessing because it is the one thing that seems to get these cases closed. The situation is desperate; I have heard the comment that Congress made a mistake giving scientific issues to judges instead of juries because the judges don't understand them either yet create at least the initial impression that they will be decided professionally. Why not have the uncertainty sooner rather than later, some suggest, and thereby terrify litigants into settling, which may well represent a better outcome than any other option.

In fact, the sum and substance of what I hear in most presentations concerning these cases is that it simply pays to settle them. I myself favor alternative dispute resolution (ADR). I settle a lot of such cases in my work as a mediator, arbitrator, or consultant. But evaluating cases for ADR too often concerns not rights or wrongs but rather the economic interest in settlement. ADR practitioners generally focus on how much money one is going to lose in a litigation by paying legal fees; how much time one is going to lose (one's own time, one's experts' time, and so on) by insisting on a ruling; and the value of any additional uncertainties created by anything but an agreed resolution. Many cases settle because one side is financially better off settling than trying to win, regardless of the merits, which is hardly a comforting way of explaining to people why they should be happy to settle. Although it is necessary, from the viewpoint of our legal and economic system, it remains disheartening that people can profit so handsomely and readily on intellectual property claims that are meritless or brought solely for their harassment (settlement) value.

The deficiencies of our litigation system are heightened, moreover, by the sheer wealth that high-tech commerce is creating. Wealth attracts lawyers like blood attracts sharks. But there are business sharks as well as lawyer sharks, and the business sharks are really as much if not more to blame than the lawyers. Indeed, if this were a chess match, the lawyers would be largely the pawns. Class action litigation is a reality even in the intellectual property area, not only because of the value of the intellectual property at issue but because companies—especially competitors—will often respond to attorneys who peddle these cases by financing them. Individuals who know something about a particular company's intellectual property, some technical weakness perhaps, are able to find the financing to make a case against that company. That is a harmful and demoralizing process, especially when we see that exploiting the technical weakness has come to be regarded as a perfectly legitimate means of competing. One major American company funded three inconsistent cases attacking the same patent: that is, three cases by three different plaintiffs, in the hope that one of them might turn out to be a winner and give the funding company access to the defendant's intellectual property.

I found another case even more disturbing, though the activity could in no sense be considered improper. A big pharmaceutical company was sued by a plaintiff company that makes drugs but does no research. The plaintiff company, instead of funding the research it takes to get pharmaceuticals approved, hires expert attorneys and patent specialists to investigate patents that have been granted and become valuable. When this company finds a valuable patent with a weakness, it finances litigation aimed at attacking that patent with a view toward obtaining a favorable settlement or license or the right to sell the pharmaceutical as a generic drug. The case in which I was involved concerned perhaps the most successful drug in the twentieth century, and the weakness involved—for which defendant paid dearly—was truly a technicality. The plaintiff did not claim that the pharmaceutical was not an "invention" that had saved countless people but only that one of the complex series of patent filings involved was a few days late because of an extra (and superfluous) foreign filing.

I do share the belief that we derive great benefit from a legal system, even a costly and burdensome one. We must address, though, what can be done to minimize the loss, the uncertainty, and the frustration that creative people endure when they develop ideas worthy of intellectual property protection but thereby become targets of opportunity in which the law is used as a substitute for economic competition. We need to craft equitable defenses to prevent losses of wealth fairly earned. And we need to make the system of litigation in this area of commerce one in which the benefits of a successful defense, or of a reasonable settlement offer by either side, are significantly enhanced.[1]

1. See, for example, the proposal to amend Rule 68 of the Federal Rules of Civil Procedure to include attorneys' fees as "costs" that are collectible if a settlement is refused that is later determined to have exceeded what was recovered.

Part Three

Measuring and Extracting Value

Steven M. H. Wallman

The Importance
of Measuring
Intangible Assets:
Public Policy Implications

Intellectual capital issues, as opposed to intellectual property issues, are increasingly being recognized as important. For too long, the measurement of intellectual capital was ignored or belittled, its presentation and discussion precluded or subject to potentially crushing liability, and its management considered too difficult. In some cases, intellectual capital seemed to be viewed more as a liability than an asset. In this chapter, I outline where I believe attention to intellectual capital issues should be directed in the future. I explain why I believe these issues are important and why I believe they matter, not only to the high-tech community but also to investors around the world.

First, let me discuss briefly why exploring intellectual capital is, or at least should be, highly relevant to the Securities and Exchange Commission (SEC), where I work. I need to note here that the commission's interest in intellectual capital issues is evolving. Some in the commission believe that there is a benefit to be had in providing information to investors concerning intellectual capital; others are concerned that too much of this type of information—information that may be difficult to verify—will be presented. To some degree, those disparate views regarding the presentation of intellectual capital stem from fundamentally different views of what securities regulation is all about.

Securities regulation helps make our system of capitalism work. The current structure works well—the U.S. primary and secondary markets are clearly the deepest, the most liquid, the fairest, and the broadest in the world. Although this success is not all a result of securities regulation or the Securities and Exchange Commission, some of it is.

The primary and secondary markets are inextricably intertwined. Capital raising, capital formation, and capital exiting, for venture capitalists and others, depends on having a good secondary market. To make secondary markets work, there must be information. And, to enable investors to buy securities efficiently and in relatively small blocks, that information must be available, useful, and reliable. There is no consensus, however, at the margin (and intellectual capital is currently at the margin), on what information is actually useful and reliable. Adding to the difficulty, there frequently are conflicts between the two goals of usefulness and reliability. Reliable information—in the sense of its being clearly provable and unequivocally accurate—is not always the most useful, and some of the most useful information is not always the most reliable.

When having to choose between reliable information and useful information, the commission has traditionally focused on, and been most concerned with, ensuring the reliability. For example, until the mid-1970s the commission precluded issuers of securities from presenting information in prospectuses that was regarded as forward-looking because such information was viewed as potentially misleading. (Attempting to predict the future suggests some certainty to forward-looking information, which is known to be inherently uncertain.) Notwithstanding the commission's views, the investing public specifically desired more forward-looking information but because of the commission's rules, the public was forced to obtain it through other, indirect means—such as through analysts who obtain information from the company. The commission eventually changed its rules so that presenting such information was no longer prohibited, but neither was it encouraged. The new rules created a regulatory safe harbor, which was generally regarded as wholly inefficacious at providing protection from obvious liability risks. The safe harbor was not used, and the information was not forthcoming directly from companies to smaller investors. A generation later, priorities and views have changed considerably. Within the past few years, Congress enacted a statutory safe harbor that encourages issuers to provide forward-looking information to the public. (Interestingly, that information now receives greater protection from liability than any other information presented in prospectuses, even though it still remains, obviously, inherently unreliable.)

The experience with making available forward-looking information underlies an increasing articulation by investors, and an understanding by lawmakers and regulators, of the utility of *useful*, as opposed simply to *reliable*, information. Nevertheless, old habits die hard. When the issues of intellectual capital and the presentation of measures of new drivers of wealth production are considered, we again hear arguments that information relating to these types of assets and measures should either not be permitted or not be encouraged—because of their unreliability.

But, as with forward-looking information generally, the demand for useful information regarding the new drivers of wealth production and new measures of intangible assets is growing. For example, studies now indicate that trends in the book value to market value for many companies have been decreasing substantially, relatively speaking, over the past few decades.[1] In the early seventies, approximately 40 percent of a company's assets were not accounted for on a company's balance sheet, relative to its market capitalization. Today, well over twice that amount is invisible in terms of traditional financial statements prepared in accordance with generally accepted accounting principles (GAAP). And that percentage is increasing rapidly (even ignoring the recent increases in equity market valuations over the past few years). This means that the traditional balance sheet and financial statements embody less of the value of the company than they have in the past. Similar trends manifest themselves elsewhere. Studies reviewing the impact of corporate earnings announcements on corporate stock prices have shown that, again over the past few decades, the impact of such announcements has receded from about $2.50 of market capitalization change for every $1 of earnings change to approximately 70¢ of market capitalization change for every $1 of earnings change.[2] Thus, the value of reported accounting earnings as a determining factor in driving stock prices has slipped to almost a quarter of what it was some years ago. The result is that accounting earnings information is now about a quarter as valuable to investors in terms of the "market share of relevant information" as it was then. Similar results, and conclusions, are drawn when considering cash flow or other traditional accounting financial statement items.

At base then, investors are concluding that current audited financial statements information—useful as it is—is not as relevant for making informed capital-allocation decisions as it once was.

1. Professor Baruch Lev, "The Boundaries of Financial Reporting and How to Extend Them" (forthcoming).

2. Ibid.

Instead, investors are arriving at investment decisions based on other information and other measures. Those new drivers of wealth production include factors such as perceptions of the quality of the workforce, the value of intellectual property, and the company's long-term strategy, as well as understandings of the level of customer and employee satisfaction, the company's investment in workforce training, its standing in the marketplace with regard to market share, and other factors. All these are measures that investors indicate are important and that are included in the market capitalization of companies. Yet none of these measures is easily qualified. Certainly, none of them is presented well in official filings, if presented at all, or required to be disclosed.

Since investors are using this information but obtaining it indirectly, as they once had to do with all forward-looking information, we need to address how this information should be treated under the current system of mandated and voluntary disclosures of information deemed useful and reliable for investment decisions. Today significant effort is expended creating, maintaining, and enforcing a disclosure system predicated to a large degree on the usefulness of GAAP financial statements. This effort is expended at the commission, as well as at the Financial Accounting Standards Board. And this effort is focused on attempting to ensure that GAAP financial statements are appropriately measuring what investors believe is important. Juxtaposed against that effort, however, is the conclusion that GAAP financial statements have steadily been losing their ability to present useful information. Consequently, there must be a rethinking of basic premises: What information should the commission in fact be encouraging or requiring to be disclosed and why?

A preliminary question concerning the presentation of additional, more-useful information is whether issuers, in fact, want to present this additional information. Clearly, just as some issuers are advocating expanded voluntary disclosure of this information, others suggest strongly that it should not be encouraged or even permitted. Under the current system, some companies are trading at remarkable market values. An examination of their earnings, balance sheets, and hard assets, however, does not allow for such market capitalization. In truth, it is difficult to conclude on the available information that these valuations are realistic or reasonable. Obviously, investors are ignoring the published and attested financial statements and relying on estimates of other drivers of wealth production. An interesting point, however, is that such estimates can be too high as well as too low. If investors had information reflecting the measures of those other drivers of wealth production, such information might suggest that some companies with extraordinarily high valuations do not deserve them. Some issuers would thus find it competitively advantageous not to have that information presented.

In addition, companies in the converse position believe that they are not receiving a sufficiently high valuation in the marketplace because of the market's lack of understanding of their intellectual capital or other factors they believe contribute to their growth. Those companies believe that, if the market could better understand the value of their well-motivated or trained workforce or their internally generated intellectual property or their high levels of customer satisfaction, they would receive far higher levels of market capitalization, thereby reducing their cost of capital.

Regardless of the competitive considerations behind differing views of the desirability of presenting additional information, it should be clear that, if better information can be better presented, capital and resources will be better allocated in the economy. That societal benefit is worth striving for.

Nevertheless, if the commission were to consider requiring disclosure of such additional information, many companies, even many of those who advocate the expanded presentation of information, would argue that it cannot be mandated. The current consensus, with which I agree, is that such information is still too unreliable to require it for all public companies. As our society moves toward a knowledge-based economy, however, the information presented to investors under traditional practices is becoming increasingly unreliable and perhaps even misleading. In other words, limiting disclosures to information that, although reliable, presents less than the true picture of a company distorts the true picture. Or, put differently again, our current system—through its continual devotion to a traditional "reliability" standard—is actually producing increasingly less-reliable information, if viewed as the total picture.

Thus, there is an interesting trade-off between reliability—meaning measurement certainty with attestation and the possibility of inter- or at least intraindustry comparability—on the one hand, and usefulness and accuracy, or, put another way, reliability—in the sense of a full presentation that is not misleading due to the exclusion of other material information—on the other. Given this trade-off, the task ahead is to determine how best to develop measures of wealth production drivers of the future.

Wealth production drivers in the past were obvious. Half a century ago, the likely future wealth production capacity of a steel mill was determined by how large the plant was, what the revenues were at the moment, and what the margins or earnings were for those revenues. Predictions of future earnings, barring some calamity, were not difficult given this information, provided there was some feel for the level of future demand. With regard to new economy companies (meaning those companies relying primarily on intellectual capital as the primary drivers of wealth production), how to measure their drivers of wealth production is far less clear. What is needed, therefore, are better measurement techniques for those drivers.

Those who oppose presenting more information regarding new drivers of wealth production aver that the information will always be too unreliable and that better measures are impossible to construct. In response, consider for a moment the stock option accounting debate that began twenty years ago. Obviously, stock options have value; if they did not, nobody would want them. The goal sought by those proposing a charge to earnings for the value of stock options was better information. The questions then were how to measure their value and how to best present that value. Twenty years ago, nobody knew how to measure that value. But now option valuation models are robust and reliable, and those who helped develop the models have won Nobel Prizes for their work.

Notably, agreeing that the information is available in the sense of having reasonably consistent valuations does not answer the question of how best to present the information. For now, stock option valuations are presented at the discretion of the issuer simply as a footnote. But what is important is that investors have the information. If the market in fact finds the information to be material, then the information will be employed, even if it is in a footnote. Two decades ago, those valuations would not have been possible and the information would not have been presented. Today the valuations are required in every public company's financial statements.

Similarly, today objections arise to the inclusion of information that clearly relates to drivers of wealth production in new economy companies because, again, that information is believed to be unreliable. Obviously, some of those measures—employee satisfaction, customer satisfaction, and brand loyalty—today *are* unreliable. But the circumstances are no different from those circumstances that ruled regarding stock options a generation ago. If the private sector and others work on it, it will be possible to develop measures, standardize survey techniques, and construct valuation mechanisms to ensure that such measures are, eventually, sufficiently reliable.

The initial task then is to continue our efforts to determine what are the true and most useful drivers of wealth production for knowledge-based companies—to discover what, in fact, correlates with profitability, earnings, and market share improvements in the future. Once that information is ascertained, the task will be to develop measures of those drivers of wealth production, to standardize those measures so that they are comparable when used over different time frames and in different companies, and to construct a common language for the presentation of that information, which can then be presented, without difficulty, to investors. To the extent that some believe that information can be presented now, there is reason to encourage, not discourage, its disclosure. By allowing its presentation, and having the ability to test against those measures in the future, we increase our ability to develop learning in the area. Valuations of stock options proceeded because entire areas of finance and capital formation depended on them, and many smart minds were employed to try to solve the riddle. We face a similar issue with intellectual capital and intangible assets in connection with an increasingly knowledge-based economy. The inquiry here must be maintained and encouraged, not discouraged. Then, if such information can be presented well to investors, it will be possible to come full circle. Good information presented to investors reduces the risk of investing, which means a reduction in the cost of capital. That clearly is a societal benefit. The goal and the steps to arrive at it are clear.

But, as we have seen in recent debates on those issues, some maintain that no consensus can, or should, be achieved concerning the identification of these drivers of wealth production or their measurement and presentation. They maintain that there will never be a sufficient level of reliability (requiring precision as the minimum acceptable level of reliability) to make their presentation useful. In contrast, I believe that such a consensus will be obtained in the not too distant future on the desirability of doing more to create appropriate pressures in these areas. We will see.

Other institutional factors will also have to be taken into account and resolved as this debate concerning the use of additional information develops, including, for example, the issue of liability for misleading information. As I mentioned earlier, a safe harbor now exists for forward-looking information; that safe harbor may not exist for information relating to the measurement of intangible assets to the extent that information is considered a current measure as opposed to a forward-looking statement. A possibility of excessive liability could block the information's presentation to the extent that it possesses an inherent unreliability. Few issues are as contentious as liability issues. Consequently, resolving that matter may take some time.

In addition, some are concerned that measuring a driver of wealth production and converting that measurement into an asset may result in increased tax liability. Currently, some states tax hard assets used in the production of wealth but not currently unmeasured intangibles. Because measuring them may lead to taxes that are not currently paid, there is an incentive to fail in measuring those assets animated by this taxation possibility. That consideration must be addressed in efforts to develop and refine those measures.

Clearly, we will have to learn to walk before we can run. For some time now concerned companies have been exploring how best to obtain intellectual capital information and use it for internal purposes only. The next step will be voluntary presentation of such information to the public. Then, if a true consensus can be achieved—which is obviously many years off—one could consider requiring some of the most robust and generic of that information. Among further concerns is how to eliminate the potential for misleading disclosures due to lack of comparability in the voluntary stage. In other words, how does one ensure comparability when voluntary disclosures from company to company are based on, for example, different sample sizes or different criteria in such measures as customer satisfaction. Ensuring the temporal integrity of the information is also important, as managers may wish to present positive information that exists in one year but to withhold the results of a subsequent survey that may reflect more negative information. The answers are not too difficult but, again, need to be agreed on. Those answers can include voluntary standards adopted by those who wish to experiment in the area coupled with public disclosures of the procedures, together with the commitment to apply the standards in at least some subsequent reporting periods in the event the company determines to eliminate them or change them for years after that.

By accepting responsibility for the integrity of the disclosures, and by ensuring that investors have a firm understanding of the disclosures' limitations, these measures can be presented so as to promote the public's interest. There is a great deal of promise to come, and the steps are clear. We should begin the march.

Leif Edvinsson and Åke Freij

12

Skandia: Three Generations of Intellectual Capital

Intellectual capital (IC) management is a concept that has been evolving at Skandia over the past several years. In 1991 Skandia's Assurance and Financial Services (AFS) was looking for a way to develop and explain our strategic innovations that created long-term savings solutions for AFS customers. We had been investing our financial capital into upgrading employee abilities on several different levels. For some employees, we had been investing in their time and energy to develop new approaches to designing new and innovative financial and savings products. For others, we had been investing in their learning about how to develop more effective pathways to our agents and salespeople. And for still others, we had been investing in teaching them how to advise clients of the benefits of the new savings solutions for them, their children, and their grandchildren. All these were hidden investments from a traditional accounting point of view.

Because we knew that our investments were producing a new kind of value, one that was not visible, we had to create new tools to allow us to identify and visualize this new, "hidden" value. The tools we developed evolved out of an initial concept called *intellectual capital*. This chapter presents an overview of how intellectual capital and intellectual capital management progressed at Skandia AFS.

Since 1991 AFS has evolved away from a traditional and conservative employee-laden structure toward a virtual (networked) organization combining employees, contractors, alliances with specialized companies, and independent asset managers and distributors. During this time we have minimized the overhead of in-house functions and have thereby become able to take advantage of the benefits of the knowledge and capabilities of a range of specialists and organizations without having to incur the fixed costs of their partnership. The idea of "virtualizing" our operations—combining nested cores of employees who design and manage savings products with a range of nonemployee but nonetheless closely allied external resources—has significantly reduced overhead costs and increased productivity and value creation. Our evolved capability is like the ripples that appear in a pond when one drop of water strikes the surface; Skandia's core employees represent the initial drop of water and the ripples carry their ideas, products, and innovations to our customers through a virtual network of contractors and alliances (see diagram 1).

To manage this virtual organization, we invested heavily in information technology. The infrastructure created by these investments was designed to emanate outward, from a core system for managing the independent fund managers and their funds to a range of solutions for the delivery of products and services; those solutions enable independent but allied distributors to market our

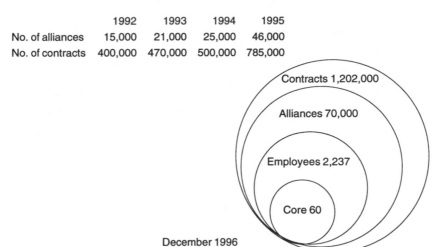

	1992	1993	1994	1995
No. of alliances	15,000	21,000	25,000	46,000
No. of contracts	400,000	470,000	500,000	785,000

Contracts 1,202,000

Alliances 70,000

Employees 2,237

Core 60

December 1996

Diagram 1. Skandia AFS as an Imaginary Organization

products to Skandia investors. Using this approach, we have created what we call "specialists in cooperation." The corresponding growth in our business has been tremendous, from $300 million in 1991 to $65 billion in 1997. AFS is now ranked fourth in the world in global investment-related insurance products.

The IC Function at AFS

In 1991, when the IC function was inaugurated by Skandia management, Leif Edvinsson was hired as director of intellectual capital. The IC function was established as a means of creating an effective interface among information technology, business development, and human resources. Edvinsson and his team defined IC as a combination of what they called human capital and structural capital. (Structural capital, in turn, included customer capital, intellectual property, and intangible assets, among other items.) Intellectual capital, together with the firm's financial capital, was defined as constituting the firm's market value.

Another way to view Skandia's perspective on its market value is as the future earnings capacity of the firm. For Skandia, as for many firms in the worldwide marketplace, their intangibles (or hidden value) have the most significant impact on the future earnings capability of the corporation.

The First Generation—Visualize and Measure

The first task of the IC function was to act as a missionary for IC within Skandia and eventually build a knowledge community involving both internal and external individuals and organizations. This community or network would include people from a wide range of functions: human resources, information technology, finance and accounting, and business development. One of the earliest tasks of this process was to find a new language for our conversations that included new words and definitions to describe the new and emerging concepts surrounding intellectual capital.

First we visualized the then current intellectual capital content in AFS operations and created an inventory of intellectual capital within the firm. That list, which evolved to encompass approximately fifty key items, was developed by the team and then intensively reviewed within the firm. From that initial "stock of intellectual capital," we looked for relationships between IC and the market value of AFS.

This early effort led to a prototype "balanced IC report" describing our hidden value to people outside Skandia. The prototype contained data collected from customer, human, process, and financial sources and attempted to create a common set of performance indicators for AFS. The data were also compiled into a document and distributed to Skandia top management and the board.

Because of the positive response to the initial internal reports, it was decided to develop and publish an IC supplement to the firm's 1994 annual financial report. The supplement described the overall concept of IC, the firm's model for processing it, and the firm's model for proceeding with further development of IC. The development model, called the *Skandia Navigator*, is a powerful graphic description of our evolving path for further developing and leveraging intellectual capital profitably within the firm.

Other IC supplements followed. The second supplement, focusing on renewal and development, accompanied the interim financial report for 1995. The third supplement, entitled "Value Creating Processes," described the relationship between IC, market value, and the future earnings of well-documented and stable business processes. The fourth supplement, entitled "The Power of Innovation," described the process of "futurizing" at Skandia, through the firm's newly created future centers. The fifth supplement focuses on customer value, visualizing a range of examples of value creation through each of the major components of customer capital: customer base, customer relationships, and customer potential. "Intelligent Enterprising" is the name of the latest published supplement.

The Second Generation—Flow and Multiply

The Skandia Navigator was created to guide us in creating innovative management and business development processes (see diagram 2). The Navigator is a management tool that aids in operative planning and strategic innovations. The five focuses of the Navigator are financial, customer, human, process, and renewal and development. The Navigator, like the North Star used by our Viking ancestors, is used by our company's leaders to keep the holistic view of business growth and sustainability.

The Navigator model has provided management with a balanced overview of our company's activities and our collective accessible intellectual capacity. Having used the Navigator model in day-to-day decision making, we feel better able to leverage both our structural capital and the capital of our strategic partners.

Targets: 1997   Weighted goal fulfillment: 90%

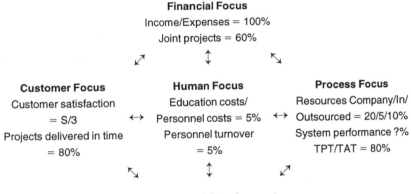

Financial Focus
Income/Expenses = 100%
Joint projects = 60%

Customer Focus
Customer satisfaction
= S/3
Projects delivered in time
= 80%

Human Focus
Education costs/
Personnel costs = 5%
Personnel turnover
= 5%

Process Focus
Resources Company/In/
Outsourced = 20/5/10%
System performance ?%
TPT/TAT = 80%

Renewal and Development
IT Development Costs = 85%
Number of projects using new technology = 5

Diagram 2. Skandia Navigator Model

Applying IC in the management of AFS leverages or multiplies the usefulness of our intellectual resources. To illustrate the results of the "multiplier effect" (i.e., globally recycling structural capital in various ways and multiplying it with local talent), we offer the following brief examples of using structural capital within AFS:

- Skandia start-ups in continental Europe (Switzerland, Germany, and Austria), begun in 1990, 1991, and 1994, achieved radical decreases in lead time to market and in money spent on the start-up.

- In a joint venture with several banks, we created a "reverse knowledge transfer," integrating some of our core processes into the new organization's business flow. In return, our partners offer a best-in-class product that complements our portfolio distribution channels.

- In our Spanish subsidiary, a tight focus on core value-creating processes has allowed a company of approximately one hundred people (some 40 percent of whom are involved in IT) to become one of the largest life assurance providers in Spain through cooperation with a savings bank network. Parenthetically, the company has one of the lowest cost ratios in the European insurance sector.

• In the United States our "specialist in cooperation" concept, with brokers as well as banks, has helped American Skandia rank among the market leaders in the variable annuity niche.

The Third Generation—Navigate and Futurize

In our early work, we created some initial drafts of simulations of IC value and the flows and correlations among the IC components. The work on these was inconclusive and went into a dormant stage following initial reviews and discussion. We are now looking at this effort again to see if we can develop management's capability, based on its actions, to use simulations to quantify the investments and changes in IC. We have drawn on work done by Intellectual Capital Services in England and the ICM Group in the United States as part of our basis for this effort. Our current exploration, called the IC Index Simulation, is under development for use within Skandia and is part of its continuing efforts to evolve the ideas and frameworks for IC that were laid out in 1992.

Skandia Future Centers.   Skandia sees the future as an asset. With this in mind, our next step was to establish the first Skandia Future Center (SFC) in Vaxholm, outside Stockholm. The aspiration is to train managers to be proactive by prototyping on future opportunities, adding to continuous renewal and development, and turning Skandia into an IC innovation company. Key activities at the Future Center so far include:

• The creation and training of Future Teams composed of Skandia people from around the world, representing a spectrum of talent. Throughthe SFC these teams are searching for the driving forces and key questions around future technology, demographics, the world economy, and new concepts in leadership.

- Three Generations Workshops, where employees from different age groups collaborate to share insights and foresights on various issues.

- Seminars on future accounting, featuring distinguished speakers such as Professor Baruch Lev of the New York University Stern School of Business Center for Research on Intangibles.

In the first twenty-four months since its opening in May 1996, SFC has had more than eight thousand visitors. In our continuing search to learn more about intellectual capital, Skandia is now aiming to establish what we call Universal Networking IC to increase the active collaboration with future-oriented organizations and individuals that create knowledge by sharing experiences. A next step in this process may be to establish a "Future Innpost" in California.

Where Is Skandia Now?

With more than five years of experience in managing intellectual capital, we have accrued an extensive amount of learning (we have created intellectual capital about intellectual capital). A list of our accomplishments in this area includes:

- IC reports to shareholders, once every six months, summarize important learnings and highlight the added value of our approach. (Two of these reports are in CD-ROM format.)

- The Navigator model has been adopted as a corporate management tool.

- The AFS Division Intranet-based Business Information System, called Dolphin, uses the Navigator model for its global management reporting structure in real time.

- Knowledge was developed at the Skandia Future Centers on how to build new organizations.

- The percentage of non-Swedish investors in Skandia rose to more than 70 percent. At the same time our valuation rose by an even higher percentage.

- The firm sponsored the world's first Mind Sports Olympiad in London, including a "Knowledge Café" with the theme "IC of the Future."

In addition to the above, we have also improved the AFS financial reporting processes, both in speed and in quality. We believe this combination of business results and continuous strategic renewal with supplementary IC reporting allows us to reduce the risk premium formerly demanded by investors for their financial investment in Skandia, thus adding to shareholders' value.

IC in the Future

Intellectual capital management at Skandia is a work in progress that involves the simultaneous practice of knowledge management and change management. To date we have accomplished this by emphasizing bench learning and stretching known management practices while carefully nourishing what we see as our future earnings capabilities. Because we see future value in the intangibles of knowledge creation and competence renewal, we see intellectual capital management as a

- Process and a journey into the unknown
- Continuous quest to learn which issues will shape the future
- Necessary action for corporate competitiveness and survival
- Quest to become more enterprising, not just more knowledgeable

We at Skandia hope that by telling our IC story we will encourage others to develop IC models for themselves. There is still much to accomplish, not only to put IC information on the same level of importance as accounting and financial information, but also to develop new models for IC practice and development. A number of institutions, companies, and groups are on similar routes of progress: Dow Chemical's development of intellectual asset management, former commissioner Steve Wallman's work at the U.S. Securities and Exchange Commission, and the ICM Gathering's intercompany learning about extracting value from intellectual capital. We encourage and support those and other activities that nourish new knowledge and applications for intellectual capital.

Gordon P. Petrash

13

Intellectual Capital Accounting as a Management Tool

Decades ago Joel Barker foresaw the significant contribution to corporate value generated by intellectual property and intangible assets. Barker, a futurist at Infinity Limited, predicted that corporate intellectual property would become more valuable than physical assets. Once so recognized, the importance of intangible assets has been rising steadily for the past thirty years and has accelerated in recent years. It is no coincidence that this acceleration coincides with the rapid growth of industries in the information technology center. The goal of this chapter is to address the need to find a better way to account for the intellectual capital of a corporation and a way in which this new intellectual capital accounting can contribute to effective management.

Tobin's Q, a formula developed by James Tobin of Yale University, provides a way to measure the value of corporate intangibles. Tobin proposed that if the market value of a corporation were divided by its book value, the results would yield a competency or service value ratio, that is,

$$\text{Tobin's Q} = \frac{\text{Market Value}}{\text{Book Value}} = \text{Service Value Ratio}$$

At Dow Chemical we have learned that this service value can also represent the intangible assets or the intellectual capital of a corporation or both. Dow's Tobin's Q, approximately three to one, indicates where investors think our source of strength exists. Similarly, the dollar value of intellectual capital can be derived by subtracting corporate book value from market capitalization. More than half the market value of Dow Chemical in 1996 was intellectual capital (see figure 1). Of course, this is not how the general public would tend to think of Dow's assets, but it is an accurate conclusion, nonetheless.

During the 1980s the shift in the market value to book value ratio highlighted the inadequacies of book value accounting. Today's analyses of this point are often led by data on Internet companies. Cisco Systems, as a dramatic example, had a book value of $4 billion and a market capitalization of $50 billion (1998, $100 billion).

Market analysts, investment and retirement fund managers, and large investors have, for many years, been calculating the value of corporations using a multitude of approaches, including complicated formulas and qualitative judgments. All employ the vast amount of information available on corporations, both public and private, including annual reports and required public disclosures (such as building permits, environmental impact studies, regulatory compliance reports, Securities and Exchange Commission [SEC] filings, and Occupational Safety and Health Administration performance records). Large amounts of information are also

$$\frac{\text{Corporate}}{\text{Market Value}} - \frac{\text{Corporate}}{\text{Book Value}} = \frac{\text{Intellectual}}{\text{Capital Value}}$$

$$\frac{\$24{,}530.4 \text{ million}}{(@ \ \$80/\text{share})} - \frac{\$8{,}364.86 \text{ million}}{(@ \ \$33/\text{share})} = \$16{,}165.54 \text{ million}$$

Figure 1. Intellectual Capital Accounting, Dow Chemical Company, 1996

available through employees, sales brochures, trade shows, indus-try conferences, patents, investor relations departments, and the media. Customers, suppliers, distributors, and competitor inter-actions are also ready sources of information. The bottom line is that there is a wealth of information available regarding any com-pany. Analysts and investors can assess this information to deter-mine the intellectual capital of a corporation, its "hidden value," and use it to generate market values that are substantially different from those suggested by traditional accounting.

Steve Wallman, while a commissioner at the SEC, observed an inequity in the way this intangible information is made available to interested parties. Influential analysts and large fund managers have easier access to corporate executives and information that is not typically made public. Strategic objectives, projected performance measures, new and emerging business opportunities, and the abil-ity of an organization's workforce to create and implement cor-porate strategy are just a few of the data points that can be con-veyed through these channels. Corporations and executives are always eager to impress significant investors because of their poten-tial impact on the stock price. The small investor is not treated the same way; his or her information is usually well filtered, inter-preted, or not made available in a timely manner. Formal account-ing of intellectual capital, in short, is one way to level the playing field. The SEC and the Financial Accounting Standards Board have studied and continue to study this issue.

Nonetheless, the challenge of measuring intellectual capital is that few existing measures and indexes that can be widely accepted and effectively used. Absolute quantifiable numbers and values break down when dealing with intangibles. There is just not enough accounting precedent to draw from to allow consistent and accurate valuations.

Yet most of what organizations measure in the area of intellectual assets falls into the process/indicator category. Frequent mention is made of strength and depth of customer relationships, capabilities and loyalty of employees and suppliers, robustness and utility of the organizational knowledge base, market recognition of brand names and processes surrounding development, and utilization of intellectual property.

The Dow Experience

Our experience at Dow has led to the following observations relevant to new intellectual capital measures:

- Intellectual capital measures are necessary—in today's business environment few initiatives can progress without pertinent measures.

- Everything can be measured—selecting the *relevant* measure is the challenge.

- Keeping measures pertinent, current, and accurate is critical.

- The process of measuring has value—trying to develop measures is an effective way of building consensus and determining the key variables critical to success, as well as relationships among them.

- If you can visualize it, you can measure it, and if you can measure it, you can manage it for continuous improvement.

- Measures are tools to enable "somebody" to make decisions.

- The most effective measures are those that are simple, drive strategic intent, and are actionable.

- Measures of intangibles are highly sensitive to context: time, location, and complementary assets.

- Intangible measures stated in ranges are more appropriate than absolute measures.

- Measures that show direction and velocity (similar to vector analysis in physics) are much more effective than static, historical data points.

- Many so-called quantitative measures are in fact compilations of qualitative inputs.

- There are two types of measures: (1) *value* measures—the end result—and (2) *process* measures—indicators that allow prediction of achieving value measures.

Several of Dow's business units are using indicator and value target measures to better integrate intellectual asset management into their business strategies (see figure 2). Consider the value targets of percent of current sales protected by intellectual assets. If 50 percent of sales in a particular business are protected by intellectual assets that provide competitive advantage (ability to command a higher price or gain greater market share), the business strategy must address the maintenance and renewal of these assets. This effort, in turn, can cut across all functional areas, including finance, marketing, production, and development.

The most important value target is the sum of net present value (NPV) of the business attributable to intellectual assets (IA) for value growth and value preservation, each calculated separately (see figure 2). This metric can be dramatically affected by factors such as the failure of a customer to renew a contract, competitive breakthroughs, development of blocking technologies, or even

Value Targets
- NPV of value growth and value preservation attributable to intellectual assets (IA)
- Percent of current sales protected by IA (that business is using)
- Percent of IA that business will use *not* aligned with technology plans
- Percent of new business initiatives protected by IA that business will use
- Percent of business-relevant competitive IA that requires specific response
- Value contributed to the business by significant IA management actions

Measurement Indicators
- Projected costs until expiration
- Percent of annual intellectual assets management (IAM) costs of research and development (R&D) budget
- Ratio of NPV apportioned to IA to net present cost of R&D per period
- Percent of competitive samples analyzed that initiate business actions by purpose (e.g., enforcement, benchmarking, product development)
- Percent of business using IA
- Percent of IA business will use more than five years after priority filing
- Qualitative value classification as a percent of projected costs (e.g., what percent of portfolio costs are for defensive cases, potential license cases, key cases)

Figure 2. Examples of Dow's Pilot Value Targets and Indicators

litigation. The measure clearly reflects current assumptions about IA strengths, risks, and opportunities. Most critically, requiring businesses to document their assumptions creates organizational memory that can be used to guide, analyze, or evaluate future decision-making processes.

Another important indicator is the ratio of NPV apportioned to IA to net present cost of research and development (R&D) for a given period (see figure 2). Using this ratio as a form of return on investment helps the business visualize R&D as a capitalized investment rather than an expense. This analysis treats intellectual asset management costs as a part of the R&D capitalized investment. The data can be evaluated to set an internal competitive standard for intellectual asset management, resource allocation, and planning.

Despite our success in finding good management value in taking into account intellectual capital, much work needs to be done. The effort will take time and experimentation. This should not stop organizations from recognizing and utilizing best practices in managing intellectual capital. Instead, it should encourage innovation.

Value creation through the management and utilization of intellectual capital is a necessary strategic objective of every company. Improved management processes that are aligned with strategic objectives and that fully leverage intellectual assets are a source of competitive advantage. Meanwhile, the fast pace and sophistication of global competition are making differentiation more difficult. Successful products and services are quickly imitated by aggressive competitors; profit margins are increasingly under pressure. Shorter product life cycles, employee movement from company to company, and customer demand for "more, better, and cheaper" products and services are all part of a complicated equation that challenges organizations in all industries. This is particularly true in regard to the need to "stand out" in a crowded field. In the midst of this turbulence, firms can find and sustain uniqueness through their own style of managing, including the development of and accounting for intellectual capital. Their future, in fact, depends on it.

Patrick H. Sullivan

Extracting Profits from Intellectual Capital: Policy and Practice

Intellectual capital is a topic of increasing interest to firms that derive their profits from innovation and knowledge. In many cases, these knowledge firms find that the marketplace values them at a price far higher than their balance sheets warrant. What is the true value of a company like Microsoft? It is more than the tangible assets: The company's value is in its intangible intellectual assets as well as its ability to convert those assets into revenues. The market premium for Microsoft and other knowledge companies is in their intellectual capital as well as the firm's ability to systematically leverage it. But, surprisingly, few managers in knowledge firms can define intellectual capital—what it is, where it resides in their firm, and how they manage it in order to produce profits for their shareholders.

Companies that make their profits by converting knowledge

into value are called *knowledge companies*. As a practical matter, those companies whose profits come predominantly from commercializing innovations are at the core of the knowledge company definition. Companies such as Microsoft, 3M, and Netscape are firms whose knowledge or intellectual capital are their major assets. They are clear-cut examples of knowledge firms. Other firms, whose profits come largely from commercializing their innovations but whose commercialization requires large and expensive business assets (such as manufacturing facilities and distribution networks), are also considered here to be knowledge firms as far as the management of their intellectual capital is concerned.

This chapter describes how a number of major international corporations have been successfully extracting profits from their intellectual capital and the innovative way in which these companies have been viewing their intellectual capital (IC) and some of the methods they have developed for harvesting profits (as well as other forms of value) from this new form of capital. The companies referenced in this chapter make up an informal interest group called the ICM Gathering, all of whose member companies are actively managing their intellectual capital (see exhibit 1). The ICM Gathering companies meet to discuss and share ideas and methods around the extraction of value from intellectual capital.

What is intellectual capital? Is intellectual capital, as one company defined it, "what walks out the door at the end of the business day"? Is it the people? A firm's know-how? Intellectual capital, as assessed by the companies in the ICM Gathering, is the sum of a firm's ideas, inventions, technologies, general knowledge, computer programs, designs, data skills, processes, creativity, and publications. The ICM Gathering thus developed a definition of intellectual capital that has served them well ever since: *Intellectual capital is knowledge that can be converted into profits*. For these companies, intellectual capital is made up of two major elements: human capital and intellectual assets.

Air Liquide (France)	Monsanto
Avery-Dennison	Neste (Finland)
Dow Chemical Company	Rockwell International
DuPont	Rosenbluth International
Eastman Chemical	S.A.Armstrong (Canada)
Hewlett-Packard	Skandia, AFS (Sweden)
Hoffman La Roche	Xerox
ICM Group	

Exhibit 1.   Membership of the ICM Gathering

- *Human capital* consists of a company's individual employees, each of whom has skills, abilities, knowledge, and know-how. To take advantage of any of those, the employee (an individual "unit" of human capital) must be physically positioned wherever that skill, ability, or bit of knowledge is to be used. Within each employee resides the tacit (uncodified) knowledge the firm seeks to utilize.

- *Intellectual assets* are created whenever the human capital commits to paper (or any other form of media) any bit of knowledge, know-how, or learning. Once "written," the knowledge is codified and defined. At this point, the firm can move the intellectual asset, rather than the individual, to wherever it is needed. Examples of intellectual assets include plans, procedures, memos, sketches, drawings, blueprints, and computer programs, to name but a few. Any items in this list that are legally protected are called *intellectual property*. Intellectual property includes patents, copyrights, trademarks, and trade secrets.

Think of the intellectual capital of the firm as shown in exhibit 2. Imagine that the large shaded box represents the firm's intellectual capital. Inside the box are its two major elements: human capital (people) and intellectual assets (paper). The portion of the

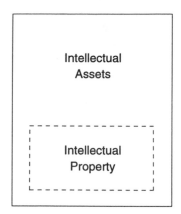

Exhibit 2. A Model of Intellectual Capital

firm's intellectual assets that are legally protected is called intellectual property.

Note that the firm does not own the human capital. Employees are not owned by the firm; they may quit, be fired, take leaves of absence, or in many other ways sever their working relationship with the firm. The firm *does*, however, own its intellectual assets: These were created by the human capital in the firm's employ and are now the property of the company. With this in mind, it is in the firm's best interest to encourage employees to codify their knowledge so that the firm may have more opportunities to leverage it into profits.

But intellectual capital by itself is not sufficient for a knowledge firm to succeed. The intellectual capital must be supplemented by yet a third "capital," representing the firm's infrastructure. This final element making up the model of a knowledge company, then, is called *structural capital* and includes all the items found on the balance sheet: financial assets, buildings, machinery, and the infrastructure of the firm. Structural capital also includes the complementary business assets that are often necessary to convert an innovative idea into a salable product or service. (Complementary business assets include such necessary business elements as manufacturing facilities, distribution capabilities, and sales outlets.) Adding structural capital to intellectual capital provides a much more accurate picture of what constitutes a knowledge company (see exhibit 3).

What Companies Are Doing

Companies that operate according to the model presented in exhibit 3 may focus their intellectual capital management activity on different portions of the model. For example, two major chemical companies see the major focus of their IC work in the intellectual asset portion of the model; their unprotected intellectual assets are the most likely source of new or innovative products. Hence, their focus is in identifying and managing their intellectual assets. Other firms, such as tightly managed computer and product companies, have innovation management systems that allow them to focus their IC activities on selecting only the best technologies to be patented and commercialized. This puts the focus of their IC activity at the frontier between intellectual assets and intellectual properties.

Companies desiring to create a large portfolio of ideas need to encourage their human capital to codify knowledge and know-how; from this knowledge they can select the most promising ideas for commercialization in the marketplace. Such firms operate at the interface between human capital and intellectual assets. Still other firms are involved in all of the foregoing and place themselves at the juxtaposition of human capital, intellectual assets, and intellectual property (see exhibit 4, which illustrates where a number of the ICM Gathering companies focus their intellectual capital management activity).

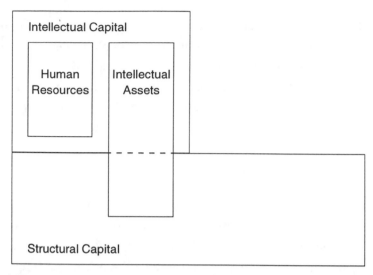

Exhibit 3. Model of a Knowledge Company

Value and the Economic Paradigm

To the economist, value is a measure of the utility that an item brings to its owner. Utility is often viewed as a stream of benefits, stretching into the future, that an owner foresees as the rent he receives from owning the item. Utility may be measured in a number of ways. To the visual artist, utility may be the pleasure his or her work gives to the viewer. To the designer, utility may be the functionality of a design. To the accountant, utility may be measured in the accuracy of historical expenditure data. To the economist, however, utility is most often measured in dollar terms.

Economists typically view a future stream of benefits in dollar terms and can discount and sum these amounts to determine the current dollar equivalent of a future stream of income. This dis- counting and summing calculation is the determination of the net present value of a future stream of benefits. Looked at through

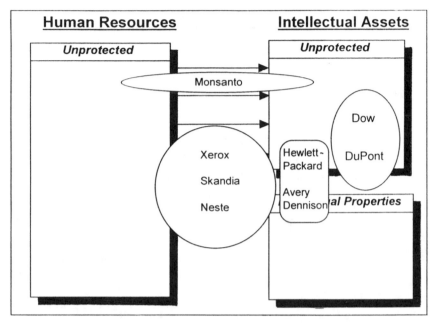

Exhibit 4. How Some ICM Gathering Companies Map Themselves

economic eyes, then, the knowledge firm would be expected to create knowledge for future commercialization and extract current profits from existing knowledge. Hence, we have come to describe the knowledge firm's two basic IC functions as *value creation* and *value extraction*.

- *Value creation* is primarily an activity that involves the firm's human capital. It is the set of activities that creates new knowledge through learning or knowledge acquisition. It also includes those activities associated with systematizing or institutionalizing the firm's processes for knowledge creation.

- *Value extraction* involves harvesting the level and degree of value required to achieve the strategic vision and long-term objectives of the firm.

Using the value extraction perspective, firms may be categorized as practicing one of three types of management:

1. *Intellectual property management.* Firms with significant le-
    gally protected intellectual assets (called intellectual prop-
    erty) focus on generating more intellectual properties as
    well as on leveraging them in the marketplace. First these
    firms develop a portfolio of defined intellectual properties,
    then they devise the broadest number of avenues for com-
    mercializing the properties in the portfolio. Intellectual
    property managers are typically tactically oriented, dealing
    with the near term and seeking profits sooner rather than
    later.

2. *Intellectual asset management.* Firms that seek to increase
    significantly the flow of innovations that can be considered
    for patenting and for commercialization focus their energies
    on the broader set of intellectual assets, the unprotected as
    well as the protected. Their management systems and pro-
    cesses are more complex because they deal with many more
    kinds of commercializable assets than just legally protected
    ones. Most often firms that operate with IAM are large and
    sophisticated, with access to the vast internal resources
    needed to identify, evaluate, and leverage the intellectual
    assets. Intellectual asset managers operate both tactically
    and strategically, with near- to midterm profits from the
    company's intellectual assets in mind, as well as longer-
    term strategic positioning.

3. *Intellectual capital management.* A few firms operate accord-
    ing to the strategic opportunities offered by the IC view of
    their firm. For example, the intellectual capital of the
    knowledge firm (its driving force) can be displayed exter-
    nally in a manner that describes and defines the company's

ability to harness its hidden value as a powerful tool for leveraging itself into the future. Further, the IC perspective helps determine the degree to which the intellectual capital of the firm is balanced and aligned with the firm's vision. Experience shows that most knowledge firms have significant imbalances between the actual deployment of their intellectual capital and a deployment that would move them more rapidly toward their vision.

Although worldwide only two or three dozen firms are systematically extracting value from their intellectual capital, hundreds of firms would like to do so. What stops companies in the second group from moving into the first is not knowing where and how to begin. Most companies wishing to develop the capability for managing their intellectual capital have little or no understanding of what it takes. Members of the ICM Gathering all report that they receive dozens if not hundreds of calls each year from companies asking to visit and to learn how ICM is done. Anxious to share what they've learned, they agree to a meeting. But as they describe all the things necessary—knowledge of company context, decision processes, work processes, databases, and know-how—the visitors' eyes soon glaze, overwhelmed by what they are hearing. They thought that the secret to intellectual capital management was one or two key concepts and maybe two or three pieces of software. Finding out that installing an ICM capability involves defining the firm's business philosophy, its vision and values, decision processes involving senior executives . . . well, it is just too much!

Managing intellectual capital, like many worthwhile business activities, involves a commitment. It involves developing a capability that results from a logical and systematic set of activities, beginning with a crisp understanding of the firm's purpose and direction and carefully crafting mechanisms to produce a desired set of results. Below I discuss each step in the process and provide suggestions about how steps may be accomplished most successfully.

The Vision

To begin with, the firm must know where it is going. What is its vision for itself in the future? What kind of firm does it aspire to become? Any journey without a destination may be interesting, enriching, and educational, but it will be neither direct nor without frustration. Remember Alice and the Cheshire Cat—*when you don't know where you are going, then any path will do*. The first step is to make sure that a long-term vision exists.

Once a company's formal vision statement is available, or a working vision where a formal statement is not available, the next step is to know the company's strategy for achieving that vision. Many companies have a well-known and articulated strategy; others do not. For those lacking a formal strategy, a statement describing the firm's de facto strategy may be created. For purposes of the ICM capability-building "project," a working strategy adequately substitutes for a formal one.

The Context

Companies, like individuals, exist in a world of their own; that is, each company has a unique set of aspirations, strengths, weaknesses, resources, culture, values, external realities, internal dynamics, personalities, politics, and worldview. No two companies have the same context, even companies in the same or similar business or industry. Coke and Pepsi, both alike in many ways, have different contexts. They may share many of the same external realities but differ in their internal realities. No two firms are alike in context. And it is the firm's context that determines much of what is considered possible, achievable, or even valuable. Context is why an idea that is rejected at one firm as silly or unworkable is seen by another as creative, insightful, or valuable. A firm wishing to create a capability for managing its intellectual capital does well to articulate its context, for context will determine what kinds of capability the firm will support.

Context is usually made up of three major elements: the business description, the external realities, and the internal realities. For each of these, few firms have an accurate (or politically acceptable) description. Most often, a firm's "party line" describes the view it wishes people to accept as contrasted with a description of what is. The exercise of defining the firm's context is an exercise in defining "what is."

Business Description

Most firms have literature describing themselves, their products or services, and their markets. Unfortunately, for many firms, these do not accurately describe the firm's true business. Some years ago Standard Oil (Esso) decided it wasn't really in the oil business, it was in the energy business. Exit Esso stage left, enter Exxon stage right! Rockwell International, a manufacturer of semiconductor chips and chipsets for fax modems, recently decided it was not in the fax modem business but rather in the personal communications business. Deciding on the firm's true business is an important precondition to understanding the role of intellectual assets.

The External Context

The forces in the external environment of the firm that drive change in the economy, the industry, and the business make up the external context of the firm. Most firms can describe the forces that most immediately affect their business: changes in the price of raw materials, the general state of the economy, competing products, or competitive thrusts. But few know or can define the forces that underlie these near-term forces for change. The external context of the firm includes the macroeconomic, legislative, regulatory, technological, and sociopolitical forces that create the firm's business environment. We need to define, describe, and know the nature of those forces and their impact on the firm. Once known, those forces can be categorized by their major and minor effects and how they are expected to be felt in the immediate, mid- or long term. The key external forces for change, and their leading indicators, must be determined and monitored.

The Internal Context

The internal context is in many ways easier to determine because much of it is already known, if not yet fully gathered together. The internal context usually includes

- The firm's vision, strategy and business goals (as stated above)
- The firm's values and culture
- An assessment of the firm's strengths and weaknesses to perform in the business it is truly in
- Strategies available to the firm, not only those it is pursuing but alternate strategies it could pursue to achieve its vision
- Current performance against goals
- Potential usefulness of IC/intellectual assets/intellectual property in achieving the company's vision and strategy
- Current posture of the company on ICM (favorably disposed, strongly against, etc.)

Having defined the three major elements of context for the firm, it is particularly helpful to document what has been learned. Some firms have created a context document or internal report that captures this information. Such a report might outline information in the following way:

- The strategic vision of the firm
- Definition of the business the firm is in
- Macroenvironmental forces
  - Overview of macroenvironment
  - Key forces for change
- Definition of the firm's products and services
  - Where each is in its product life cycle
- Definition of the basis for competition
  - Cost
  - Differentiation
    - Dimensions of differentiation
- Description and definition of the technology strategy
- Current firm performance
  - Measures of performance

The Role(s) for Intellectual Capital

Once the firm's vision and strategy are known, the role(s) for intellectual capital can be defined. For many technology-based knowledge companies, the role of the human capital is to create patentable innovations that are consistent with the company's line of products and services. For these companies, the role for value extraction is constrained to defensive use: protection and exclusive exploitation of protected innovations. In addition to assuring exclusive use, defensive use of the firm's intellectual assets includes assurances of freedom to practice a technology in the future as well as avoiding litigation.

But increasingly firms are realizing that intellectual capital can be part of a strategic offense. Firms may use intellectual capital to generate new or otherwise unanticipated streams of revenue. Firms may use the portfolio to generate income they otherwise might have forgone. They may license core or strategic technologies into new markets that do not compete with their strategic or core markets. They may license or sell outdated strategic technologies in existing markets. They may license both core and noncore technologies in nonstrategic markets. Companies may also create de facto technology standards by cross licensing with business or technology competitors to create a market for yet-to-be-developed technologies. They may simply license out company technology because its widespread use may create a de facto standard, thereby forcing competitors to seek a license to produce products or services consistent with the new standard. Finally, many companies, having learned that they cannot afford to maintain the range of competencies and skills required to sustain their product line, are creating strategic alliances with firms that have the needed capabilities. Successful negotiations with such alliance partners are often enabled by the presence of strong portfolios of intellectual assets and intellectual properties.

Still another role for intellectual capital may lie in using it to strategically position the firm. Making the outside world aware of the firm's capabilities, its stocks of IC as well as its ability to leverage them, may position the firm in a marketplace or provide access to capital in the financial markets that otherwise might either not be available or at least not be available on favorable terms.

Whether the roles for intellectual capital are determined to be tactical or strategic, immediate or long term, internally or externally oriented, intellectual capital can play many roles in firms who have carefully decided where they wish to go. Such decisions make it easier to determine how intellectual capital, as well as other strategic assets of the firm, may be used to achieve the desired results.

The Management Capability

Once the roles for intellectual capital are determined, it becomes incumbent on the managers of the firm's intellectual capital to develop the internal capabilities for exploiting it in meaningful ways. Beginning with the technology-based knowledge company, this section describes where and how to begin creating the capability for managing intellectual capital.

BEGIN WITH THE IP PORTFOLIO

This section pertains to the companies having one or more portfolios of intellectual properties. For such companies, the place to begin is with the best-defined portfolio of intellectual properties. Typically this is the portfolio of patents.

Defining the Portfolio. Managing intellectual properties means first defining the properties to be managed. For companies owning patents or the rights to patents, these constitute the company's portfolio. The first question to be asked is what does the portfolio contain? Are the patents known? (Surprisingly, there are many companies who cannot define the patents they own.) Companies should be able to describe their portfolio in a number of ways: numbers of patents; the groupings of patents by technology, by intended business use; and the remaining life in the patents by income-generation capability and by time-horizon of expected use.

Designing the IPM System. Begin by describing the IP management system the firm ultimately wishes to create. Include the basic functional elements as well as the decision processes, their supporting work processes, and databases. The system design at this stage should be at the overview level. (Detailed design information is not necessary at this early stage, and could even be nonproductive.) The overview IPM system design developed here becomes the template the firm works toward implementing (see exhibit 5).

Defining the Portfolio Database.   In addition to hard copies of each patent, effective patent management demands a computer file containing useful information on each patent, including information needed for decisions at several levels: portfolio management, tactical business decisions, and strategic business decisions.

Establishing the Competitive Assessment Activity.   Fundamental to managing the firm's intellectual property is knowing what the competition is about. This means that the firm needs to know, for both its business and its technology competitors, what it has produced, what its current position and capabilities are, what its strategies are, and what action can be expected from it in the future. Competitive assessment should be performed by people with business as well as technical and analytic backgrounds. Many technology firms try to convert technologists into business analysts on the assumption that business analysis is relatively easy if one has a scientific or analysis background. Make no mistake, business analysis requires the kind of special training found in business or economics programs at a university. Anything less than this level of training is not recommended.

Creating a Patent Policy for the Firm.   In an ideal world, businesses would only develop innovations that are in line with the strategy or that enable the vision. Our world is, unfortunately, less than ideal. Innovators produce what they produce, and these innovations are not all necessarily on target for the vision or the strategy. To make decision making easier, firms have found that a policy establishing guidelines for what the firm wishes to patent is desirable. Patent policies span a range of possibilities. For example, a company might patent

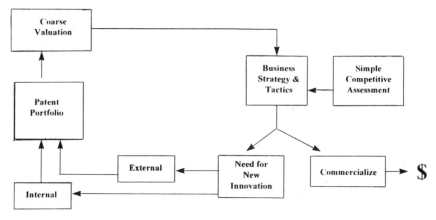

Exhibit 5. Simple IP Management System

- So as to have a portfolio with which to negotiate business agreements (licenses, joint ventures, alliances, et al.) with other companies
- Most things that have a chance of technical success
- Only those discoveries that have a strong chance of technical success regardless of potential business application or use
- Only those discoveries that have a clear application to your own company's products or processes
- Those patent discoveries that might block or delay similar discoveries by competitors
- Most things that are patentable
- Only the occasional discovery of exceptional importance
- Nothing

Regularizing the Patent Generation Process. All technology firms have some kind of process that produces innovations targeted for patenting. Not all the innovations produced are of patentable quality; even if they were, the firm might not wish to invest in patenting them. Although the patenting policy provides one level of decision-making guidance, many more innovations may clear the policy guideline hurdle than the firm wishes to patent. The decision to patent is best made in the context of the firm's business strategy, the amount of budget it has reserved to cover the costs of patenting, and the set of patentable innovations available for consideration. Firms wishing to ensure an adequate flow of innovations into its patent decision process create information processes that highlight innovations under development. This makes it easier for firms to know whether sufficient numbers of innovations are in process to meet their strategic needs, whether too many are in progress in one technology area and not enough in another, or whether enough innovations are in progress at all. The firm's existing processes for knowing what is in the pipeline and for making the patent decision must be regularized and efficient enough for the firm to know that it has a sufficient number and quality of innovations to meet its needs.

Developing a Valuation Process.   Creating the capability for people within the organization to develop both qualitative and dollar-based estimates of the value of the firm's intellectual assets should provide a range of valuation methods providing dollar values ranging from coarse valuation to fine.

Developing a Value Extraction Analysis Capability.   For each technology with the potential for commercialization, several questions must be asked and answered before the company can decide to invest in commercialization, including, Which combination of conversion mechanisms should the firm use to extract the most value from the innovation? Should the firm sell the innovation, license it, joint venture to obtain necessary complementary assets, enter into a strategic alliance to obtain access to markets, integrate everything, or donate the technology for a tax benefit? Each technology requires an analysis to determine how many conversion mechanisms the firm can use to obtain the best profits.

Create a Licensing/Joint Venture/Alliance Capability.   Once the firm has decided to commercialize an innovation, it needs to make the commercialization happen. In many cases this means commercializing the innovation through licensing, joint venturing, or entering into a strategic alliance. Firms must develop an office or a capability that will be able to expeditiously develop license, joint venture, and strategic alliance agreements and execute them for the firm.

MANAGING INTELLECTUAL ASSETS

By this point, firms having created the foregoing capabilities have also developed a systematic approach that they can expand to manage their intellectual assets. An intellectual asset management capability typically involves expanding and enhancing the portfolio(s) and the competitive assessment function.

Developing Portfolios of Nonprotected Assets.   A portfolio (and databases) for nonprotected intellectual assets with commercial use or interest might include licenses (both in- and outlicenses), nondisclosure agreements, joint venture agreements, outsourcing contracts and service agreements, IA aspects of mergers and acquisitions, and customer lists.

Developing IT Links between Portfolios.   Links between the IA portfolio databases might include company names, names of individuals, technologies, products, and services.

Expanding Competitive Assessment.   Developing the IA level of competitive assessment may involve gathering information about the specific marketplace positions and long-term strategies of competitors to determine the specific value of current and potential portfolios based on their effect on competitors (e.g., infringements and design-arounds, as well as predicted competitor response to potential strategic thrusts).

Creating Litigation Avoidance Analytic Capability.   Knowing when and how a company is at risk of infringement litigation is important. Perhaps of even greater importance is the degree to which potential litigants may be infringing on a firm's intellectual property or knowing if a competitor has previously signed a non-disclosure agreement or is party to a contract or supplier agreement. All this information is part of a viable litigation avoidance capability.

MANAGING INTELLECTUAL CAPITAL

Firms managing their intellectual capital are strategically focused in managing *both* the human and the "paper" assets of the firm. For technology companies, the building block capabilities are already in place. But nontechnology companies need to create all of the following:

Competitive Assessment. Here competitive assessment focuses on the business and technology competitors but, in addition, focuses on the technology of competitive products, services, and markets, in particular on the competitors' human capital as well as on their technology.

Human Capital Management. In managing the firm's human capital it is important to know the current and ideal use of its human resources. What is the ideal allocation or alignment of the firm's human capital for achieving near-term goals? Long-term goals? What is its actual current alignment? What is the value creation focus of the human capital? What is the know-how the human capital has created? How is this know-how defined? How may it be described? How does the firm access it? Commercialize it? How can or how has the firm developed systems to institutionalize the management of its human capital?

Human Capital Measurement. How does the firm define, describe, and measure its intellectual capital? What kinds of knowledge does the firm's human capital generate? What is the breadth and what are the levels of knowledge created?

Intellectual Capital Reports. What kinds of reports does the firm have or wish to have about its intellectual capital? Internal reports? Actual or potential external reports? Do these include measures of key intellectual capital activities? Do they include valuations of the firm's human capital?

Summary

This chapter set out to explain how a set of companies, all actively managing their intellectual capital assets, might view intellectual capital and what actions they might take to extract more value from their intangible assets. In describing the methods for creating definitions, frameworks, and capabilities, the chapter has presented a general method for managing intangible assets.

Intangible assets, when viewed as a business asset that can be harvested, may be categorized by a time horizon. For example, the foregoing has shown both tactical and strategic uses and value for intangibles. The tactical may involve the immediate or near-term conversion of assets into cash; the strategic or long-term may involve using intangibles to position the firm in its external environment.

Tactical value extraction requires the close coordination of a range of intellectual capital activities that revolves around the technology or technologies to be commercialized. These activities are conducted at the level of intellectual property management (IPM) or intellectual asset management (IAM).

IPM concerns the activities, decision processes, work processes, and databases used for commercializing individual *patented technologies or innovations.*

IAM considers the broader set of intellectual assets that include both legally protected and nonprotected intellectual assets. It too concerns the activities, decision process, work processes, and databases used for commercializing and *obtaining additional extracted value from the firm's intellectual assets and innovations.*

Strategic value extraction by knowledge companies is typically concerned with the firm's future or its long-term value extraction needs. Firms involved with strategic value extraction activity are usually involved with aligning their intellectual capital with the firm's long-term interests or concerns. The strategic value extraction activities usually concern using the intellectual capital of the firm as a basis or building block on which to define the vision; aligning intellectual capital resources with the vision and strategy to enable their achievement quickly and efficiently; reporting externally to the financial markets on the firm's strategic uses of intellectual capital; and the implications of these uses on the firm's long-term ability to create value for shareholders.

Whether tactical or strategic, long- or near-term, extracting value from intellectual capital is an emerging field of management. A number of large international corporations have made major investments in extracting profits from their intangible assets. Other firms can follow in their footsteps. Creating the capability for extracting value from intellectual capital is not difficult, but it does require a commitment to creating a nontraditional view of the firm that supplements the standard business framework. It involves creating a series of interlocking capabilities, each consistent with the firm's general business model and each uniquely focused on the firm's intellectual assets.

This approach to developing profits for knowledge companies, although novel, is working in sophisticated companies. It can work for others as well.

Appendix—Bibliography on Intellectual Capital

INTELLECTUAL CAPITAL

Brooking, A. *Intellectual Capital*. London: International Thomson Business Press, 1996.

Edvinsson, L., and P. Sullivan. *Developing Model for Managing Intellectual Capital*. *European Management Journal* 14, no. 4 (August, 1996).

Edvinsson, L., and M. S. Malone. *Intellectual Capital, Realizing Your Company's True Value by Finding Its Hidden Brainpower*. New York: Harper Collins, 1997.

Hudson, W. J. *Intellectual Capital, How to Build It, Enhance It, Use It.* New York: John Wiley & Sons, 1993.

Klein, D. A., and L. Prusak. "Characterizing Intellectual Capital." Multi-Client Program Working Paper, Ernst & Young, March 1994.

Parr, R., and P. H. Sullivan. *Technology Licensing—Corporate Strategies for Maximizing Value.* New York: John Wiley & Sons, 1996.

Petrash, G. *Dow's Journey to a Knowledge Value Management Culture. European Management Journal* 14, no. 4 (August 1996).

Stewart, T. *Intellectual Capital: The New Wealth of Organizations.* New York: Doubleday, 1997.

Stewart, T., "Brainpower," *Fortune,* June 3, 1991, p. 44.

Stewart, T. "Your Company's Most Valuable Asset: Intellectual Capital," *Fortune,* October 3, 1994.

Sullivan, S. *Insights into Commercializing Technology. Les Nouvelles,* March 1993, pp. 30–35.

Teece, D., "Profiting from Technological Innovation: Implications for Integration, Collaboration, Licensing and Public Policy. *Research Policy* 15 (1986): pp. 285–305.

Knowledge Management

Manville, B., and N. Foote. "Strategy as If Knowledge Mattered," *Fast Company.*

Nonaka, I., and H. Takeuchi. *The Knowledge Creating Company.* New York: Oxford University Press, 1995.

Williams, R. L., and W. R. Bukowitz. *Knowledge Managers Guide Information Seekers. HRM Magazine,* January 1997, pp. 77–81.

MEASUREMENT

Organization for Economic Cooperation and Development (OECD). *Measuring What People Know: Human Capital Accounting for the Knowledge Economy.* Paris: OECD, 1996.

Conference Board. *New Corporate Performance Measures,* Report Number 1118-95-RR, Conference Board, 1995.

Kaplan, R. S., and D. P. Norton. *Translating Strategy into Action: The Balanced Scorecard.* Boston: Harvard Business School Press, 1996.

Lucas, C. "Visualize, Measure and Manage." Working paper, Dow Chemical Company, 1996.

Sveiby, K. E. *The New Organizational Wealth, Managing & Measuring Knowledge-Based Assets.* San Francisco: Berrett-Koehler Publishers, Inc., 1997.

Wallman, Steven M. H. *Regulation for a New World. Business Law Today,* November/December 1996, pp. 8–13.

Wallman, Steven M. H. Preface to *Securities Regulation in Cyberspace* (Bowne & Co., 1997).

Wallman, Steven M. H. *Technology Takes to Securities Trading. IEEE Spectrum*, February 1997, pp. 60–64.

STRATEGY

Hamel, G., and C. K. Prahalad. *Competing for the Future*. Boston: Harvard Business School Press, 1994.

Hamel, G., and C. K. Prahalad. "Strategic Intent." *Harvard Business Review*, May–June, 1989, pp. 67–78.

Imparato, N., and O. Harari. *Jumping the Curve, Innovation and Strategic Choice in an Age of Transition*. San Francisco: Jossey-Bass Publishers, 1996.

Lewis, J. D. *The Connected Corporation*. New York: Free Press, 1995.

Porter, M. *Competitive Strategy—Techniques for Analyzing Industries and Competitors*. New York: Free Press, 1980.

Porter, M. *Competitive Advantage—Creating and Sustaining Superior Performance*. New York: Free Press, 1985.

Porter, M. "What Is Strategy?" *Harvard Business Review*, November–December, 1996, pp. 61–78.

Prahalad, C. K., and G. Hamel. "The Core Competence of the Corporation," *Harvard Business Review*, May–June 1990, pp. 79–91.

Savage, C. *Fifth Generation Management*. Boston: Butterworth-Heinemann, 1996.

Sullivan, P. H. "Strategic Vision—Creating the Future," unpublished paper, 1986.

TECHNOLOGY MANAGEMENT

Clark, K. B., R. H. Hayes, and C. Lorenz. *The Uneasy Alliance—Managing the Productivity-Technology Dilemma*. Boston: Harvard Business School Press, 1985.

Foster, R. *Innovation—The Attacker's Advantage*. New York: Summit Books, 1986.

Hayes, H. H., S. C. Wheelwright, and K. B. Clark. *Dynamic Manufacturing— Creating the Learning Organization*. New York: Free Press, 1988.

Rogers, E. M. *Diffusion of Innovations*, 3d edition. New York: Free Press, 1983.

Smith, D. K., and R. C. Alexander. *Fumbling the Future—How Xerox Invented, Then Ignored, the First Personal Computer*. New York: William Morrow & Company, 1988.

Stobaugh, R., and L. T. Wells Jr. *Technology Crossing Borders: The Choice, Transfer, and Management of International Technology Flows*. Boston: Harvard Business School Press, 1984.

VALUES

Hall, P. Brian. *Values Shift: How Individuals and Leaders Develop*. Rockport, Mass.: Twin Lights Publishers, 1995.

Tim Draper

Intellectual Capital
Measurement
for Start-Ups:
The Best of Intentions, the
Worst of Outcomes

I am in the venture capital business.
Our industry is a catalyst in creating jobs, wealth, and the American dream for entrepreneurs and does not want intellectual capital bureaucrats meddling in the very capitalism they are supposed to protect. In 1996, venture capitalists used $9.5 billion in funds to fuel new investments. This dollar amount is an increase of 25 percent over 1995. The growth in 1997 has been just as significant.

Venture capitalists are growing, thriving, and creating profits, returns, and jobs and do not need fixing. Valuing intellectual capital has never been a problem to us; if it were listed on the balance sheet, it could only cause confusion.

Why Measure Intellectual Capital?

If you are an accountant, you want to give investors a reasonable picture of what a company looks like financially at any given moment. Well, as an investor, I think the idea of intellectual capital being a part of that reasonable picture is untenable.

To whose benefit is it to track intellectual capital? The "unintellectual" public? the tax man? the investment banker? the Securities and Exchange Commission (SEC)? FASB? It will benefit none of the foregoing. It appears to me that tracking intellectual capital is an effort to fill the gap between book value and market capitalization. It will do no such thing; more likely it will provide fodder for lawsuits.

Further, who decides how intellectual capital is defined, what is measured, and how it is measured? (a newly created bureaucracy?). How often is the accounting for intellectual capital updated? on a daily basis to keep step with its every change? every time a neuron moves? or when one of the supposed intellectual capital measurements changes? Who does this updating on either the government or corporate level? accountants and lawyers? How is this information disseminated? as a supplement to annual and quarterly reports? as a daily bulletin on the Internet? Oh, and by the way, who pays for all this? the taxpayers? the corporations? Do I now have to put an "intellectual capital" accountant on my payroll?

These questions and many others need to be seriously scrutinized, and any government involvement in trying to account for and legislate intellectual capital is a horrific idea.

I believe that the purpose of an established company's measurement of intellectual capital is to help it intelligently plan for the future. Looking at particular assets, such as customer relationships, innovations in the pipeline, knowledge base of each department, and so on, is valuable when planning strategic leaps into new areas of growth. This exercise is also beneficial in highlighting areas of weakness that need strengthening and in comparing oneself to the competition to determine relative position in all these categories.

But aren't we already doing this? Mandatory intellectual capital measurement would require us to expose this process to the public and to our competitors. Anyone could peer over our shoulder and watch our business through a microscope. Can you imagine actually measuring the 164 intellectual capital items Skandia currently has listed, including "number of customers lost," "number of days spent visiting customers," and "sales closes divided by sales contacts"? or actually using corporate time and money to calculate percent of telephone accessibility by customers and percentage of employees with a secondary education or higher? Enforcement of this level of tracking and disclosing irrelevant statistics would be the iceberg that sinks the *Titanic* juggernaut of corporate America.

Who Would Profit from This New Bureaucracy?

Maybe the true question is, Who would profit from the bureaucratic enforcement of intellectual capital? Dataquest has predicted that, over the next decade, the intellectual capital consulting business will grow to $4 billion a year. For $2 to $3 million Ernst & Young will create a four-pronged approach—known at the consultancy as "culture, knowledge, content, and stewardship"—to discovering and utilizing a company's corporate intellectual capital.

Better yet, I could shovel my investors' money at "intellectual capital" lawyers, instead of using it to fund new companies. Since revenues from patent licensing and litigation are expected to reach $100 billion by the end of 1997, what would happen if intellectual capital fees were added to this staggering amount? A huge bonanza indeed! but not for consumers, customers, investors, employees, or me. Whole new departments would have to be created within corporations to track intellectual capital, and a knowledge bureaucracy would be created within these corporations. We would take our focus off the customer.

Clearly, the benefactors of intellectual capital measurement include those that many of us in capitalistic societies try to minimize exposure to, including lawyers, auditors, bureaucrats, corporate cost centers, and consultants.

A Dangerous Vision

Commissioner Wallman is a cheerleader for intellectual capital reporting. He wants a separate supplement attached to annual—and perhaps even quarterly—reports that would measure customer satisfaction and loyalty. He believes that J. D. Powers (another potential benefactor of intellectual capital bureaucracy) could perform industrywide surveys and could gauge both relative and absolute levels of customer satisfaction. It could also slow productivity by spending time interviewing employees for things like employee satisfaction. In the April 7, 1997, *Forbes ASAP*, which covers the topic of intellectual capital, Mr. Wallman is quoted as saying, "They can be very simple measures like how many days of absenteeism there are, to measures that relate more psychologically gratifying issues of how happy people are at work and things like that."

Huh?

He further elaborates, "The government, I think, has a valid role to play in standard-setting, enforcing appropriate disclosures, eliminating externalities, ensuring antifraud, and things of that nature."

Mr. Wallman believes that in two to four years new methods, new theories, and new constructs will be discovered. In about five to ten years he believes that this financial reporting will be available on the Internet, including employee satisfaction or customer satisfaction measures. In addition, a person could put together a customized financial statement based on reporting lines one thought were valuable and make a decision on that data to invest or not invest. He states: "I might value some intangibles more highly than you might, or less highly, or not at all. But at least I would have access to it, and would be able to place it into my own grid and assign some multiple that made sense to me."

If this is the future, stop the clock!

The Purpose of Financial Reporting

Let us go back to the basics of financial reporting and the purpose for which it has been utilized for the past five hundred years. In a nutshell, financial statements are prepared for owners, lenders, regulators, and employees to present meaningful information about a firm's business activities. Period.

When intellectual capital supporters want to start measuring and disclosing minutiae, such as per capita annual cost of training and support programs for full-time employees, we are in serious trouble. Highly regarded investor and columnist John Rutledge believes, and I agree, that balance sheets are for stuff, not people and ideas. He has said that balance sheets were never intended to measure the value of a company and that they are not used for that purpose by serious investors. A balance sheet item for intellectual capital would force us to decide how to define our ideas and thoughts, then measure and value them. The thought police would have definitely arrived.

Rich Willis, a marketing consultant, has stated that managers err when they treat information like a hard, measurable asset. He gives five sound reasons for this:

1. The value of information changes with time, usually at an incredible speed in high technology.

2. Value is in the eye of the beholder.

3. The value of information can be negative.

4. Information's value is dependent on others' knowledge of similar information.

5. The value of information is unrelated to its cost.[1]

He is right.

Netscape and Parametric Technology

Let's take a case in point. How would Mr. Wallman value the intellectual capital of Netscape in, say, June 1994? Whatever number he chose would be wrong by about $4 billion, roughly seven orders of magnitude. How can he value the thoughts in a founder's head? Or how could he decide how a population of customers would respond to this innovative front end to the Internet?

Parametric Technology is another example. When I first interviewed Sam Geisburg in a hole in the wall outside Boston, I saw that he had developed a software program to change objects to 3-D and 2-D simultaneously. Everything I saw could have been described as intellectual capital. There was nothing else. (Even the computer was leased.) I valued the company at $3 million. Silly me. At the initial public offering Parametric Technology was valued at $90 million, and Parametric Technology's market capitalization today is $7 billion. The intellectual capital was always there with the founder. It just took eight years and a lot of hard work to surface.

Intellectual Capital for Start-Ups

As an investor at the seed-level stage of start-ups, I do not measure intellectual capital as the difference between book value

1. Rich Willis. *Forbes ASAP*, April 1997, p. 36.

and market value. In the conceptual stage, there is no book value or a negative one if costs have already been incurred. Since the company is not in the marketplace, there is no current market value to measure. Therefore I have my own criteria for "intellectual capital" that I use to measure the potential of the company as a successful profit center. I base the process entirely on measurements that have nothing to do with the usual balance sheet standards such as tangible assets, liabilities, and so on because there is no land, there are no receivables, there is no revenue.

All I have to go on when deciding to fund a start-up is the intellectual capital of its management. I try to give extra credit to those who have had superior education, to those who have succeeded in their past endeavors, and to those who have great enthusiasm for their work. And even then, with my thirty years of investment experience (since the age of ten) and that of my partners, our firm's decision is frequently wrong.

We are completely wrong fully one-third of the time, and another one-half of the time we are disappointed; we are pleasantly surprised one-sixth of the time. At Draper Fisher Jurvetson, we review thirty-five hundred business plans a year, of which two hundred get serious consideration and fifteen to twenty, or less than 1 percent, actually get funded.

In other words, out of the thirty-five hundred business plans we examine, only two or three are successful each year. Although we have never accurately predicted the intellectual capital of a start-up, we are nevertheless very successful as investors, mostly because of how far wrong we are in the winners. We strive to provide entrepreneurs with the support they need to create profitable, growing businesses, while providing investors with outstanding investment returns. The company has an eight-step due diligence process; at any stage, if one or more of these appear weak, we make the decision not to invest. Here is the process:

1. *Read Plan / Assess Team.* We request a business plan description and complete résumés of management from all entrepreneurs. The general partners meet with the best of these entrepreneurs, attempting to identify key traits that have been associated with entrepreneurial success in the past, such as high energy, a must-win attitude, intellectual brilliance, high personal integrity, relevant experience, a strong work ethic, and the ability to prioritize and focus.

2. *Evaluate Market.* In addition to relying on our own experience, Draper Fisher Jurvetson has developed relationships with many market experts, including CEOs and other key employees of many successful companies in the technology arena. Each of these contacts represents a valuable source of information about his or her own market, and we call on these contacts for candid references. As we evaluate markets, we need to become convinced that a company can attain niche leadership over time.

3. *Examine Business Model.* We examine the models on which business plans are built and have developed a distinct bias toward business models calling for high gross margins and relatively low capital intensiveness. Such businesses have higher internally sustainable growth rates than most and are the best candidates for superior return on equity invested.

4. *Check References.* We require each entrepreneur to supply a list of references so that the general partners may get a better sense of the entrepreneur's past experience, strengths, weaknesses, and work habits. Draper Fisher Jurvetson makes it a point to get references outside this list as well to avoid only "cherry-picked references." We believe that these checks are important to develop a complete and accurate picture of the team.

5. *Call Potential Customers.* We make it a practice to call a number of prospective customers to get a sense of how they might respond to the envisioned product. Early on we attempt to develop and promote a sense of customer orientation in all entrepreneurs in whom we invest.

6. *Evaluate Product / Technology.* As part of our analysis, we need to be convinced that the product is unique and that use of the product does not require a substantial change in customer behavior. To evaluate technology, Draper Fisher Jurvetson does not rely on in-house expertise alone but contacts appropriate specialists to evaluate the feasibility of developing the entrepreneur's vision. Generally, we believe that assuming technology risk is part of the job of the early-stage venture capitalist.

7. *Evaluate Risks / Rewards.* We evaluate the pro forma financials, the likelihood of an exit after a five- to seven-year holding period, and the upside and downside prospects for the company. We insist that, given realistic expectations, we must be able to make at least ten times, preferably one hundred times, our money on each initial investment.

8. *Decide.* When Draper Fisher Jurvetson decides to make an investment, the general partners draw up a term sheet for negotiation. Valuation, board seats, requirements for additional investment, vesting schedules, salaries, and so forth are all discussed, and terms are agreed to. Generally, we will require a board seat and preferred stock. Although the result of the negotiation must clearly meet our needs, we believe that the needs of the entrepreneurs must also be met. From the point of view of the investment onward, we strive to match our interests with those of the entrepreneurs so that we can work together as true business partners.

Now consider this process in relation to the categories used by Skandia, a pioneer in the intellectual capital movement, in pursuit of its measurement of intellectual capital. The categories are:

1. *Intellectual Capital.* The sum of structural capital and human capital, indicating future earnings capacity, or knowledge that can be converted into profit.

2. *Human Capital.* The accumulated value of investments in employee training, competence, and future.

3. *Structural Capital.* The value of what is left when the human capital—the employees—has gone home. Databases, customer lists, manuals, trademarks, and organizational structures are a few examples or financial and physical assets. Found on balance sheet as "Total Assets."

4. *Customer Capital.* The value of the customer base, customer relationships, and customer potential. Component of structural capital. The value of contracted customer relationships.

5. *Organizational Capital.* Systematized and packaged competence, plus systems for leveraging the company's innovative strength and value-creating organizational capability.

6. *Innovation Capital.* Renewal strength in a company, expressed as protected commercial rights, intellectual property, and other intangible assets and values.

7. *Process Capital.* The combined value of value-creating processes.

Questions

Clearly the executives at Skandia who created these categories and definitions have tried to think through them carefully and have done their best to create valid yardsticks for measurement. One question I have—out of many—is what is the true value of this exercise? I am also unclear about the concept of systemized and packaged competence. What is it, how is it measured, and what value does its measurement offer? Much of this information appears to me to be nebulous to the point that it could be manipulated and greatly mislead annual report readers.

Where would each of Draper Fisher Jurvetson's due diligence measures fit? Would key traits that have been associated with entrepreneurial success in the past, such as high energy, a must-win attitude, intellectual brilliance, and so on, be human capital? Would IQ be measured? Would past effectiveness be measured? How is a quantitative value placed on these traits for each person on the management team? And, more to the point, what is the true value in doing so? Is team chemistry a human capital measurement? What if a team member leaves? Does that particular intellectual capital score plummet? Clearly, there is danger in outside interference in measuring or requiring quantitative measurement and required public disclosure of these and other factors.

My Formula for Intellectual Capital

Parametric Technology yielded more than a five hundred to one return to Draper Fisher Jurvetson on its original investment ($3 million valuation, $90 million IPO, $7 billion today's valuation); Hotmail, a company started by two twenty-six-year-olds, returned over one hundred times the original investment two years later; and Combinet, started by a very experienced entrepreneur, has returned forty times the investment. All three of these companies were enormous successes, with very different beginnings. How can you measure gut instinct?

Here is my formula for intellectual capital: IC = Best Guess.

Intellectual capital is priceless or worthless depending on the random actions of millions of people. Any number an accountant puts on the intellectual capital of a company would be wrong.

Not only wrong but misleading. My guess is that by any measure the value of the intellectual capitals of Digital Equipment or Novell would be higher than that of Yahoo! or America Online, but I would take the intellectual capital of the on-line services over the hardware dinosaurs in a heartbeat.

And how would some poor accountant determine that some key hire of a competitor would make obsolete the intellectual capital of a company within twelve months? A brilliant engineer can change the entire direction and outcome of an industry in some fundamental and extraordinary way; any of those events could get that accountant (and the company) sued for misrepresenting the company's true intellectual capital.

In instances in which an industry is very stable (perhaps an overregulated industry like utilities or telecommunications), intellectual capital can be valued accurately because of that stability. But what happens when that industry becomes deregulated or acquires a new and perhaps unregulated entrant whose intellectual capital starts to take over the market? What then, Mr. Wallman? Any assessment of intellectual capital is going to be far off the mark. What it comes down to is valuing something precisely that you know will be misleading and precisely wrong.

And when it comes down to it, what investor is going to give any credence at all to that number? Fortunes are going to be made on intellectual capital that no one ever heard of. And changes to stock prices based on a company's intellectual capital will pale by comparison to a new marketing concept or the result of a big negotiation.

Crystal Ball and Calculator, Anyone?

So what do we gain by making our corporations fill out yet another complicated, government-mandated form? I say we as a society, as business professionals and as investors, lose.

We lose the productivity of the individual who filled out those forms. He could have been the one who would dramatically increase the intellectual capital of the company, but instead he spends his time filling out forms for some fictitious investor (no true investor would give the value assigned to intellectual capital much credence) and figuring out whether the intellectual capital of his company is $90 million or $91 million in a $5 billion company. Meanwhile, his company loses its market to a foreign competitor who never had to fill out the form.

One argument says that investing is inherently unfair because some people understand a given company's intellectual capital value better than others. Let's face it—some people have more intellectual capital than others. Does that mean they should not use it to make proper investment decisions? This is capitalism. You win some, you lose some. People make choices and live with the consequences.

I find it hard to understand the benefit of having another line item on a balance sheet that is precisely calculated but is misleading at best and consistently wrong. Investors will not have any better idea of whether a given stock is undervalued or overvalued based on this additional figure.

In the venture capital business, we constantly make judgments on the intellectual capital value of start-ups. But we do not make those judgments on the amount of money they have invested in research and development or even the skunk works project going on in the back room but rather on our best guess about the future of the company. How hard will the key team work? How well will they get along? How will the customers respond? How big is their marketplace? Is their business model sound? How lucky are they?

What we explore, then, is the nearly random effect of trillions of neurons in the heads of the company's people, their competitors, and their customers and all the decisions that each person makes. If I have learned anything in the past thirty years, it is that none of the likely scenarios ever happen. What usually happens is something no one could have predicted. So why should companies be held accountable for something no one could have predicted in the first place? In short, asking an accountant to predict the future or the company to be held accountable for things completely out of its control only means that class action lawyers will have a field day.

The future is uncertain. It is a surprise. There will be winners and losers. Let company officers report their vision of it without repercussions. As long as they accurately show you what they have done, they shouldn't have to justify what they have thought. Don't protect me, the private investor, from making mistakes like the one I made on Parametric Technology.

I am going to tell you a secret. This game is won in the marketplace. Apple still has better intellectual property than Microsoft. Would the SEC value Apple's intellectual capital higher? or Microsoft's because of the larger research and development budget? Either way the value would be wrong.

Apollo had better intellectual property than Sun Microsystems, but Sun became the standard by winning in the marketplace. Relational Technology had better technology than Oracle, but Oracle did a better job of marketing to the customer.

More regulation, such as that proposed for intellectual capital and intended for the good of the individual investor, of which I am one, is not in anyone's best interest. The road to hell is paved with good intentions.

If all creativity that goes into trying to make companies fit into a box were focused instead on something out of the box, what an economy we'd have! Imagine if that bureaucrat or lobbyist or form-filler-outer could instead create what Sam Geisburg has created.

Good, simple, consistent accounting tied to physical items is all that we need. A good team, good products, and good education are invaluable. Let us not tamper with this successful formula by requiring corporate America to become involved in intellectual capital regulation, which will only hurt corporate profitability and national competitiveness. Leave corporate America's intellectual capital alone.

Part Four

The Burgeoning
Challenge
in Genomics

Clarisa Long

16

Patents and Innovation in Biotechnology and Genomics

The nature of an industry's technology determines the role and effect of intellectual property rights. Different forms of intellectual property rights, and different scopes and levels of protection, are appropriate for different technologies. In some industries, if patent rights were strongly enforced, firms using their *own* inventions would risk an infringement lawsuit. Thus, tacit practice in such industries is not to use intellectual property rights as a means of capturing returns from innovation. In other industries, however, firms heavily rely on intellectual property rights such as patents to recoup their investment in research and development. In such industries, the benefits of research are captured largely in a product's final use value by the firm responsible for its development.

Biotechnology and the Role of Patent Protection

As with any industry, biotechnology possesses a set of characteristics that strongly affects the nature and type of intellectual property protection most appropriate for it. Companies in the biotechnology and pharmaceutical industries rely heavily on patent protection to enable them to profit from their research and development. Innovation in biotechnology and pharmaceuticals particularly depends on strong patent rights because they are the only effective way in which firms can appropriate sufficient returns from their investment. In contrast, companies in other industries, such as semiconductors and computers, reap returns mainly by being the first to implement an innovative technology. They do not expect strong enforcement of intellectual property rights; rather, they expect that rivals will adopt their inventions after a lag in time.

The biotechnology and pharmaceutical sectors are characterized by enormous research and regulatory approval costs, by unusually high degrees of risk and uncertainty in bringing products to market, and by final products that can be imitated at low cost. Those industries also tend to have multiple researchers with the same knowledge base who are faced with the same opportunities and, therefore, are more inclined to make a race out of the discovery, publishing, and patenting processes. The pharmaceutical and biotechnology industries also have depended almost exclusively on the discovery of new knowledge and the development of completely new products. As a result, patents tended to correspond to only one product. Until now, this innovation model contrasted sharply with most sectors, where innovation focuses on incremental product improvements or advances in system design. As with any industry, the incentives created by intellectual property rights have much to say about the pace and direction of the innovative process. The available evidence suggests there is little doubt that proper incentives will allocate resources in the desired direction.

A system of intellectual property rights can provide incentives to innovate. By rewarding creativity, it encourages innovators to spend their time and resources in research and development efforts. It also stimulates the investment needed to market an invention. By exchanging formal property rights protection for the inventor's disclosure of the information needed to reproduce the invention, such a system reduces the likelihood of duplicated efforts and increases the chance that further advances in technology will arise from the disseminated information.

The entire edifice of intellectual property rights is built around a simple dilemma: Without legal protection not enough information will be produced, but with legal protection not enough information will be used. Economic theory hypothesizes that the private market will underproduce information because a producer cannot appropriate the full value of the information without protection.[1] Information is the classic example of a public good. The cost of producing a unit of information does not vary with the number of people who will use it, and use by one person does not deprive another. From the standpoint of intellectual property rights, these two concepts can be expressed as *indivisibility* and *inappropriability*.

Information is indivisible or nonrivalrous, which means that it is undepletable: Use by one person does not deprive another of using the same information. The information producer incurs the same costs regardless of how many people use the information; the use of the information by others does not interfere with the producer's use; and the information can be used endlessly. This obser-

1. See Thomas S. Ulen and Robert Cooter, *Law and Economics*, 2d ed. (Reading, Mass: Addison-Wesley, 1996) p. 118.

vation is not new. Almost two centuries ago, Thomas Jefferson noted that

> If nature has made any one thing less susceptible than all others of exclusive property, it is the action of the thinking power called an idea, which an individual may exclusively possess as long as he keeps it to himself; but the moment it is divulged, it forces itself into the possession of everyone, and the receiver cannot dispossess himself of it. Its peculiar character, too, is that no one possesses the less, because every other possesses the whole of it. He who receives an idea from me, receives instruction himself without lessening mine; as he who lights his taper at mine, receives light without darkening me.[2]

Because information is intangible, harm to the information producer arising from the failure or lack of legal protection is harder to quantify and thus does not create as much public outrage as would theft of tangible personal property.

The inappropriability aspect of this model states that, in the absence of enforceable property rights, producers of information-intensive technologies will be unable to reap the market value of the information. The information itself has only a marginal value to the producer; the real value lies in selling it to the public. But sale of the technology reveals the information it contains to competitors and potential copyists, each of whom can copy the information and thereby re-create the value of the property at a price lower than that of the original producer. Unless enforcement measures allow the innovator to appropriate the value of the informa-

2. Edward C. Walterscheid, "Inherent or Created Rights: Early Views on the Intellectual Property Clause," *Hamline Law Review* 19 (1995): 81–105 (pages 101–02 contain the quote in the letter from Jefferson to Isaac McPherson, August 13, 1813). As secretary of state, Thomas Jefferson was on a board composed of the secretary of state, the secretary of war, and the attorney general that had the responsibility for examining patent applications. Patent Act of 1790, Chap. 7., 1 Stat. 109-12 (April 10, 1790).

tion, innovators will find the incentive to produce information diminished.[3]

This model does not present the complete picture, however. Scientists, especially those engaged in basic research, are motivated by more than just the desire to appropriate the market value of their inventions. Within the scientific community, collaboration is a necessary part of the research process and publication is the currency of reputations. Both collaboration and publication may preclude later attempts to patent an invention, but they also provide incentives to produce information, even in the absence of intellectual property rights.

If the market underproduces information because of indivisibility and inappropriability, the state can intervene to overcome the market failure by producing the information itself, subsidizing the private production of information, or granting intellectual property rights.[4] The Human Genome Project, the National Institutes of Health's National Center for Biotechnology Information, and GenBank are examples of producing biotechnological information; tax breaks and direct funding for genetic research are examples of subsidizing; and pharmaceutical patents are an example of the state granting intellectual property rights.

An often overlooked point is that these policy prescriptions, from an economic perspective, are complementary means to the same end—optimal amounts of discovery and innovation—even though they are often viewed as conflicting. Although each may have policy consequences that affect the desirability of its use, all three are intended to solve the basic appropriability problem of

3. The U.S. International Trade Commission estimates that patent infringement alone reduces the annual investment in research and development by $750 million to $900 million each year. Pharmaceutical Research and Manufacturers' Association (PhRMA), *Opportunities and Challenges for Pharmaceutical Innovation* (Washington, D.C.: 1996), p. 3.

4. Ulen and Cooter, *Law and Economics*, p. 118.

genetic information that leads to the underproduction of such information by private sources without additional incentives.

When an innovator cannot appropriate value, whether monetary or nonmonetary, from releasing the information contained in an innovation into the market, then the innovator has a strong incentive not to reveal the information and to use it as a trade secret instead. A trade secret is information that (1) "derives independent economic value, actual or potential, from not being generally known to, and not being readily ascertainable by, other persons who can obtain economic value from its disclosure or use," and (2) the innovator takes reasonable means to keep secret.[5] If the information contained in a trade secret is misappropriated, the trade secret holder may sue, but if the information is discovered independently by a second innovator, the trade secret holder has no recourse. Even if the trade secret holder believes that the information may have been misappropriated by a competitor, litigation still may not be the answer because the trade secret holder will have to reveal the information in the process of proving his or her case.

The received wisdom is that, if we wish, as a policy matter, to disseminate information expeditiously, patents are preferable to trade secrets because the inventor must disclose the relevant information underlying the invention in exchange for the patent. In highly innovative fields like biotechnology, however, information has a short half-life. Information that is relevant and interesting today is passé tomorrow. If trade secrets are a thoroughly dissatisfying means of disseminating information, patents are not an ideal way either. Even if information is disseminated through a patent

---

5. Uniform Trade Secrets Act § 1 (1985). Because the law of trade secrets has never been federalized, requirements for trade secrets and trade secret protection vary by state.

specification, it can be stale by the time the patent document is published.

Bargaining with the State

The Patenting Process

Patents, the primary means of protecting biotechnological inventions, grant the exclusive right to prevent others from making, using, selling, or offering to sell an invention for twenty years.[6] A patent does not confer on the patentee the right to make, use, or sell; rather, it confers the right to use the power of the state, in the form of access to the courts, to prosecute violators. In exchange for that right, the patentee must reveal to the world, in the form of an extensive and detailed public document, the antecedent basis of the invention, a detailed description of the invention, all the information necessary to reproduce the invention, and the best means of using it.[7] With a few statutorily recognized exceptions, others who wish to use the idea can be required to pay the property rights holder.

Not all discoveries are patentable. The range of patentable innovations is thus just a subset of all research outcomes. In the United States, patentable subject matter is "any new and useful process, machine, manufacture, or composition of matter, or any

6. 35 U.S.C. §§ 154, 271 (1994 & Supp. I). The legislation implementing the trade agreements resulting from the Uruguay Round of multilateral trade negotiations under the General Agreement on Tariffs and Trade (GATT), codified as Pub. L. No. 103-465, has altered the patent term from seventeen years from the date of issue to a term ending twenty years from the date of the filing of the patent application or, under some circumstances, the date of earlier filed applications that are referenced in the later filed application.

7. 35 U.S.C. § 112 (1994).

new and useful improvement thereof."[8] The Supreme Court has construed this language broadly to include "anything under the sun that is made by man," including genetically engineered living organisms and DNA sequences.[9] Although products of nature may not be patented as such, patents have been issued on such products in human-altered form. For example, DNA sequences may be patented in an isolated and purified state because they exist in nature in an impure state. The requirement that a patentable invention be useful excludes from protection certain scientific discoveries that, although interesting as a subject of further research, cannot yet be used for any practical human purpose.

In addition to being new and useful, an invention must also be nonobvious. One may not patent an invention that is already available to the public either because it was previously known or because it is readily discoverable through obvious advances. As genetic research discovers more innovations, the nonobviousness requirement narrows the scope of protection that subsequent inventors can get for genetic information.

The patent laws require that patentees reveal "a written description of the invention, and of the manner and process of making and using it, in such full, clear, concise and exact terms" so as to enable others to re-create the invention.[10] Patent applicants who attempt to withhold vital information about the invention from their applications, in the hopes of extending the exclusive use of their application after the statutory period, run the risk of having their patents invalidated *ex post*. If competitors believe the invention is not fully disclosed in the patent, they can challenge its validity before the United States Patent and Trademark Office (PTO) and appeal decisions by the PTO to the United States Court

8. 35 U.S.C. § 101.

9. *Diamond v. Chakrabarty*, 447 U.S. 303 (1980).

10. 35 U.S.C. § 112 (1994).

of Appeals for the Federal Circuit (CAFC). If the PTO or the CAFC concludes that the applicant misled the PTO in filing the application (e.g., by hiding relevant information), then the PTO or the court will invalidate the entire patent. The punishment for such "inequitable conduct," as it is known, is huge: complete invalidation. The anticipated value of the patent, therefore, directly correlates with the incentive to act honestly when submitting the application. The more important the technology, the broader the scope of the claims; the greater the anticipated stream of future revenue, the greater the incentive for the patentee to be scrupulously honest and reveal all relevant information.

Under the "first to invent" system used in the United States, in which ownership rights are granted to the applicant who can prove prior invention (even if that applicant is not the first to file an application to patent the invention), independent discovery by a rival does not deprive a prior inventor of property rights but may raise the cost of defending the patent. Because applying for ("prosecuting") a patent is an expensive and time-consuming process, and because enforcing and defending a patent can cost patentees up to millions of dollars in litigation fees, patenting is a strategic decision.[11] Not all patentable innovations are actually patented. Sometimes researchers may choose for strategic reasons to release information into the public domain, or withhold it from the public domain, without seeking intellectual property protection.

Thus, the grant of patent rights involves an individual bargaining with the state. The bargain is a simple one: Information about the invention is exchanged for the ability to use the power of the

---

11. The American Intellectual Property Law Association (AIPLA) has recently estimated that the "cradle to grave" costs of prosecuting a relatively straightforward patent in the United States range from $14,420 to $23,540. American Intellectual Property Association, "Cradle to Grave Costs for a U.S. Patent," *AIPLA Bulletin*, March–April 1996, p. 446.

state to enforce the patentee's right to prevent others from using the innovation without the patentee's consent. This bargaining process is a true negotiation, which is why an experienced patent prosecutor can reduce transaction costs for his or her client in the long run. If, at the end of the negotiation, patent applicants are dissatisfied with the scope of protection the state offers them, they can withdraw their patent request. Although this means that they can't use the legal system to keep others from using their invention, they also don't have to reveal the information to the world.

The EST Patenting Controversy

A good system of intellectual property protection knows when to create ownership rights and when not to. This applies to biotechnological innovations as much as anything else. When property rights are uncertain or too narrow or broad or differentially applied, or when otherwise neutral laws are manipulated to achieve policy ends, transaction costs are created, incentives are distorted, innovation is retarded, and faith in the neutrality of the law is undermined. Recently the patentability of one class of biotechnological inventions has been subject to great uncertainty, resulting in tensions among industry, government, and academia.

The controversy began in June 1991, when the National Institutes of Health (NIH) filed patent applications on partial gene sequences, called expressed sequence tags (ESTs), that it had discovered.[12] ESTs are short DNA sequences some 150–400 base pairs long. They can be used as a probe to determine the location of a gene on a chromosome, but they do not reveal the biological role of the gene or the reason a particular tissue expresses the gene. The specification of the NIH's patent application disclosed more than just the ESTs, but it did not identify the full-length

12. Arthur L. Caplan and Jon Mertz, "Patenting Gene Sequences," *British Medical Journal* 312 (April 13, 1996): 926.

sequence of newly discovered genes, teach the biological activity of all the genes, or identify the proteins coded by those genes. The NIH asked for a broad scope of patent protection, sometimes covering the entire gene and the proteins it coded for, when in fact the underlying function of the gene was unknown.

According to its statement, the NIH based its decision to file patent applications on ESTs on its desire to be able to transfer federal technology to industry by licensing the sequences if they were found patentable.[13] By filing patent applications on the sequences, the NIH was able to publish the results of its findings while preserving any potential intellectual property rights. If it published its research results without filing patent applications on the ESTs, then under the U.S. patent statute it might preclude itself from filing patent applications on future discoveries involving ESTs because the later invention was either obvious or was already in the public domain. Under 35 U.S.C. §102(b) (1994), an applicant is barred from receiving a patent on an invention if it was "described in a printed publication in this or a foreign country or in public use or on sale in this country, more than one year prior to the date of the application for patent in the United States." This one-year statutory bar creates tension between the incentives to publish research results and the ability to apply for a patent on the results of that research. Again, an invention is also unpatentable if it is deemed obvious, given the state of the prior art.[14] The NIH was concerned that such uncertain status of future patent applications would render the private sector less willing to perform research in this area.[15]

13. Christopher Anderson, "NIH Drops Bid for Gene Patents," *Science* 263 (February 18, 1994): 909–10; Bernadine Healy, "Remarks of Dr. Bernadine Healy at the Fourth Annual PHS Technology Transfer Forum," Washington, D.C., November 14, 1991.

14. 35 U.S.C. § 103 (1994).

15. See *Testimony of Dr. J. Craig Venter before the Senate Judiciary Subcommittee on Patents, Copyrights and Trademarks*, September 22, 1992; but see Association of Biotech-

An uproar ensued, including unfavorable reactions from other governments. The controversy was whether ESTs, or for that matter entire genes, could be patented when their function in the body was unknown and whether the NIH should seek patents on innovations produced by publicly funded research.[16]

Proponents of patenting sequences for unknown functions argued that disclosing the sequencing information without attempting to patent the sequences might foreclose "future patenting by anyone who discovers the full gene by identifying its function and . . . mak[ing] the newly discovered genes unattractive to private industry for use in product development."[17] The Association of Biotechnology Companies stated that it supported the NIH's decision to file patent applications on the ESTs "as a means to preserve its options on how to best utilize the technology for the public benefit."[18]

Opponents of patent protection for ESTs expressed both legal and social objections. They argued that because the patent application did not indicate the biological function of the sequences claimed, the patentees would be able to claim the rights to all products arising from the use of the gene. Some also noted that allowing patents to be issued would run counter to the norms of science, including Nobel laureate Paul Berg, who said that "patent-

---

nology Companies, *Statement on NIH Patent Filing for the Human Genome Project*, May, 1992 ("Whether future patent claims are obtainable . . . is not the concern of the NIH, which should not become engaged in schemes designed to ensure future exclusivity").

16. Reid G. Adler, "Genome Research: Fulfilling the Public's Expectations for Knowledge and Commercialization," *Science* 257 (August 14, 1992): 908; Rebecca S. Eisenberg, "Genes, Patents, and Product Development," *Science* 257 (August 14, 1992): 903.

17. Bernadine Healy, "Special Report on Gene Patenting," *New England Journal of Medicine* 327 (August 27, 1992): 664–68.

18. Association of Biotechnology Companies, "ABC Supports Filing of DNA Patents, Opposes Biological Diversity Treaty," press release, May 17, 1992.

ing bits and pieces of sequence that are meaningless functionally
. . . makes a mockery of what most people feel is the right way to
do the Genome Project."[19] Others argued that allowing patent
protection for such genetic information would encourage data
hoarding, prevent further research on the DNA sequences, and
result in a deluge of applications flooding the patent office. The
Industrial Biotechnology Association objected to the NIH's seeking
patents on genetic sequences for which the biological function was
unknown; it did not object to scientists in the private sector doing
the same thing.[20] The British Medical Research Council found itself
in the odd position of criticizing the NIH for filing patent applications on ESTs, yet resorting to filing applications on approximately
twelve hundred of its own sequences as a defensive action. (The
council eventually withdrew its applications.)

The PTO is not used to being at the center of controversy. The
weight of public opinion seemed to run against ownership of these
genetic sequences, and yet the PTO had been granting patents on
DNA sequences since 1981. Also, the wave of complex and time-
consuming applications was being submitted to the PTO when it
was overworked, understaffed, and trying to update its technology. This was further complicated by the fact that the applicants
overreached, asking for a scope of protection in excess of what
they were entitled to.

The PTO responded by creating a legal fiction: The ESTs were
unpatentable, it said, because they lacked utility. Patents cannot be
issued on useless inventions; as a scientific matter, however, the
ESTs were useful inventions. The policy goal behind the EST controversy was to make sure that inventors, who had admittedly

19. Leslie Roberts, "NIH Gene Patents, Round Two," *Science* 255 (1992): 912.

20. Industrial Biotechnology Association, "IBA Position Paper: Recommended Federal Policy Concerning Human Genetic Sequences Discovered by Federal Researchers,
Contractors, and Grantees," Washington, D.C., 1992.

overreached, didn't receive a broader scope of protection than they deserved, based on the genetic information they revealed. Although there were perfectly legitimate ways to do this, stating that the DNA sequences lacked utility was not one of them.

In February 1994, after the PTO rejected the sequences on the grounds that their usefulness was unknown, among other things, the NIH abandoned its patent applications for the 6,869 sequences for which it had by then sought intellectual property protection.[21] But the NIH was not alone in trying to patent gene fragments, nor has the patenting controversy ended with the NIH's abandoning its application.

In February 1997, a PTO official announced that the it had "decided to allow claims to ESTs based on their utility as probes" for larger DNA sequences.[22] This decision, however, only renewed the controversy over the patentability of ESTs, with the PTO reporting that dozens of applications to ESTs filed by private sector firms are still pending. Indeed, because of difficulties involved in evaluating the patentability of this large number of sequences, the PTO estimates that, if it did nothing else, it would take its biotechnology staff an entire year to evaluate the applications.[23] Although it has held hearings on the subject, patent applications claiming thousands of nucleotide sequences continue to overwhelm the PTO.

It remains for the PTO to determine the scope of protection to grant to ESTs. Even if the PTO ultimately ends up rejecting an application, it must first check each genetic sequence claimed against the sequences stored in five major databases to verify that

21. Anderson, "NIH Drops Bid," p. 909.

22. Eliot Marshall, "Companies Rush to Patent DNA," *Science* 275 (February 7, 1997): 781.

23. Gretchen Vogel, ed., "Gene Fragments Patentable, Official Says," *Science* 275 (February 21, 1997): 1055.

the sequence is not already in the public domain. To do this, the PTO uses two supercomputers, each with sixteen thousand processors in parallel, and a sensitive program that can catch DNA sequences that are only minor modifications of existing sequences. Patent examiners also carefully review the applications. Allegedly, as many as 18,500 sequences have been claimed in a single application. The PTO estimates that it costs five thousand dollars and takes approximately sixty to sixty-five hours to examine one hundred sequences.

Although the genomics industry has thrived, it has been handicapped by the uncertainty surrounding ESTs, just as a real estate developer would be if clear title to land were unavailable and uninsurable. The longer the property rights remain uncertain, the more difficult they will be to sort out. The ultimate message of the EST controversy may have been stated in an Office of Technology Assessment report released almost a decade ago. Focusing on the obstacles to research that stemmed from uncertainty about legal title to biological materials, the report concluded, "regardless of the merit of claims by the different interested parties, resolving the current uncertainty may be more important to the future of biotechnology than resolving it in any particular way." At some point, an imperfect solution, expeditiously reached, becomes preferable to a perfect solution that takes a long time to reach. Only time will tell whether this point has been reached in the case of ESTs.

The Challenge of Genomics to Intellectual Property Rights

A number of important considerations will affect the future interplay between intellectual property rights and the cutting edge of biotechnology innovation. Biotechnology research is shifting its focus from the gene to the genome. The genome of an organism is all the genetic material in its chromosomes; genomics is the study of genomes. In this field, databases and software are playing an increasingly important role in innovation and are often incorporated into the final product. In the next few years, biomedical advances and new drug products will depend as much on incremental improvements in databases or redesigns of existing software systems as on blockbuster breakthroughs.

Applying advanced computing power to biotechnology is becoming a driving force in innovation and the development of new products and services. New information technologies have created tools and methods that are transforming the research enterprise and becoming central to the process of innovation. Most significantly, in addition to the products derived from their use, genomic information and research tools based on information technologies have themselves become marketable. Thus, value will be determined by the ability to use the information, not mere ownership of it.

In the past few years, the growth, interpretation, and organization of masses of data on a previously unimagined scale have become a hallmark of modern biotechnology. Over the next decade, the great challenge to biotechnology will be interpreting the sheer complexity of genomic data. Collaboration among scientists will be more essential than ever before, yet investors and researchers worry that this very collaboration could place information into the public domain and thereby jeopardize future attempts at intellectual property protection for the very valuable results of their research. For example, genome maps are vital to genomic research. In the case of the human genome, no individual entity can create a complete map by itself, and such maps are essential to eliminate duplication of effort as multiple labs research the same regions of the genome. But maps are useful only to the extent that they are accurate and complete, and they can be completed only when information is released into the public domain.

Intellectual property rights must also coexist with the norms of scientific research. "While a convincing case can be made for the value of patents in securing investment and attention from those who hold them, limiting access to portions of the human genome to a small set of scientists simply because they identified the sequences first is unlikely to lead to the maximal intellectual exploitation of this resource."[24] Critics worry that attempting to patent the products of genetic research will decrease the cooperation and collaboration among genome scientists necessary to create gene maps.[25] Critics, also noting the potential for conflicts of interest among scientists, are concerned that patenting will change the ethos of the basic research community.[26] The intersection of genomics with intellectual property rights is already profoundly reshaping the balance struck among the interests of biotechnology researchers, investors and other market actors, and the public good. The recent debate about the patentability of ESTs and the interplay between intellectual property protection and the norms of scientific inquiry are illustrative.

Intellectual property rights will remain necessary to attract private investment in biotechnology, especially in highly innovative and fast-paced fields like genomics. U.S. research-based pharmaceutical companies now invest more money in research than the NIH's entire budget. Biotechnology and biomedical research fare much better than other scientific disciplines in the federal budget, but even a 9 percent increase in federal dollars from 1993 to 1997 does not come close to meeting the needs of basic research in biotechnology. Private investment is the only realistic means whereby some of that shortfall can be covered for the foreseeable

24. Caplan and Mertz, "Patenting Gene Sequences," p. 926.

25. See, for example, Leslie Roberts, "Genome Patent Fight Erupts," *Science* 254 (1991): 184.

26. See, for example, Christopher Anderson, "Genome Project Goes Commercial," *Science* 259 (January 15, 1993): 300; National Institutes of Health–Department of Energy Subcommittee for Interagency Coordination of Human Genome Research, statement, January 3, 1992.

future, and such investments will not be forthcoming without adequate and effective intellectual property rights.

Government institutions and universities have become new entrants in innovation markets by design and by financial necessity. Beginning with the Bayh-Dole Act in 1980, federal policy has permitted and encouraged universities to obtain intellectual property rights on government-funded research as a means to stimulate technology transfers. The number of new university patents has grown from about 280 a year before 1980 to more than 2,600 a year in 1997.

Highly information-intensive fields of biotechnology, like genomics, are cumulative effects technologies. Basic research and product development increasingly depend on continuous interaction. Perhaps more than in any other industry, research tools in biotechnology have both basic and commercial applications. Intellectual property rights, or the lack thereof, in either area will affect the other.

From a legal perspective, granting private property rights to biotechnological innovations may increase transaction costs as researchers and other users confront the problems of determining and securing ownership rights efficiently. The licensing issues will be further complicated because the industry is made up of a changing collection of many different entities and institutions. Each of these public and private actors has its own informal norms and standards about licensing intellectual property rights. Finding common ground may prove difficult.

Litigation costs also are likely to impose significant transaction costs in biotechnology. Differing conceptual approaches, business strategies, and legal standards can be used to protect various forms of new technologies. The confusion may lead to periods of over- and underprotection for biotechnological information or, as in the case of ESTs, long periods of uncertainty about rights. Uncertainty about ownership rights and access to information during the period in which the legal and political system tries to catch up to fast-moving and novel technological changes will have a chilling effect on innovation.

Intellectual property must adapt to the globalization of technology and markets. The United States' biggest successes in international markets have come in those products and services in which U.S. firms have been vigorous technological innovators. American pharmaceutical, biotechnology, and information service firms are three such world leaders.

The most successful economies in the decades to come will be those that can best harness their brain power to generate economic growth. Thus, governments increasingly view the conditions for achieving robust economic growth and job creation, such as strong intellectual property rights and high levels of spending on research and development, as national imperatives. The key lies in turning research-based discoveries and improvements into competitive goods, services, or information for global markets. As Winston Churchill once observed, "the empires of the future will be the empires of the mind."

Thomas J. White and John J. Sninsky

Genomics and Intellectual Capital

17

The imminent deciphering of the heritable information content of human beings and other organisms portends a need to reconsider the valuation of genetic information as a form of knowledge per se, and the methods of obtaining and using it. One approach to this subject has been to concentrate on flaws in the present system of assigning intellectual property rights and on proposals for revising it.[1] Another has been to nationalize the "ownership" of the DNA of the citizens of a particular country or members of an indigenous population as a unique "property." A third position is that "natural" DNA, genes, and cells are unpatentable subject matter. All these positions fundamentally misunder-

---

1. L. C. Thurow, "Needed, a New System of Intellectual Property Rights," *Harvard Business Review*, September–October 1997, pp. 95–103.

stand or distort both the inherent nature of genetic information and the meaning of variation among individuals and populations within a species. As the premier embodiment of intellectual capital, genetic information as a form of information encompasses both unprotectable knowledge and a discrete kind of predictive information that warrants economic incentives for those who discover it.

The complete set of instructions for making an organism is called its *genome*. It contains the master blueprint for all cellular structures and activities for the lifetime of the cell or organism. Found in almost all cells, the human genome consists of DNA organized into structures called *chromosomes* that constitute the basis for heredity. The Human Genome Project is an effort to make a series of descriptive maps or diagrams of each of the twenty-four human chromosomes at increasingly finer resolution and to determine the complete order and chemical structure of the DNA in each of the chromosomes.[2] The ultimate goal of genome research is to find all the genes in the DNA sequence and to develop tools for using this information in the study of human biology and medicine.

This global endeavor, primarily funded by the United States at an estimated total cost of $3 billion, is scheduled for completion in 2005. Although the experimental aspects of this research involve physical and chemical methods of analysis, the ultimate output of the project is information instead of physical materials that would need to be archived and exchanged among laboratories. This information database, consisting of about 3 billion units (called *bases*) constituting a "DNA sequence," is also not from a single individual; different sections of it are obtained from multiple people, and some specific sections are repeatedly analyzed from multiple people to see if there are variations that can be associated with certain

2. Human Genome Project Information: *http://www.ornl.gov*.

diseases. On average, two people will show some variation every 300–500 bases, but much of it is neutral and does not cause disease. But by analyzing people from families with a history of disease, such information contributes to a knowledge of genes that may cause inherited diseases, such as cystic fibrosis or hemophilia, or that may contribute to one's risk for more common disorders such as heart disease, diabetes, arthritis, asthma, and osteoporosis.

These multifactorial diseases are influenced by both environmental and genetic causes. For example, some of the environmental factors associated with heart disease are smoking and a diet high in salt, cholesterol, and fat. But genetic factors also contribute to an individual's risk for hypertension, high cholesterol, and blood clots or thrombosis. As multiple genes are identified for each of these facets of heart disease, they will represent potential targets for drug discovery, diagnosis, and new treatments. And as the relationships between genetic variation (mutation) and disease are elucidated, this knowledge may be medically useful in predicting the risk for disease in otherwise healthy people or in making a differential diagnosis where current methods are inadequate, such as distinguishing the dementia caused by a stroke from that due to Alzheimer's disease. This knowledge may be helpful in making a prognosis, in selecting patients who are likely to benefit from available or experimental treatments, in selecting appropriate drugs based on the likelihood of efficacy or fewer adverse effects, and for monitoring a patient's response to therapy.

To the extent that any of these potential outcomes occur, the complete human DNA sequence may represent the ultimate intellectual capital. However, the idea that "noticing what an existing gene does is simply not equivalent to inventing a new gene"[3] is fundamentally misguided. People with genes that cause some kinds of disease may eventually be treated with novel therapies based on

---

3. Thurow, "Needed, a New System."

"existing" genes that provide "normal" or nondiseased functions (i.e., one is not inventing new genes but using existing genes in a new way). Second, the normal or non-disease-causing gene, is by definition not going to be exclusive to any particular nation or ethnic group. Hence, when its sequence is known, the gene can be recovered from almost any individual anywhere in the world—not just from the original group where the genetic variant associated with disease, or better health, is first identified and characterized. In contrast to the conventional wisdom,[4] there is no incentive for keeping such information secret; what will be economically important to the discoverer is the knowledge and ability to produce a form of diagnosis or therapy that provides a medical benefit.

The Computer and Biotechnology Industries

An analogy can be made between two of the most important tools used in the computer and biotechnology industries. The first is *bandwidth*, a commonly used term that refers to the amount of information processed by computers and is frequently characterized in levels: narrow, mid, and broad bandwidth. For example, using a standard computer modem permits the narrow-bandwidth flow of information to a computer from a network; mid bandwidth is sometimes represented by an ISDN line, and broad bandwidth is typified by cable television lines or fiber optics. Further, microprocessor chips are rated in terms of millions of instructions per second (MIPS). For example, the new processors have MIPS nearly equivalent to the number of bases in the human genome. The number of transistors per chip follows a prediction made in 1971 by one of the founders of Intel, Gordon Moore, that the number of transistors per chip would double every 18–24 months (this also applies to clock speeds). Figure 1 shows the increase in transistors

4. Ibid.

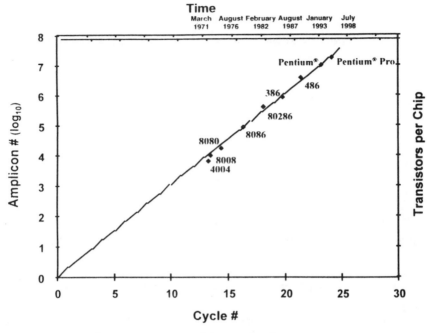

Figure 1. PCR and Microprocessors: Information Tools

per chip for various Intel chips as a function of time between 1971 and 1998. Each generation of Intel chip falls on the exponential graph.

The biotechnology industry and the Human Genome Project in particular have had a second equally powerful tool for the generation of information since 1985: the polymerase chain reaction (PCR). This is a technique for producing large amounts of a specific DNA sequence from small amounts of tissue, blood, or other specimens. Described as being to genes what Gutenberg's printing press was to the written word, PCR, starting with a single molecule of DNA as a template, can produce a trillion copies of it in a series of steps called *cycles* (see figure 1). The bandwidth analogy highlights the information content of PCR assays rather than their molecular biological nature. To the medical laboratory, it is the information content of the result rather than the intricacy of the procedure that is important. PCR's enormous productivity as a tool for generating information has had a major impact on clinical medicine, genetic research, forensic medicine, and evolutionary biology. Furthermore, though the method was published in the open scientific literature as rapidly as possible, it was also patented and has provided substantial value to the owners of the patents.

As PCR has matured commercially, there has been a corresponding increase in the bandwidth of its output. The initial PCR reactions targeted small fragments of DNA of approximately 100 units (base pairs). These have subsequently been expanded to much longer fragments (e.g., 30,000 base pairs), and the ability to simultaneously amplify multiple fragments now permits different segments of a gene or multiple genes to be interrogated in a single assay. One can think of this simultaneous amplification of different segments as the equivalent of multitasking in computers. It is also easy to see how a gene sequence can be thought of as "instructions" per base. The first commercial PCR assays were also qualitative (i.e., measured only the presence or absence of a pathogen). But with the development of simple and robust quantitative assays, one could determine not only whether the sequence from an organism was present but the number of copies of the virus or pathogen as well. Finally, improvements in sequencing methods, typified by "designer sequencing enzymes" and DNA chips (e.g., Affymetrix's), allow one to determine the actual sequence of the amplified material from multiple genes in a single test, providing even more information. The Affymetrix chip, for example, employs photolithography, a procedure commonly used in the computer industry, as a means to generate the DNA chips. Since the resolution of the first DNA chips uses instrumentation already superseded by contemporary computer technology, we can envision additional future exchanges of intellectual capital between these industries as well as the replacement of rapidly obsolete tests with improved versions.

The analogy can be extended further. A highly variable pathogen such as HIV, the virus that causes AIDS, mutates so rapidly that there are now many different variants found throughout the world, sometimes differing by as much as 20 percent of their sequence. The range of variants detected by a PCR assay can be thought of in the three categories mentioned above. For example, the first commercial quantitative assays could be thought of as mid-bandwidth because they detected the variants of the virus that are most common in North America and Europe. More recent versions now detect the sequence variation (or information content) in viruses from all over the world, even from countries such as Cameroon and Burkina Faso. Similarly, initial assays could quantify virus in amounts from about five hundred to a million copies; recent versions broadly detect from ten to a billion copies. Finally, by providing virus quantification, analyzing the viral mutations that cause drug resistance, and determining the genetic information in certain human genes that influence prognosis and susceptibility to infection, the most advanced assays provide even more information for making treatment decisions for infected persons.

The enormous increase in knowledge arising from the sequencing of the entire genomes of various viral and bacterial genomes, leading to the identification of new human gene targets for drug discovery, is already providing a competitive advantage to those pharmaceutical firms that have committed significant resources to that effort. Even without a clear resolution of some of the patentability issues, the lead provided by earlier identification of key genetic functions to target for new drug screens and designs provides significant differentiation among competitors. Furthermore, new bioinformatics companies, dedicated to the interface between the computer and biotech industries, are springing up to be the first to develop the tools to "mine" the vast databases of sequence information and to predict the functions of the genes for further characterization. The magnitude of the data from different organisms, individuals, disease states, and treatment regimens that must be compared requires the development of new visualization tools and algorithms, many of which are being conceived in other disciplines as divergent as physics and meteorology. The Cancer Genome Anatomy Map, an interdisciplinary program to establish the information and technological tools needed to decipher the molecular anatomy of a cancer cell,[5] is a perfect example of the hybridization of biotechnology and computer technology into "intellectual capital." Its goal is to achieve a comprehensive molecular characterization of normal, precancerous, and malignant cells that is broadly accessible to the scientific community over the Internet.

Patent Issues and Genetic Testing

The search for the genetic causes of multifactorial disorders increasingly involves investigators, and thus inventors, from multiple institutions (academia, government, and industry) with the inevitable multiple ownership of patents on individual genes. Even a single gene for a disease such as cystic fibrosis may have more than six hundred mutations, and although it was identified in 1989, a U.S. patent has still not been issued on the original discovery— much less on any of the additional disease-associated mutations. Since a complex disease such as asthma may also have many genetic influences, an analysis of many or all of the predisposing genes and their possibly multiple mutations will be necessary for a complete diagnosis. Each inventor or institution will be likely to own some but not all of the patents on the genes and mutations for a particular disease. Therefore, unless nonexclusive licenses are granted for diagnostic services and products, no medical institution or manufacturer will be able to offer a complete diagnostic product or panel of related products for comprehensive genetic testing. In this respect, exclusive licenses for drug development contrast with

5. Cancer Genome Anatomy Project: *http://www.ncbi.nlm.nih.gov/ncicgap/*.

the requirement for nonexclusive licenses for diagnosis in order for genetic information and capital to reach commercialization. It will also be essential for investigators to be realistic about compensation for a discovery that represents the most nascent stage of a drug or diagnostic product.

Access to Pathology Specimens for Genetic Analysis

If DNA sequence information can be considered a form of intellectual capital, then the potential to obtain such information from the retrospective genetic analysis of archival clinical or pathology specimens raises the conflicting issues of advancing medical knowledge, the privacy of medical information, and the need for informed consent for such testing. Today pathology specimen collections in hospitals and medical schools around the world constitute an international resource of genetic and medical information. For specimens stored from patients whose clinical history, treatment, and outcome are already known, the predictive value of genetic analyses could be demonstrated or disproved much more quickly than if prospective studies were conducted. Proposed legislation to require prospective informed consent for such retrospective analyses of archival specimens would result in the loss of valuable medical information useful in the development of new tests, drugs, and procedures, and would require many years to repeat clinical studies, assuming it were even possible. An alternative policy could protect the privacy of medical records by unlinking patients' names and other identifiers from their records and any specimens used for retrospective analyses. For many biopsy specimens taken for microscopic and biochemical analyses, informed consent was frequently obtained at the time the specimens were collected for possible use in teaching and research on the causes of disease. Thus, as long as the retrospective research on anonymous samples is reviewed and approved by an institutional review board, and privacy of the results and medical history is protected, contemporaneous and separate patient consent for each analysis of a new gene on an archived or remnant specimen should not be required.

Regulatory Hurdles to Genetic Testing

A final issue involves regulatory barriers to the use of genetic information for diagnostic purposes. The Human Genome Project has immense potential to encourage the early diagnosis, prevention, and treatment of chronic conditions. An analogous example is the successful use of phenotypic information on blood pressure and cholesterol levels to initiate treatment with antihypertensive and cholesterol-lowering drugs in order to prevent heart attacks and subsequent surgery. However, currently no molecular diagnostic products for genetic diseases have been cleared by the FDA for use in the United States, and it is unlikely there will be any for at least several more years, despite many recent advances in the identification of genes that cause even relatively common diseases such as cystic fibrosis. Even though it has been ten years since the fundamental PCR patents issued in the United States, only four FDA-cleared diagnostic products are available commercially for the infectious agents responsible for tuberculosis, for the sexually transmitted disease caused by chlamydia, which can lead to sterility and pelvic inflammatory disease, and for viral load testing for HIV. The six molecular diagnostic companies together have only seven FDA-approved products based on DNA amplification for a total of only four organisms, yet Roche alone has over twenty-four products approved outside the United States in other highly regulated countries such as France and Japan. With the typical regulatory review process taking about four years for a test of a major public health problem like tuberculosis, it is improbable that the FDA is going to approve any genetic tests for complex diseases such as osteoporosis any time before the next century.

Consequently, the sequence information useful for genetic medicine is already finding another route into practice via specialized services offered by medical schools and teaching hospitals. Professional associations now provide over the Internet a list of more than six hundred genetic diseases and the contacts for laboratories offering testing services. Since these tests are independently developed by each laboratory, they often lead to inconsistent and unstandardized results. Ironically, they are therefore less controlled for the quality of their results than would be the case with an FDA-cleared kit. Clearly, for the novel genetic intellectual capital arising from the Human Genome Project to achieve a place in routine diagnostic medicine, reform of the FDA process for reviewing medical devices is essential.

Conclusion

The atlas of the human genome will revolutionize medical practice and biological research into the next century.[6] All human genes will eventually be found, and accurate diagnostic tests will be available for most inherited diseases, including those multifactorial disorders that are also influenced by environmental factors. In addition, the mechanisms by which those genes cause disease will be discovered and targeted for new therapies and preventive measures. Starting from a partial sequence, the Human Genome Project is already metamorphosing into additional new projects to identify the functions of genes and pathways and to characterize the chronometric and tissue-specific differences in those functions. This knowledge will help us understand how our species evolved from a series of common ancestors and how humans develop from

6. Human Genome Project Information: *http://www.ornl.gov.*

a fertilized egg into an adult and subsequently age. In one sense then, the project will help to recapitulate phylogeny *and* ontogeny.

The power of these methods has also led to the complete sequencing of ten microbial genomes to date; fifty more are in progress.[7] This means that the genomes of the twenty-five major bacterial and parasitic pathogens could be available within the next few years.[8] The future targets for vaccines and drug development for these diseases will then be available to all scientists and companies. The project will also continue to diversify into other projects to sequence the genomes of plants and animals such as those of the key agricultural industries. In addition to presenting new opportunities for intellectual capital, ethical issues will arise from the use of this knowledge that will require both public education and an informed legislature to derive the potential benefits to medicine and humanity.

7. World Wide Web site: *http://www.tigr.org*. E. Pennisi, *Science* 277 (1997): 1432–34.

8. B. R. Bloom, *Nature* 378 (1995): 236.

Part Five

Emerging
International Regimes

Clarisa Long

Investment, Technology Transfer, and Intellectual Property Protection in Latin America

There's an old saying that it's easier to steal somebody else's ideas than to come up with your own. Latin American nations often seem to justify piracy of international intellectual property by telling their citizens that "we cheat the other guy and pass the savings on to you." For decades, Latin American governments have explained their failure to enforce intellectual property rights on the grounds that observing world-class standards of intellectual property protection would impede national development and place their own citizens at a competitive disadvantage. The industrialized world, they argue, was able to achieve its current level of development partly because it was unfettered by strong intellectual property rules. Although this is historically true, the context and circumstances have changed. As Latin America is coming to realize, the absence of intellectual property regimes is placing it at a competitive disadvantage on the world stage. Nations that cheat innovators fail to attract capital investment, are unsuitable partners for technology transfers, and have no savings to pass on to their citizens.

Intellectual Property Protection in Latin America

Intellectual property rights in the form of patents, copyrights, and trademarks are granted by national governments and are enforceable only in the country in which they are granted. Once granted, they can be traded or licensed like other forms of personal property. The scope of intellectual property rights granted, and the degree to which those laws are enforced, closely reflects what a nation considers to be its best interest. Latin American nations are no exception.

Latin America has one of the lowest standards of intellectual property protection of any region in the world.[1] The level of protection in industrialized countries is generally high, whereas intellectual property protection in Latin America varies widely, with many products excluded from protection altogether. Although the United States extends patent protection to seeds and plants, for example, the intellectual property laws of many Latin American countries explicitly or implicitly exclude biotechnology products and most agricultural inventions. The enthusiasm with which intellectual property rights are enforced by Latin American

---

1. See Edgardo Buscaglia and Jose-Luis Guerrero-Cusumano, "Quantitative Analysis of Counterfeiting Activities in Developing Countries in the Pre-GATT Period," *Jurimetrics Journal* 35 (winter 1995): 221–41. I use the term *intellectual property* to describe all types of intellectual and industrial property, including patents, trademarks, copyrights, trade secrets, and mask works. In many Latin American countries, however, the term is limited to copyrights. Patents and trademarks are considered *industrial property* rights.

governments varies even more than the level and scope of protection.

Latin America does not possess a legal tradition of protecting intellectual property rights.[2] Frequently, Latin American politicians perceive the costs of enforcing intellectual property rights as hampering their chances for reelection and, among other things, reducing campaign contributions made by lobbies representing local pirate industries.[3] By contrast, they deem the benefits of defining and enforcing intellectual property rights to be more distant and less tangible.[4] As a result, whereas the industrialized world regards the protection of intellectual property as a fundamental right, comparable to rights over physical property, Latin American countries have traditionally treated the protection of intellectual property as an economic policy variable.

The most valuable intellectual property on the world market today is information-intensive technology in which the main value of the product is determined by the cost of research and development (R&D) needed to produce it.[5] High-technology products such as computer software and hardware, biotechnology, and phar-

2. See ibid., p. 229.

3. For example, the pharmaceutical industry in Argentina is represented by its lobby, the Industrial Center of Argentine Pharmaceutical Laboratories (CILFA). CILFA's total contributions to members of the Senate and Chamber of Deputies places it among the five most generous pharmaceutical industry lobbying groups in the world. See Tomas Sercheri, "La Corrupcion y la Contribuciones de CILFA," *La Razon*, May 17, 1995, p. 18.

4. See Carlos Primo Braga, "The North-South Debate on Intellectual Property Rights," in *Global Rivalry and Intellectual Property*, ed. Carlos Newell (Ottawa: Institute of Research on Public Policy, 1991).

5. The Organization of Economic Cooperation and Development (OECD) classifies a product as knowledge intensive whenever investment in research and development is more than 10 percent of the total cost of producing the product. See OECD, *Economic Arguments for Protecting Intellectual Property Rights Effectively*, TC/WP(88)70 (Paris: OECD, 1993).

maceuticals are extraordinarily information intensive. In the pharmaceutical industry, the discovery process is extraordinarily resource intensive; once an effective drug is on the market, the compound is comparatively easy to reverse engineer.[6] A copyist does not even need to invest much energy or creativity in figuring out how to copy most information-intensive products because U.S. law requires that the inventor reveal to the world how to make and use the product in exchange for a grant of intellectual property rights.

The problem is compounded by the fact that piracy is easier than ever before since digitized information can be copied with the touch of a button. (In contrast, when the value of an innovation is determined by its physical structure, not by the cost of R&D, the marginal cost of copying is much higher.) The ease of copying is a relatively new development in the history of technology. Until a few decades ago, a person who attempted to pirate and mass-produce copies of a book in violation of copyright laws faced reproduction and publication costs that were not significantly lower than those of the original publisher. The nature of information-intensive technologies, however, makes even their low-tech variations easy to copy. For example, a cassette tape duplicator, made in the United States and available in Brazil for US$4,000, can make three copies of a cassette tape simultaneously in ninety seconds.[7]

Latin American countries have traditionally been forced to import information-intensive goods and services. With the exception of Brazil and Mexico, primary goods are still the main component

6. Research and development expenditures on pharmaceuticals were estimated at $15.8 billion in 1996. Pharmaceutical Research and Manufacturer's Association (PhRMA), *Opportunities and Challenges for Pharmaceutical Innovation* (Washington, D.C.: PhRMA, 1996), p. 9.

7. Jeb Blount, "Hands of Steal," *Latin Trade*, November 1996, p. 56.

of these countries' gross domestic products.[8] As a result, no local constituencies exist to lobby for strong protection of intellectual property rights for information-intensive products, and high-technology products such as software and pharmaceuticals do not enjoy effective patent or copyright protection in most Latin American countries. Latin American nations often claim that they fear strong protection would allow the industrialized world to hold a monopoly on innovative technologies, particularly in the field of biotechnology, and produce drugs and agricultural products that it would sell to the developing world at a high price.

Until recently, modern intellectual property rules were not applied by Latin American governments, even when the benefits of intellectual property protection were recognized by business interests and by the countries generating the essential technologies needed for development.[9] Even now, although formal protection may be available on paper, enforcement is largely nonexistent and even the best enforcement efforts are weak. Thus, Latin America is plagued by two problems with respect to intellectual property: the lack of formal laws providing an adequate scope of protection and the failure to enforce existing laws against violators. Both are necessary for a functional intellectual property system.

In contrast to the philosophy of the United States—that intellectual property rights are to be granted as a reward for creativity and innovation—Latin American nations have used intellectual property rights to regulate technology transfer and minimize royalties to the industrialized world. For example, in most Latin

8. World Bank, *1996 World Development Report* (Baltimore: Johns Hopkins University Press, 1996).

9. Carlos Primo Braga, "The Developing Country Case for or against Intellectual Property Protection," in *Strengthening Protection of Intellectual Property in Developing Countries*, ed. Wolfgang E. Siebeck, Robert E. Evenson, William Lesser, and Carlos Primo Braga (Washington, D.C.: World Bank, 1990), pp. 69–87.

American countries the same government agency that registers patents also regulates foreign direct investment and technology transfer. Seeking to maximize scarce foreign exchange, those countries maintain a weak system of intellectual property protection so as to minimize the outflow of royalty payments.

Argentina, as a net borrower of ready-made know-how from more technologically advanced economies, is a good example of preferring short-term benefits to long-term gains. In Argentina, information technology has only recently been incorporated into much of the private sector, and small- and medium-sized enterprises still predominantly rely on adapting second-rate technologies to local conditions.[10] Many reasons explain this state of affairs. In Argentina, and indeed throughout Latin America in general, technological innovation has always been misrepresented as productive capacity embodied in physical capital. Public policy has not been devoted to enhancing future technological capabilities for the generation and absorption of applied knowledge. Policy makers have simply not understood the importance of enhancing future technological capabilities.

To the extent that Latin American countries do grant formal protection for intellectual property, they often take away with the left hand what they have bestowed with the right. Three techniques used by Latin American nations to weaken the protection afforded by intellectual property rights are (1) issuing compulsory licenses, (2) allowing parallel imports, and (3) applying a working requirement test.

---

10. See Michael Gadbaw and Timothy Richards, eds., *Intellectual Property Rights: Global Consensus, Global Conflict?* (Boulder and London: Westview Press, 1988), pp. 189–90, for a discussion of the state of technological adaptation in Argentina. John Barton argues that countries generating advanced technologies have contributed to this state of affairs by imposing legal restrictions on technology exports based on national security concerns. See John Barton, "The Economic and Legal Context of Contemporary Technology Transfer," manuscript, Stanford University, 1992.

Latin American countries have traditionally imposed compulsory licensing agreements as a precondition for granting and enforcing intellectual property rights. This means that, if a foreign patentee wants to sell a patented product in such a country, the patentee is required to license the right to make, use, and sell that product to local firms, often on fixed-rate royalty terms. Local intellectual property holders are only marginally affected by such conditions because, at present, less than 1 percent of royalties from the licensing of intellectual property is generated by Latin American nationals.[11] Most Latin American countries also attempt to undercut the market power of a foreign national by allowing parallel imports—that is, by allowing competitors who have acquired the right to use a patent abroad to sell a copy of the patented product locally in direct competition with the original owner of a patent. Finally, a working requirement test means that, unless the holder of a patent uses or produces the innovation within the national territory, other producers wishing to use the patented technique will be entitled to a license even without the patentee's consent. If an inventor ceases to use a patented technology (to "work" the technology) for even a short period of time or uses the technology in a way that runs counter to the wishes of the political system, the patent is revoked and the invention declared public property.

Latin American countries have been lax in their justifications for granting compulsory licenses and have also favored mandatory fixed royalty payments in accordance with a national policy of minimizing foreign exchange outflow. Many Latin American governments have used the working requirement test and other barriers to avoid anticipated bottlenecks in the domestic production of "essential" products. They also argue that, unless they impose restrictions on foreign holders of patents, intellectual property

11. See Primo Braga, "The North-South Debate on Intellectual Property Rights."

protection will allow foreign companies to displace domestic producers, exploit market power, and charge higher prices to consumers.

What has readily become apparent, however, is that these methods of undercutting intellectual property protection achieve short-term benefits at the expense of long-term gains. The lack of protection has generated a hostile environment for foreign and domestic investment that hampered the economic growth potential of countries within the region.[12] Investors do not want to bring their latest and best technology to countries whose legal systems systematically fail to protect intellectual property rights. Ultimately these policies discouraged industrialized countries from investing information-intensive technologies in the region. Latin America failed to realize that a relationship existed between protection of intellectual property and high levels of technological investment.

For a long time, it did not matter, at least from the perspective of many Latin American nations. Under the import substitution approach to development, Latin American nations encouraged investment in domestic manufacturing as a substitute for imports. In such an environment, protected from international trade, firms could survive by investing in second-rate technologies. Put simply, strong intellectual rights were not associated with development.

The failure of the import substitution model of development left Latin America with no choice but to incorporate world-class technologies. This in turn meant they would have to converge toward the intellectual property standards prevailing in nations benefiting from information-intensive technologies. In the past decade, Latin America has been moving toward the adoption, mod-

---

12. See Buscaglia and Guerrero-Cusumano, "Quantitative Analysis of Counterfeiting Activities in Developing Countries," p. 229.

ernization, and harmonization of intellectual property laws. As world markets became increasingly integrated, the need for harmonization of territorial intellectual property laws will continue to grow.

The development and commercialization of technology are crucial components of economic growth.[13] With the globalization of the world economy, Latin American countries are finding that maintaining competitiveness is a critical factor in development. Because information-intensive intellectual property is generally produced only after considerable financial investment, the actual, perceived, and expected losses due to inadequate intellectual property protection influence the willingness of firms to transfer information-intensive technology to Latin American countries.[14] The more information intensive the technology, the greater the reticence to transfer it in the absence of adequate intellectual property enforcement. For example, firms with intellectual property rights to information-intensive technology such as chemicals, pharmaceuticals, machinery, and electrical equipment are significantly influenced by the strength of the regime of intellectual property protection in Latin America.[15] Firms in the transportation equipment, metals, and food industries, however, are not as dissuaded from

13. See Nathan Rosenberg and L. E. Birdzell Jr., *How the West Grew Rich: The Economic Transformation of the Industrial World* (Bombay: Popular Prakashan, 1990); Dominique Foray and Christopher Freeman, eds., *Technology and the Wealth of Nations* (Boston: Little, Brown, 1993), pp. 23–34.

14. Edwin Mansfield, "Unauthorized Use of Intellectual Property: Effects on Investment, Technology Transfer, and Innovation," in *Global Dimensions of Intellectual Property Rights in Science and Technology*, ed. Mitchel B. Wallerstein, Mary Ellen Mogee, and Roberta A. Schoen (Washington, D.C.: National Academy Press, 1993), p. 147. See also Edwin Mansfield, "Intellectual Property Protection, Foreign Direct Investment, and Technology Transfer," discussion paper 19, International Finance Corporation, World Bank, Washington, D.C., 1994, p. 1.

15. Mansfield, "Intellectual Property Protection," p. 1.

investing in Latin American countries as are the more information-intensive sectors.[16]

The Harmonization of Intellectual Property Laws

With so much at stake, it is no wonder that industrialized countries, led by the United States, have begun lobbying for intellectual property rights in the Latin America to be on par with those in the industrialized world. Past experience has shown that no nation can protect the intellectual property of its nationals in the international arena through domestic policy alone. In contrast, international treaties specifically devoted to intellectual property rights protection have been largely ineffective in dealing with piracy in the developing world.

One method of encouraging legal reform has consisted of tying intellectual property issues to other foreign policy issues, such as international trade. The agreement on Trade-Related Aspects of Intellectual Property Rights, Including Trade in Counterfeit Goods (TRIPs), which was part of the Uruguay Round Agreements Act of the General Agreement on Tariffs and Trade (GATT), is the most comprehensive multilateral agreement on intellectual property to date. For the first time, TRIPs explicitly made the protection of intellectual property rights part of a broad multilateral trade agreement. Argentina, Brazil, Chile, and Mexico have agreed to raise their standards of intellectual property protection pursuant to TRIPs.

TRIPs achieves several important objectives for international

---

16. Edwin Mansfield, "Patents and Innovation: An Empirical Study," *Management Science* 32 (1986): 173–81. See also Edwin Mansfield, "Intellectual Property Protection, Direct Investment, and Technology Transfer: Germany, Japan, and the United States," discussion paper 27, International Finance Corporation, World Bank, Washington, D.C., 1995, p. 2.

intellectual property protection. It mandates that the standard of intellectual property protection in developing countries, including all of Latin America, be raised; it promotes the transparency of rules governing intellectual property; it applies the principles of national treatment and most-favored-nation treatment to intellectual property enforcement; and it requires that all signatories establish and enforce a common paradigm of intellectual property rules. TRIPs provisions are a great step toward international harmonization of international intellectual property standards.

Nondiscrimination

One of the most important features of TRIPs is that of nondiscrimination: GATT member states must not favor the intellectual property rights of their own citizens against the intellectual property rights of citizens of other members, and they must not favor the rights of citizens of one member country over those of another.[17] The practical result is that products produced within Latin American nations by local firms are equivalent to imports of the same product. This principle of nondiscrimination formally establishes that importing an innovative technique, product, or process to Latin American countries is equivalent to producing it domestically.

Duration of Intellectual Property Rights

The duration of a patent term within TRIPs has been standardized at a minimum of twenty years from the date of filing;[18] copyrights are standardized at fifty years on sound recordings and at least fifty years on motion pictures and other works.[19] Trademark protection is established for seven years and is indefinitely renew-

17. TRIPs agreement, Articles 1 and 3.
18. Ibid., Article 33.
19. Ibid., Article 12.

able as long as the trademark is in use.[20] TRIPs requires that contracting states expedite administrative procedures for granting patents to avoid a de facto reduction in the effective life of a patent.[21]
To the extent that this provision proves effective, it will be a boon
for information-intensive firms, which have continually been frustrated by the long backlogs in granting intellectual property rights
throughout Latin America.

Scope of Intellectual Property Rights

Throughout Latin America, the list of products that have been
declared ineligible for intellectual property protection is long, including software, pharmaceuticals, and the products of biotechnology (e.g., genetically engineered organisms). TRIPs expands the
existing scope of protection for trade secrets, computer programs,
and databases. In the case of pharmaceuticals, although TRIPs extends the scope of what is patentable, it excludes natural or artifi-
cially produced biological material, animals, and plant varieties.[22]
TRIPs also confers on patentees the following exclusive rights: the
exclusion of third parties from the acts of producing, distributing,
selling, or importing a product subject to a patent; the exclusion
of third parties from the acts of using, selling, and importing a
patented process and full protection of the product obtained
through the patented process; and the flexibility to sell or license
patent rights. Although protection for information-intensive products is not airtight, TRIPs represents an increase in the previous
level of protection.

20. Ibid., Article 18.
21. Ibid., Article 33.
22. Ibid., Article 27. Those exclusions represented a victory for Latin America in
the eyes of some negotiators.

Licensing

This is an area in which international disputes are common. TRIPs has failed to resolve these conflicts because it allows nations to grant compulsory licenses for "adequate remuneration" after considering each case "on its individual merits" and after attempting to negotiate "reasonable commercial terms" with holders of intellectual property rights.[23] TRIPs specifies that compulsory licenses must be nonexclusive and of limited duration, but it undercuts this by mandating that appeals of compulsory licenses be subject to the jurisdiction of the nation imposing the license. The result is that, even after TRIPs, Latin American countries can continue to require compulsory licenses.

Transition Period for Less-Developed Countries

TRIPs allows developing countries a ten-year grace or transition period in which to extend intellectual property rights to those industries that had not been previously subject to intellectual property protection.[24] TRIPs does not require "pipeline" or retroactive protection for patents that are covered under the new proposed laws but were not protected under the old laws. Both the grace period and the lack of pipeline protection are particularly troubling issues for investors in the pharmaceutical sector in countries such as Argentina, where an enormous industry producing pirate pharmaceuticals has developed and where displacement of workers and capital is an economic and social concern.[25]

23. TRIPs agreement, Article 31(a), (b).
24. Ibid., Article 66(1).
25. A comprehensive picture of these and other issues can be found in "Patents Farmaceuticas," special edition of the *Revista del Derecho Industrial* 35 (May–August 1990) (Ed. Depalma, Buenos Aires). See also Alberto Bercovitz, "Historical Trends in the Protection of Technology in Developed Countries and their Relationship to Protection in Developing Countries," UNCTAD/TT/Misc./75.

Enforcement Mechanisms

TRIPs attempts to cure the problems in international market transactions of high-technology goods and services. It also provides benefits to those developing countries that have had limited access to high technologies because of their lack of technological capabilities. By providing clear and enforceable rules, plus dispute settlement mechanisms, TRIPs promotes the institutional capacity of developing nations to absorb complex technologies.

In short, the principles enunciated in TRIPs are moving Latin America toward harmonized standards of intellectual property protection, but the speed of the convergence can be extremely slow. TRIPs has a ten-year transition period to allow developing countries to comply with increased standards of protection for intellectual property rights. How quickly increased standards of protection will be adopted, and what form those standards will take, remains an open question. The onus is on Latin American countries to carry out the process of intellectual property reform.

The Future of Intellectual Property Rights in Latin America

Incentives to adopt or alter a particular intellectual property scheme can come from within, or from without, a culture. The speed with which developing countries adopt standards of intellectual property protection in compliance with TRIPs will depend largely on local domestic conditions and political pressures.

Slowly, Latin American countries are addressing the issues of increased standards of protection and enforcement of intellectual property rights, but their efforts have met with mixed success. One commentator describes the scene:

> Venezuela recently created its first "authors' rights task force" to pursue violators of copyrights, but the country's own national copyright registry burned down soon after. Argentine President Carlos Menem,

targeting a 1933 law, decreed protection for computer programs, but a court said software couldn't be copyrighted. Paraguay indicated an intention to revise its pre-digital [intellectual property rights] laws and raided pirate factories, but the plants reopened within weeks.[26]

Peru's National Institute for the Defense of the Standards and Protection of Intellectual Property (INDECOPI) claims to be protecting the rights of intellectual property holders, but the incidence of piracy in that country does not appear to be diminishing.[27] Intellectual property holders in Peru must pay for the costs of prosecuting violators, in addition to paying the bribes Peruvian police have demanded in exchange for conducting raids.[28] Neither Argentina nor Columbia nor Chile provides intellectual property protection for pipeline pharmaceuticals that were in development before TRIPs took effect.

Among Latin American countries, Brazil, for one, appears to have made significant gains: In June 1996, Brazil passed a patent law that expanded the scope of subject matter that could be patented and granted pipeline protection for pharmaceuticals. But in so doing, it came under fire from the Roman Catholic Church, which objected to patenting living organisms created by biotechnology.[29] Although Brazil now has the highest level of intellectual property protection in Latin America, piracy is still a problem; estimates credit Brazil with over one-third of the market for pirated cassette tapes in Latin America.[30]

Brazil's reasons for raising its standards of intellectual property protection are simple. From a domestic policy perspective, Brazil's

26. Blount, "Hands of Steal," p. 52.

27. Ibid., p. 57.

28. Ibid., p. 58.

29. Ibid., p. 54. The United States Supreme Court in 1980 declared in *Diamond v. Chakrabarty* that the products of biotechnology were patentable. 447 U.S. 303 (1980).

30. Blount, "Hands of Steal," p. 56.

reforms correspond with the failure of the import substitution approach to development in Latin America. More than any other country in the region, Brazil until recently practiced an extreme version of this approach to development. From the early 1930s until the late 1980s, Brazil and other Latin American nations encouraged investment in domestic manufacturing as a substitute for imports, suppressed agricultural prices, expanded the size of public sector enterprises, and attempted to stimulate savings and investment through taxation and credit allocated by the public sector, all in the belief that amassing domestic physical capital was the key to development. Import substitution industries grew behind protective walls based on subsidies and tariffs in a milieu where many other determinants of the rate of economic growth, such as investment in human capital and the role of microeconomic incentives, were completely ignored by policy makers.

Protection of import substitution industries caused domestic prices and costs far to exceed international prices and created few incentives for efficiency. These protected industries produced substitutes for imports but usually depended on the import of raw materials and technology. Import demand grew rapidly as these firms imported capital goods to accelerate investment. The anti-export bias, combined with the import substitution program, caused a scarcity of foreign exchange, which in turn created a structural barrier to investment in expensive first-rate technologies. Within this environment protected from international trade, however, firms could still survive by investing in second-rate technologies. This import substitution strategy was applied to the domestic pharmaceutical and computer industries in Brazil.

The import substitution approach to development fell out of favor during the international debt crisis of the 1980s, when Latin American policy makers realized that internal markets and import substitution were not enough to assure sustainable growth.[31] The demise of the import substitution model left Brazil in particular, and Latin America in general, with no other option for economic growth than to eliminate trade barriers and promote competitive exports through the incorporation of world-class technologies. As a result, countries such as Argentina, Brazil, Chile, and Mexico are being forced to reconsider many of their legal institutions, including their national intellectual property laws. International economic and political forces have forced Brazil to converge toward the intellectual property legal frameworks prevailing in nations generating standard technologies.

At the same time, the privatization of state monopolies and the shift toward import competition produced a vast increase in the demand for high-technology products in Latin America. The United States experienced a 215 percent increase in exports of telecommunication and information technology to the region between 1988 and 1995. For Japan and the European Union, these figures were 187 and 97 percent, respectively.[32] The vast increase in the international transactions of information-intensive goods and services exported to Latin America made it increasingly necessary to use U.S. foreign policy as the main mechanism to promote intellectual property reform in Latin America. It soon became clear that the international harmonization of intellectual property rules was a sine qua non for the transfer of complex technologies to the developing world.[33]

31. For a complete description of this process, see Edgardo Buscaglia Jr., "Law, Technological Progress, and Economic Development," Hoover Institution working paper I-93-5, International Studies Program, Stanford University (1993).

32. See Bureau of National Affairs, *International Trade Reporter* (Washington, D.C.), May 30, 1996, pp. 766–69.

33. See General Agreement on Tariffs and Trade (GATT), *Trade Policy Review* (Geneva: GATT, 1990).

The feasibility of enacting intellectual property rights reforms sooner rather than later will depend on Latin American leaders' assessment of the costs and benefits of providing enhanced intellectual property protection. Political and business leaders in the developing world realize that raising the standards of intellectual property protection will create long-term benefits but short-term costs. The political feasibility of intellectual property reform in Latin America can only occur when politicians perceive that the long-term benefits of enacting a new law are greater than the short-term costs.

Increased political stability increases the chance that Latin American politicians and business leaders will support and adopt policies conducive to long-term gains, rather than treating intellectual property as an economic variable to avoid the short-term costs of paying royalties. The present relative political stability, supported by periodic elections and a greater access to public office, has created a environment where legal reforms requiring politicians to act for the long term are more feasible than ever before. Politicians' chances of reelection make them and their parties potential repeat players in the political system, able to capture the long-term benefits derived from their proposed legal reforms.

When governments are unstable, and when politicians do not expect to gain the long-term benefits of legal reforms, they do not have the incentive to make those reforms. For example, in Argentina the costs of reform have been brought to the attention of the Congress by powerful interest groups representing the domestic pirate pharmaceutical sector.[34] Mandated royalty payments, human and nonhuman resource displacement, and possible anticompeti-

---

34. The two main trade associations representing the industry are CILFA and the Latin American Pharmaceutical Industry Association (ALIFAR). Both have strong ties to key members of the two legislative branches in Argentina. Millions of dollars in political contributions explain the influence of these associations in Congress.

tive effects are perceived by many Latin American nations as unbearable costs caused by the introduction of patent protection. By contrast, possible benefits such as enhancing technology transfers and capital formation, disclosure of new knowledge, improvements in health/safety standards, and global technological dynamism have traditionally been perceived as long-term speculative gains.

The policies supporting a weak enforcement of intellectual property rights have also been depicted as a way to avoid displacing domestic pirate industries. In the case of pharmaceuticals, well-known political and business leaders in developing countries have expressed ethical concerns about improved standards of protection. Indira Ghandi's words have come to symbolize the strong opposition to granting intellectual property rights to pharmaceutical products in developing countries. In a famous speech, given before the World Health Assembly, she said that "the idea of a better ordered world is one in which medical discoveries will be free of patents."[35] Nor is opposition to increased standards of protection limited to political leaders. The American Embassy in Buenos Aires has estimated that the pharmaceutical and software firms opposing enhanced intellectual property protection, and their associations, have consistently outspent foreign firms and their trade associations by a margin of nine to one.[36] The pirate pharmaceutical industry in Argentina, which is worth $4.6 billion, supplies the rest of Latin America with pirated copies of U.S.-patented pharmaceuticals.

Latin American governments are properly concerned that intellectual property rights will raise the cost of patented products

35. Gadbaw and Richards, *Intellectual Property Rights: Global Consensus, Global Conflict?* p. 57.

36. Mark Siegelman, "Intellectual Property Protection: Argentina," U.S. Department of Commerce, pp. 8–14.

beyond the reach of the poor. But ironically enough, this argument is often advanced by the pirate pharmaceutical industry in Argentina. The pirate pharmaceutical industry in Argentina is well organized and enjoys market penetration and market dominance, making up more than 50 percent of the total pharmaceutical market in Argentina. Contrary to expectation, pirate pharmaceuticals in Argentina are 12.1 percent more expensive, on average, than their patented counterparts. Although it is true that patents may raise prices, so too can well-organized interest groups.

Ultimately, intellectual property protection attracts international investment. Patent laws were introduced in the presence of powerful domestic pirate pharmaceutical industries in Brazil in 1996, in Mexico in 1991 (amended in 1995), and in Italy in 1978. In the Mexican and Italian cases, the perceived costs were overstated by local politicians a priori.[37] It is too soon to reach a conclusion with respect to Brazil. Ultimately, Italy and Mexico experienced increased levels of investments and employment in their domestic industries.[38] Moreover, the Mexican and Italian pharmaceutical sectors enjoyed lower average prices and enhanced foreign competition in an environment with lower market concentration ratios.[39] When other variables are held constant, a statistically significant relationship arises between the increase in the U.S. direct investment in Mexican manufacturing during 1990–92 and an index of the perceived strengthening of the intellectual property enforcement mechanisms.[40] The same can be expected for Brazil; the recent law allowing patent protection for pharmaceuticals has

37. See Buscaglia and Guerrero-Cusumano, "Quantitative Analysis of Counterfeiting Activities in Developing Countries," pp. 229–30.

38. See ibid., p. 229.

39. For more details, see Jeong-Yeon Lee, work toward a doctoral dissertation at the University of Pennsylvania, 1993; and Mansfield, "Unauthorized Use of Intellectual Property: Effects on Investment, Technology Transfer, and Innovation."

40. Lee, work toward a doctoral dissertation at the University of Pennsylvania.

been estimated to have attracted as much as $1.2 billion to Brazil in pharmaceutical investment.[41] In Latin America, intellectual property reforms would, as in Mexico and Italy, increase the flows of foreign direct investment into those sectors protected by patents.

Nevertheless, it is also necessary to reduce the cost that politicians pay for supporting better laws. Unsupervised financial contributions to members of Latin American legislatures, originating from groups representing pirate industries, are aimed at blocking the enactment of stricter intellectual property laws.[42] These contributions are currently unmonitored in Latin America (except Mexico). For example, it is estimated that Argentina's pharmaceutical lobby, the Industrial Center of Argentine Pharmaceutical Laboratories, contributes millions of dollars a year to the political campaigns of those members of Congress opposing stronger patent laws.[43] Therefore, supporting stronger standards of intellectual property protection has very real political costs. To reduce the politicians' perceived costs of supporting legal reform, it is necessary to establish a close supervision of political campaign financing coupled with stiff penalties for those members of Congress who sell their votes. The fight against corruption would also enhance the likelihood of enacting and enforcing well-defined intellectual property rights.

The impetus to harmonize standards for intellectual property protection also depends on the degree to which countries involved in a trade agreement have compatible incentives for technological development. More specifically, countries with emerging high-

41. John Schwartz, "160 Countries Set Treaties on Internet Copyrights," *Washington Post*, December 21, 1996, sec. A8, col. 1.

42. See Edgardo Buscaglia, "Corrupcion y la Oposicion a la Ley de Patentes," *El Comercio* (Lima, Peru), August 12, 1996, p. 16.

43. Ibid.

growth sectors will experience private-sector pressures to harmonize their intellectual property laws with those of countries experiencing the same changes. Because the nonagricultural trade-related sectors of a nation's economy are the most likely sectors to demand information-intensive products, they can be expected to lobby for improved intellectual property protection for nationally produced high technology and for free trade in foreign high technology. Traditional agrarian economies, in contrast, do not have the same incentive to reform their laws to protect the assets of their own or other nations' high-growth sectors.

Latin American governments are now following the bumpy road toward market-led growth and import competition after decades of failed development policies. Reservations notwithstanding, the cost-benefit perceptions of many Latin American political and business leaders about intellectual property legal reform have begun to change during the past few years. TRIPs and the expected trade gains have tipped the balance in favor of a stronger intellectual property framework; the question now is how soon Latin American nations will implement increased levels of intellectual property protection. At this stage, we can expect domestic political forces to provide the essential engine of legal reform and regional political stability to allow governments to be able to reap the long-term benefits of those reforms.

Conclusion

Progress toward higher standards of intellectual property protection and enforcement in Latin America is definitive but slow. Clearly, the road to intellectual property reform will not be easy. But Latin America has the goad of decades of failed development policies and disastrous economic planning prodding it toward adopting strategies that will allow it to develop and compete in an increasingly high-technology-driven world. In the final analysis, political and economic pressures have provided the impetus for the current wave of intellectual property reform observed in many developing nations. The marriage of convenience between intellectual property and international trade issues has caused many Latin American nations to see the enforcement of intellectual property as one way to gain foreign market access under preferential terms.

With experience as a guide, Latin American nations realize that they must provide incentives for information-intensive technology producers to invest their latest and best technologies in the region. Where local constituencies also benefit from the protection of intellectual property, the chances of improving intellectual property protection will be highest.

Crawford Beveridge

19

The Role of an Economic Development Agency in Creating the Right Environment for a Knowledge-Based Society

The future of knowledge-based economies in an increasingly litigious world has been a subject of much debate in recent times. As Lester Thurow put it in an article in *Harvard Business Review*, "Fundamental shifts in technology and in the economic landscape are rapidly making the current system of intellectual property rights unworkable and ineffective."[1] Fortunately, we in Scotland believe we are leading the way in the creation of an ideal environment in which knowledge-based industries—and the necessary associated security of intellectual property—can flourish.

Scotland is a country less than half the size of California, with

---

1. Lester Thurow, "Needed, a New System of Intellectual Property Rights," *Harvard Business Review*, September–October 1997, pp. 212–36.

a population of five million people. It is part of the United Kingdom (U.K.), having entered into a voluntary union with England
almost three hundred years ago. As part of the agreement of that
union, it kept its own legal structure, its own educational system,
and, of course, its distinctive culture. The recent referendum between England and Scotland will give the Scots their own parliament in 2000 within the U.K. system. Scotland's secretary of state
is a member of the cabinet of Tony Blair, the prime minister.

The country has been engaged in the process of creating intellectual capital for many centuries, and Scots have blazed trails in
science and engineering, from astronomy to optoelectronics, from
steam power to semiconductors. Many people will know of the
contribution to steam power by James Watt, to the telephone by
Alexander Graham Bell, and to television by Logie Baird. Yet,
although Scottish science and technology continue to be utilized
and exploited around the world, we have not paid as much attention as we might to how to exploit them in our own backyard.
What I want to describe are steps we are taking to try to change
that situation and to position ourselves for the next millennium. I
want to promote the understanding that our small nation has
grasped the essential issues relating to success in a knowledge-
based society and the policy decisions regarding the management
of intellectual capital.

And what about Scottish Enterprise, the organization I head?
Scottish Enterprise is not a government department but a rather
unique establishment (found in the United Kingdom) that exists at
arm's length from the government. We work for the secretary of
state on the basis that he funds us with a block of money to pursue
specific objectives with regard to economic development in Scotland. We are given a large degree of freedom in how we go about
that task. Our people are a mixture of career economic development specialists and people like myself who came in from industry
for a few years and will probably go back out to industry when

their task is done. Some may see this setup as an example of big interventionist, centrally planned government. Nothing could be further from the truth.

From my time in America, I remember well Ronald Reagan's comments that the nine most dangerous words in the English language were "I'm from the government and I'm here to help." Much of our role is not to do things but to clear out of the way things that should not be done; to get rid of the barriers so that the market can operate and business can do what it needs to do. So we believe that public sector organizations like ours have a significant role to play in creating—in partnership with industry and academia—the right environment. We also believe that small, flexible, and responsive nations that are committed to embracing change can succeed in the new economy.

Context for Change

Internationally competitive firms—the main drivers of economic growth, wealth creation, and job opportunities—rarely exist in isolation but are often found in local clusters of mutually supportive industries. Studies consistently show that economic growth tends to be concentrated in industries or groups of related industries in a geographic area marked by close links among customers, suppliers, academic institutions and even competitors. Strong clusters tend to have many advantages, including

- Foreign companies may be drawn to locate in areas where there is a strong cluster environment.

- New businesses spring up to service the aggregate requirements of successful local industries and incoming businesses.

- People with good ideas and specialized skills are drawn to these areas and their input increases the momentum of the local economy as it develops and expands.

Although an individual cluster provides greater diversity than a single industry, in a globally competitive economic climate of change and uncertainty, multiple clusters spread development risks even further. They represent an opportunity for a region to develop a balanced portfolio of economic assets that is capable of smoothing out some of the stresses and strains of modern market forces. The rational development of multiple clusters within a region is a complex and challenging task demanding deep industry knowledge and a detailed understanding of the drivers of strategic change in the global business environment.

Scottish Enterprise has four main roles in this cluster-based approach. The first role is to create and communicate a distinctive and challenging economic vision in collaboration with key partners and stakeholders. The second is to improve the availability, quality, and cost-effectiveness of all components of a cluster. The third is to create a context that fosters innovation and upgrading. The fourth is to reinforce the overall process of cluster development. Scottish Enterprise's ambition—to help generate jobs and prosperity for the people of Scotland—incorporates this cluster approach, which depends on a variety of key industries and enabling technologies, including biotechnology, education services, energy, financial services, food, and the information industries including electronics, software, and multimedia.

This cluster strategy's range of projects is outlined below.

- *Encouraging new ventures/start-ups.* The provision of zero-stage start-up funding for financing new companies' products has helped new optoelectronics entrepreneurs during the critical first stages of business development.

- *Attracting inward investment.* Hyundai Electronics Europe plans to establish a complex of two state-of-the-art semiconductor facilities in Scotland as part of our already strong semiconductor manufacturing cluster.

- *Building and anchoring the local customer base.* Over the years Scotland has been successful in attracting multinational electronics companies to locate manufacturing plants around the country. These original equipment manufacturers (OEMs) such as IBM and Compaq operate in a global market and, as such, demand extremely high standards of their suppliers.

- *Promoting exports.* Overseas exhibitions and trade missions are effective tools for fulfilling a number of marketing objectives: testing the market, meeting potential agents or distributors, and making contact with key customers. The Scottish Exhibition and Mission Programme, organized by Scottish Enterprise, helps companies in key clusters such as food, electronics, energy, biotechnology, and textiles to maximize the potential from these opportunities at exhibitions under the umbrella of a distinctive Scottish identity.

- *Education and training programs.* Scottish Enterprise has built and fostered strong links with industry bodies such as the Scottish Electronics Forum, the Scottish Optoelectronics Association, and the Scottish Software Federation. Through these affiliations projects are being developed to upgrade the skills of the existing Scottish workforce and educate future generations to the high standards required by the electronics cluster.

- *Research efforts in local academic institutions.* To bridge the gap that exists between pure research and production in the emerging biotechnology cluster, Scottish Enterprise helped to establish the MRC Scottish Collaborative Research Centre, which creates lab space wherein companies interested in developing some particular research through to a commercial state can come together with the scientists who conducted the original research.

- *Forums for building and exchanging knowledge.* The Scottish Oil and Gas Innovation Forum was set up by Scottish Enterprise to identify and maximize the growth opportunities for the oil and gas industry by both encouraging innovative ideas at a technological level and creating new ways companies can work together.

- *Developing existing specialist companies.* Design and development is essential to the well-being of the electronics sector worldwide. Therefore, in the development of the Scottish information industry cluster, it is essential that design capabilities be built up in Scotland which suppliers can easily access.

    To help facilitate more OEM supplier-design partnerships, Scottish Enterprise has produced a CD-ROM containing details of all existing design capabilities available in Scotland, from large representatives of the defense industry to smaller independent design houses.

- *Attracting new start-ups/inward investors.* As a virtual center of excellence, the National Microelectronics Institute's headquarters at Heriot-Watt University in Edinburgh helps strengthen the electronics cluster in Scotland by coordinating information technology links and by promoting training and technical services throughout the United Kingdom.

Success in the Knowledge-Intensive Environment

Because this cluster focus has been emerging in Scotland, the country is now one of the most successful locations for inward investment in Europe. As a result of its inward investment policies, and the spin-offs they have created for indigenous businesses, Scotland now supplies 13 percent of Europe's semiconductors, 32 percent of Europe's branded personal computers, 65 percent of Europe's automated teller machines, and 80 percent of Europe's workstations. By the same token, it would have been hard for anyone to have escaped the publicity generated by Dolly, the cloned sheep. Dolly is a product of the Roslin Institute, one of a number of collaborative research centers that cover a wide range of technologies.

These developments interact with the educational vibrancy of the nation. With thirteen universities and fifty-four colleges, many of which already have worldwide reputations, Scotland produces the highest number of graduates per capita overall in the European Union (EU), especially in engineering (where its output is the highest in the EU). Scotland's well-known tradition of excellence in education has produced a level of funding for research that is disproportionately high for a country of its size. Scottish universities receive 12.5 percent of all U.K. university research funding and 12.6 percent of U.K. industry research funding—with only 10 percent of the population.

Another happy result of our efforts has been the creation of strong networks for exchanging knowledge. In areas such as electronics, textiles, optoelectronics, oil and gas, molecular biology, interactive media, neural networks, and so on, Scottish Enterprise now supports active collaborative forums bringing together industry, academia, and government. Supporting those programs are specific interventions in design, including an Institute of Photonics (to transfer university research throughout the country's optoelectronics industry) and the United Kingdom's National Microelectronics Institute (based in Scotland and intended to link our semiconductor companies to academia), as mentioned above.

Obviously, the commonality in all this is knowledge. These knowledge-based activities are driving us inexorably in the direction of a knowledge economy.

Knowledge and Property

The challenges of intellectual property (IP) creation and utilization, in support of competitiveness and wealth generation, afford nations significant opportunities in the knowledge economy.

The problems that currently surround intellectual capital, and the difficulties in trading and protecting IP, offer a market opportunity for those nations that can simplify the process of IP trade and at the same time protect an owner's investment. Scotland has seized that market opportunity with both hands and is in the process of developing an environment in which a knowledge-based economy can not only function but also prosper. What we are talking about is nothing more or less than the reinvention of our *economy*. We have done it before—in the movement away from the heavy industries of shipbuilding, steelworking, and coal mining to the high-technology industries of electronics and semiconductors. What we are now doing is changing the environment to encourage more knowledge-based companies and projects to flourish in Scotland.

Because of the faster pace involved in product design and the need to use multiple sources of IP, the creation of a "development-friendly" environment is a major priority.

The challenges are numerous. For example,

- IP/copyright legislation tends to have its origins in the arts and creative disciplines and therefore often tends to be inappropriate for today's technology-related applications.

- The European Union is taking a strong interest in this area, as shown by Trade-Related Aspects of Intellectual Property Rights (TRIPS) discussions, and would like to see the relevant treaties updated to recognize the importance of intellectual capital. The EU is also drafting a directive that would ensure that the owners of intellectual property receive full legal protection when that property is distributed in digital form.

Time, of course, is a critical factor for success in high-technology products. In Scotland we are aiming to create a new way of working that will allow IP to be traded in a secure environment and thereby enable companies to drastically shorten product development times and gain a much higher level of usage from their existing library of IP.

Obviously, there is currently a wide-ranging debate about the future of knowledge-based societies and how intellectual property will be safeguarded in the increasingly fast-moving consumer electronics markets. Issues such as IP copyright legislation, education, physical movements of IP data, and customs and taxation issues are all being looked at carefully in order that growth not be impeded. Along with the difficult issue of security of transfer comes perhaps the more troubling issue of traceability. We are determined to produce some meaningful "watermark" that will help stop unauthorized reuse, modification, or incorporation of IP.

Scottish Enterprise aims to build on the base that we have established in many areas, including current manufacturing activities, software development, academic excellence in leading edge technologies, a deregulated telecommunications environment, and a strong record of inward investment and export achievement. Taken together, these elements constitute a strong platform from which to move Scotland toward a strong position in the global information industry, providing high-value jobs and economic growth.

Knowledge Industry Focus

Overall, this focus requires an economic shift, from being predominantly manufacturing-based toward value-added and knowledge-intensive activities, hence securing continued growth in long-term higher levels of employment. For Scotland and the U.K., the key strategic issues relating to this longer-term industry development include development of an advanced technology base, commercialization skills, and software-based activities. Additionally, a greater emphasis needs to be placed on knowledge and skill-based activities, particularly in the areas of research and development, design, telecommunications, and multimedia. Finally, attention needs to be given to the internationalization of standards for manufacturing excellence within small and medium-sized enterprises.

Major electronics companies are also facing a critical decision point regarding their approach to system design. For example, semiconductor technology is progressing to the point where, within the next two years, at 0.18 micron, up to 100 million transistors could be designed onto a single chip. Few companies have the intellectual property to effectively utilize semiconductor integration capacity of this scale by themselves; consequently, they are forced to search for alternative and complementary sources of intellectual property. Additionally, consumer markets tend to have short (around nine months) product life cycles; thus time to market is becoming increasingly critical as the consumer component grows in importance. Most important, finalizing a contract for a single block of IP between two companies can take up to twelve months. When the target market is projected to have a product life cycle of only nine to twelve months, that contracting time is uncompetitive. The way business is done will probably have to change.

As a result, Scottish Enterprise recognizes that companies are today initiating experimental, "proof of concept" projects to demonstrate how they could, at the technical integration level, create "systems on chips." Concurrently, they are attempting to determine where they should locate their next generation design centers with an eye toward an environment that facilitates the conduct of business.

Scotland's ambition is to create a physical and fiscal infrastructure where IP blocks, under a certain framework, can be developed, traded, and utilized by worldwide consumer manufacturing companies in a timely, legal, and cost-effective manner. Our concept is to provide a location that can host a sustainable "design complex" that would provide customers with fast access to highly complex designs from multiple intellectual property sources that will be required for next-generation products in the consumer markets.

We do not underestimate the nature of the barriers or the scale of business and legal change that is required to accomplish these goals, but we are keen to start the process and make it work. Intellectual property protection and management are our most difficult challenges, and the creation of a secure IP trading process is vital to successful delivery of this new methodology. Scotland is working now to create unique solutions, an opportunity provided because the law is "thin" in the United Kingdom relative to the United States. Even though Scotland already has a legal system that offers robust protection of IP without frustrating its exploitation, our culture is much less litigious than that in the United States.

Aside from strengthening intellectual property protection, we have focused on three other areas that need improvement. First, education at the university level needs to be revised to support the concept we are trying to develop. Second, Scotland is in the midst of developing its infrastructure to support the physical movement of IP data. This process, once completed, will create a great leap in data transfer and in productivity. Third, customs and taxation issues related to the value of blocks of IP and their transfer need to be ironed out to everyone's satisfaction. Scotland wants to avoid the multiple taxation of intellectual property transfers, a problem that exists throughout the rest of Europe.

In short, Scotland envisions itself as the location for next-generation IP design and innovation. The environment for multiple design and product development companies underpins Scottish Enterprise's strategy for cluster development across a wide range of industries. With our strong education system, low level of litigation, encouragement of collaborative research, and focused strategy for knowledge industries, we believe that Scotland offers an unbeatable environment in which cutting-edge intellectual property will grow and thrive. Scottish Enterprise is supporting this effort on many fronts and looks forward to its continued role in Scotland's IP success.

Appendix—Selected Readings on Intellectual Capital and Cluster Development

Collins, Luke. "Shift to Systems on Chip Signal Massive Changes Ahead." *Electronic News*, March 14, 1997.

"European Professor Demos Macrocell Intellectual Property Service at DAC: Startup Looks to Commercialise Web-Based Design Tentatively Formed to Provide Online Subscription-Based IP Information Tools." *Electronic Engineering Times*, June 11, 1997.

Fox, Melanie. "For Sale: Intellectual Property." *Cadence Plugged-In*, February 6, 1997.

"IP Unfolded." *Electronic Engineering Times*, April 1997.

"New Infrastructure Would Meld VSI, Corporate Intranets, Advanced Tools: Portable

IP Could Transform Japanese IC Design." *Electronic Engineering Times*, March 20, 1997.

Santarini, Michael. "Questions Gnaw at Core of Design Reuse." *Electronic Engineering Times*, August 4, 1997.

Steffora, Ann, and Mario Pereira. "One Good Spin Deserves Another." *Electronic Business Asia*, August 1997.

Pamela Samuelson

 20

Challenges for the World Intellectual Property Organization and the Trade-Related Aspects of Intellectual Property Rights Council in Regulating Intellectual Property Rights in the Information Age

Two international organizations, one old and one new, have as a goal promoting respect for intellectual property rights on a global scale. The World Intellectual Property Organization (WIPO) has five decades of experience in promoting international discussions about intellectual property norms and administering major international intellectual property treaties. These include most notably the Paris and Berne Conventions that regulate, respectively, norms concerning the legal protection of industrial property and literary and artistic works.[1] In

---

1. See Berne Convention for the Protection of Literary and Artistic Works, September 9, 1886, as last revised at Paris, July 24, 1971, and amended in 1979, 828 U.N.T.S. 221 (hereinafter Berne Convention); Paris Convention for the Protection of Industrial Property, March 20, 1883, 13 U.S.T. 1, revised July 14, 1967, 21 U.S.T. 1583, 823 U.N.T.S. 305 (hereinafter Paris Convention).

the aftermath of the 1994 adoption of the agreement on Trade-Related Aspects of Intellectual Property Rights (TRIPS) as an annex to the international agreement that established the World Trade Organization (WTO),[2] WIPO's prominence in the international intellectual property policy arena is under challenge by the newly created TRIPS Council. The council has responsibility, among other things, for overseeing compliance with TRIPS norms and recommending amendment to the TRIPS agreement as new intellectual property norms become accepted by the international community.[3] The roles of these two organizations are intertwined to some degree.

As established as WIPO and the TRIPS Council seem to be in today's international intellectual property policy arena, each faces a more uncertain future than some commentators seem to think.[4] Both individually and in conjunction with one another, these institutions face serious challenges. Neither should take for granted that fifty years hence it will have surmounted these challenges and achieved the level of trust, acceptance, and respect that it might wish for in the new world economic order.

For WIPO, the most obvious challenges lie in redefining its

2. See Final Act Embodying the Results of the Uruguay Round of Multilateral Trade Negotiations, April 15, 1994, reprinted in *The Results of the Uruguay Round of Multilateral Trade Negotiations—the Legal Texts* 2–3 (GATT Secretariat, ed., 1994); Marrakesh Agreement Establishing the World Trade Organization, April 15, 1994 (hereinafter WTO agreement), Annex 1C: Agreement on Trade-Related Aspects of Intellectual Property Rights (hereinafter WTO agreement), Annex 1C: Agreement on Trade-Related Aspects of Intellectual Property Rights (hereinafter TRIPS agreement), reprinted in *Results of Uruguay Round*, supra, at 6–19, 365–403.

3. TRIPS agreement, supra note 2, Arts. 68–71. See generally Adrian Otten and Hannu Wager, Compliance with TRIPS: The Emerging World View, *Vanderbilt Journal of Transnational Law* 29 (1996): 391, 409–13.

4. See, for example, *From GATT to TRIPS: The Agreement on Trade-Related Aspects of Intellectual Property Rights*, ed. Friedrich-Karl Beier and Gerhard Schricker, 1996 (hereinafter *From GATT to TRIPS*).

role in the international intellectual property policy making community. The TRIPS agreement, after all, was adopted in part because of dissatisfaction with WIPO processes.[5] Although the TRIPS Council has been tasked to work out cooperative arrangements with WIPO, internecine struggles seem almost inevitable between these two organizations. In the long run, unless a mutually satisfactory, symbiotic relationship develops between these two organizations, one is likely to achieve hegemony at the expense of the other. This will likely lead to a withering away or a considerable diminishment in the role of one of these institutions in the intellectual property policy arena.

For the TRIPS Council, the most obvious challenge lies in constructing an institutional structure that will accomplish the major goal of TRIPS: that of persuading countries to comply voluntarily with the letter and spirit of TRIPS norms. The temptation to be highly interventionistic—in overseeing national intellectual property policies and in raising ever higher the "floor" of minimum rights that TRIPS obligates WTO members to accept—should be resisted, at least in the near term. WTO members must come to trust the TRIPS Council. This will be difficult if the benefits of TRIPS come to be perceived as confined to the relatively small number of WTO members that are major exporters of intellectual property products.

The time is surely ripe for an essay on survival strategies for WIPO and the TRIPS Council in relation to these sorts of institutional challenges, as they strive to regulate intellectual property rights for the global information economy in the twenty-first century. As worthy as this topic is for consideration, this chapter will take a somewhat different tack, discussing some less obvious, more substantive challenges these organizations face. It will also provide

5. See, for example, Paul Katzenberger and Annette Kur, "TRIPs and Intellectual Property," in *From GATT to TRIPS*, supra note 4, at 15.

some suggestions about how WIPO and the TRIPS Council might enhance their prospects for achieving their mutual goals: increasing respect for intellectual property rights and reducing the trade distortions that arise from inadequate intellectual property protection in the global arena.

There are at least four respects in which WIPO and the TRIPS Council need to broaden their perspectives if they are to succeed in fostering adequate and effective intellectual property protection in the international community over the next fifty years. First, these organizations need to become more mindful of economic learning and more attentive to competition policy in formulating and applying intellectual property norms. Second, these organizations need to obtain disinterested expertise in emerging information technologies so that their efforts to aid the evolution of intellectual property norms will be built on an appropriate understanding of technological developments.

Third, WIPO and the TRIPS Council need to be alert to the possible emergence of new intellectual property paradigms for the information age. The norms enshrined in the Paris and Berne Conventions and incorporated by reference in TRIPS derive from the needs of a nineteenth-century manufacturing-base economy. The global information economy may require new norms of intellectual property.

Fourth, WIPO and the TRIPS Council should ponder the relationship between intellectual property and intellectual capital. If the true source of wealth in the information economy is intellectual capital, then perhaps intellectual property policy should be molded to enhance intellectual capital. Intellectual property policy is a means to promote the public interest and consumer welfare, not an end in itself.

An Overview of WIPO and the Treaties It Administers

The World Intellectual Property Organization is a subdivision of the United Nations, which has responsibility for, among other things, administering the Berne Convention for the Protection of Literary and Artistic Works and the Paris Convention for the Protection of Industrial Property.[6] It also oversees a number of more specialized treaties, such as those that protect semiconductor chip designs and sound recordings.[7] In this capacity, WIPO hosts meetings at which national delegations discuss possible revisions of, or supplementations to, existing treaties as well as proposals for new treaties. Once consultations have produced a relative consensus on the desirability of new or revised norms, WIPO will convene a diplomatic conference to consider draft treaties embodying those norms. The most recent example was the December 1996 diplomatic conference that considered three draft treaties: one to supplement the Berne Convention mainly dealing with digital copyright issues, one to supplement the Rome Convention to extend rights it confers on performers and producers of sound recordings, and one to create a new treaty to protect the contents of databases.[8] Treaties supplementing the Berne and Rome Conventions were concluded at this conference.[9]

6. See generally Frederick M. Abbott, "Protecting First World Assets in the Third World: Intellectual Property Negotiations in the GATT Multilateral Framework," *Vanderbilt Journal of Transnational Law* 22 (1989): 689.

7. Treaty on Intellectual Property in Respect of Integrated Circuits, as opened for signature May 26, 1989; International Convention for the Protection of Performers, Producers of Phonograms, and Broadcasting Organizations (Rome 1961) (known as the Rome Convention).

8. See, for example, Pamela Samuelson, "The U.S. Digital Agenda at WIPO," *Virginia Journal of International Law* 37 (1997): 369 (discussing the diplomatic conference and its consideration of the three draft treaties).

9. WIPO Copyright Treaty, adopted by the Diplomatic Conference. WIPO Doc. CRNR/DC/89 (December 20, 1996) (hereinafter WIPO Copyright Treaty); Agreed

One reason that international agreements on intellectual property norms have historically been difficult to achieve arises from substantial differences in national intellectual property norms and traditions. A major focus of international treaty making on intellectual property matters has, as a consequence, been on promoting the norm of "national treatment."[10] This requires nations to accord to the intellectual creations of foreign nationals at least as much protection as the nation accords to similar works created by its own nationals. It thus outlaws one form of blatant national protectionism, such as the nineteenth-century practice of the United States that protected the literary works of American authors but not those of foreign authors.[11]

Although international intellectual property treaties typically aspire to harmonize national intellectual property rules, they have generally left many issues to the discretion of individual nations, including whether to protect certain kinds of works and the scope or duration of protection certain works should enjoy. The Berne Convention, for example, leaves to national decision making whether copyright protection should be available to aesthetically designed useful articles (such as teapots or furniture),[12] requiring only that, if a nation offers copyright protection to such designs created by its own nationals, it must also protect the designs of foreign creators.[13]

Even a cursory reading of the treaties administered by WIPO

Statements Concerning the WIPO Copyright Treaty, adopted by the Diplomatic Conference on December 20, 1996, WIPO Doc. CRNR/DC/96 (hereinafter Agreed Statements); WIPO Performances and Phonograms Treaty, adopted by the Diplomatic Conference, WIPO Doc. CRNR/DC/90 (December 20, 1996).

10. See, for example, TRIPS agreement, supra note 2, Art. 3 (referring to national treatment principles in other major treaties).

11. See Copyright Act of 1909, sec. 16 (now repealed).

12. See Berne Convention, supra note 1, Art. 2.

13. Ibid., Art 5(1).

reveals that they aim to standardize at least some components of the major intellectual property regimes. The Paris Convention, for example, sets forth basic principles of patent, utility model, industrial design, and trademark protection systems.[14] Harmonization goals of past treaties have been undermined to some degree by the long-standing practice of allowing countries to accede to WIPO-administered treaties while reserving a right not to implement certain norms in the treaty. The United States, for example, is a member of the Paris Convention but does not have either a utility model law or an industrial design law as such. Nations have also been given considerable leeway in implementing treaty norms to conform to their traditions. Established state practices have historically been given considerable deference.

A distinguishing feature of the Berne Convention was its insistence that a nation's copyright law needed to meet certain minimum standards before that nation could join the Berne Union and enjoy the benefits of the treaty. These minima include granting authors of literary works the right to control reproductions of their works in copies for the life of the author plus fifty years.[15] Another minimum standard is making such protection arise automatically and not imposing any formalities, such as requiring registration of a claim of copyright as a precondition of protection.[16] The Berne Union has been somewhat loose about what constitutes compliance with Berne minima, seemingly on the philosophy that it will be easier to goad a repenting sinner along the road to redemption once it becomes a member of the fold.

The resistance to adherence to international norms can be illustrated by U.S. examples. The United States did not join the Berne Union until 1989, in large part because it did not wish to

---

14. See Paris Convention, supra note 1, Arts. 1–12.
15. Berne Convention, supra note 1, Art. 7(1).
16. Ibid., Art. 5(2).

comply with certain Berne minima.[17] The United States had, for example, a long tradition of requiring copyright notices on all published copies of a work.[18] Omission of such notices generally led to the work being dedicated to the public domain under U.S. law. Berne Union members, however, frown on such formalities, regarding them as undermining the rights of authors to reap the benefits of their creations. Although the United States dropped its mandatory copyright notice provisions in the Berne implementation legislation, it retained a rule requiring U.S. nationals to register claims of copyright with the U.S. Copyright Office before they can bring a lawsuit to complain of copyright infringement.[19] Although the Berne Convention regards registration requirements as another kind of improper formality, it accepts the United States imposing formalities on its own nationals, forbidding only imposition of formality requirements on authors from other Berne Union nations. In this respect at least, foreign authors are treated better under U.S. law than are U.S. authors.

Another Berne Convention minimum standard that the United States has resisted is Berne's requirement to protect the "moral rights" of authors.[20] Under the convention, nations must recognize the right of authors both to be identified as the creators of their works and to safeguard their works from destruction or mutilation. The United States relied principally on certain state moral rights

---

17. The United States officially joined the Berne Convention on March 1, 1989. Two actions were needed to accomplish this accession: U.S. Senate ratification of the treaty on October 20, 1988, and President Ronald Reagan's signature on the enabling legislation that substantially conformed U.S. law to Berne minimum standards. See Berne Convention Implementation Act of 1988, Pub. L. 100-568, 102 Stat. 2853 (1988). See generally Jane C. Ginsburg and John Kernochan, "One Hundred Years Later: The United States Adheres to the Berne Convention," *Columbia / Volunteer Lawyers for the Arts Journal of Law and Arts* 13 (1988): 1.

18. See, for example, Copyright Act of 1909, secs. 19–21 (now repealed).

19. 17 U.S.C. sec. 411.

20. Berne Convention, supra note 1, Art. 6bis.

laws and on a federal law regulating false designations of origin to say that it was in compliance with the attribution right requirement.[21] Far less plausible was the U.S. argument that it was in compliance with the integrity component of the Berne moral rights norm. U.S. publishers do not care for the idea of giving authors the right to enjoin them from editing out a segment of a book. Even less do motion picture studios wish to provide cinematographers or movie directors with a legal right to stop the colorization of movies or editing that the studio regards as necessary to enhance the commercial appeal of a film. Although the United States eventually amended its copyright law to grant attribution and integrity rights to authors of certain works of visual art,[22] the issue of U.S. compliance with Berne moral rights requirements remains a sore subject both internationally and in Hollywood, where directors, cinematographers, and actors remain intent on attaining recognition of their moral rights under the Berne Convention.[23]

The principal reason that the United States finally joined the Berne Convention in 1989 was not because it had been converted to the high protectionist norms that the convention lays down but because it needed to be a member of the Berne Union in order to have a stronger influence on international copyright policy.[24] This was obviously in the U.S. national interest, given the dramatic increase in exports of U.S. copyright products in the second half of the twentieth century and the vulnerability of those products to

21. "Final Report of Ad Hoc Working Group on U.S. Adherence to the Berne Convention," reprinted in *Columbia/Volunteer Lawyers for the Arts Journal of Law and Arts* 10 (1986): 513 (hereinafter "U.S. Ad Hoc Report").

22. 17 U.S.C. sec. 106A.

23. Disagreements between the United States and the European Union on this issue emerged at the WIPO diplomatic conference in December 1996 and, for a time, threatened the prospects for concluding treaties there. See, for example, Samuelson, "U.S. Digital Agenda."

24. See, for example, Ginsburg and Kernochan, "One Hundred Years Later."

the large-scale unauthorized copying that undermined U.S. export markets. The United States needed international cooperation to control such piracy, and the Berne Union was at a time the only forum where this kind of cooperation could feasibly be obtained.

Once the United States became a member of the Berne Union, it lost no time in exercising leadership there. Shortly after U.S. accession to the Berne Convention, the U.S. delegation to WIPO-sponsored meetings about a possible supplementary agreement to the Berne Convention insisted that any such agreement include a provision calling on nations to protect computer programs and databases as literary works within the meaning of the convention.[25] Because WIPO had previously proposed a sui generis form of legal protection for computer programs and because a number of countries had adopted or were considering other legal regimes for computer program protection, the U.S. proposal was far from a sure thing at the time.[26] The United States lobbied hard for its proposal, no doubt in part because it hoped that this would preserve U.S. dominance in the world market for those classes of intellectual products.

In succeeding years, as discussions on a supplementary agreement to Berne continued, the United States proposed other treaty provisions that would benefit U.S. copyright industries. Working with WIPO officials, with the committee of experts responsible for drafting treaties to consider emerging norms, and with European allies, the United States was largely successful in promoting its digital agenda in the most recent round of WIPO copyright and neighboring rights negotiations.[27] The treaties included U.S.-initiated norms calling for protection of computer programs and databases as literary works and the protection of copyright manage-

25. See, for example, Samuelson, "U.S. Digital Agenda."
26. Ibid.
27. Ibid.

ment information attached to digital versions of protected works. WIPO itself had a big stake in the successful conclusion of these new treaties, as several other recent treaty-making activities it had initiated had been unsuccessful.

The TRIPS Agreement and the TRIPS Council

Even as the United States was beginning to exercise leadership in Berne Union meetings on digital copyright and other issues, it was vigorously pursuing an alternative strategy to enhance international protection of intellectual property rights. The United States played a central role in the negotiations that led to the successful conclusion of the agreement on Trade-Related Aspects of Intellectual Property Rights as an annex to the agreement establishing the World Trade Organization.[28]

U.S. support for TRIPS grew in substantial part out of dissatisfactions with WIPO, the treaties WIPO processes yielded, and the lack of effective enforcement mechanisms to deal with national deviations from WIPO treaty norms.[29] WIPO-sponsored negotiations tended to take a painfully long time and to result in treaties with weaker norms than the United States perceived to be in its national interest.[30] Even worse was the fact that, once a norm

28. See, for example, J. H. Reichman, "Intellectual Property in International Trade: Opportunities and Risks of a GATT Connection," *Vanderbilt Journal of Transnational Law* 22 (1989): 747.

29. See, for example, Abbott, "Protecting First World Assets,"; Marshall A. Leaffer, "Protecting United States Intellectual Property Abroad: Toward a New Multilateralism," *Iowa Law Review* 76 (1991): 27.

30. See, for example, Morton David Goldberg, "Semiconductor Chip Protection as a Case Study," in *Global Dimensions of Intellectual Property Rights in Science and Technology*, ed. Mitchel B. Wallerstein, Mary Ellen Mogee, and Roberta A. Schoen (Washington, D.C.: National Academy Press, 1993), pp. 329, 335, observing that the WIPO-negotiated treaty on semiconductor chips was so weak that leading chip-producing nations would not sign it.

became part of a WIPO-administered treaty, there was no effective international mechanism to enforce it. Although the Berne Convention contemplates that one nation can challenge another nation's compliance with Berne norms before the International Court of Justice (ICJ), the treaty also permits countries to declare that they will not be bound by an ICJ ruling on Berne compliance matters.[31] In practice, this rendered the Berne enforcement system toothless. Before TRIPS, countries with grievances about another nation's noncompliance with intellectual property norms had little recourse other than bilateral negotiations to resolve disputes over these rights.

The United States hoped that TRIPS would remedy the perceived deficiencies of the WIPO-centered regime for international protection of intellectual property rights. Following Berne's example, TRIPS establishes minimum protection standards not just for copyright but also for several other classes of intellectual property rights, including rights in sound recordings and broadcasts, trademarks, industrial designs, patents, semiconductor chip designs, and trade secrets.[32] For the most part, TRIPS establishes its norms by incorporating provisions of the Berne and Paris Conventions, but it does so selectively. The moral rights provision of the Berne Convention, for example, is explicitly omitted from the TRIPS agreement.[33] In addition, the unfair competition provision of the Paris Convention is incorporated into TRIPS only insofar as it provides a framework for protection of undisclosed information (i.e., trade secrets).[34] TRIPS also establishes some norms not found in the major conventions, such as requiring WTO members to

31. Berne Convention, Art. 33.

32. TRIPS agreement, Arts. 9–39. See J. H. Reichman, "Universal Minimum Standards of Intellectual Property Protection under the TRIPS Component of the WTO Agreement," *International Lawyer* 29 (1995): 345.

33. TRIPS agreement, Art. 9(1).

34. Ibid., Art. 2(1).

regulate the rental of sound recordings, computer programs, and motion pictures.[35] In addition, TRIPS, like most WIPO-administered treaties, obliges countries to respect national treatment principles.

The most heralded accomplishment of TRIPS is, however, its dispute settlement process.[36] At long last, there is an international mechanism with which to resolve complaints about inadequacies of intellectual property protection. A state that believes its nationals have been harmed by another state's failure to protect intellectual property rights can file a complaint with the WTO alleging a violation of TRIPS. If efforts at conciliation and mediation prove unsuccessful, the TRIPS Council will convene a panel of experts to rule on the validity of the complaint. If the panel and the appellate body that has authority to review the panel's ruling uphold the complaint, the offending nation will have to choose between adjusting its law or enforcement practices and facing trade sanctions by the victor. Trade sanctions may even be levied against products unrelated to the violation of TRIPS norms (e.g., inadequate protection of sound recordings may, for example, eventually lead to trade sanctions against exports of textiles.)[37] The goal of these sanctions is not to punish the offending nation but to give it more urgent reasons to meet its obligations under TRIPS.

Lawyers understandably emphasize the formal dispute settlement process as the main accomplishment of TRIPS. However, informal dispute resolution before the TRIPS Council will generally precede the formal complaint process and, in general, will be

35. Ibid., Arts. 10–11, 14.

36. See, for example, Rochelle C. Dreyfuss and Andreas F. Lowenfeld, "Two Achievements of the Uruguay Round: Putting TRIPS and Dispute Settlement Together," *Virginia Journal of International Law* 37 (1997): 275 (discussing WTO dispute settlement process); Paul Edward Geller, "Intellectual Property in the Global Marketplace: Impact of TRIPS Dispute Settlements?" *International Lawyer* 29 (1995): 99.

37. Dreyfuss and Lowenfeld, "Two Achievements of the Uruguay Round."

preferable to formal resolutions. Notwithstanding the saber-rat-tling of copyright industry representatives from the United States and elsewhere,[38] it is a serious matter for countries to bring a formal action against other nations before an international tribunal. Threatening a formal complaint may, however, help induce voluntary compliance in some cases.

Two other roles of the TRIPS Council are worthy of mention. The TRIPS Council has responsibility for oversight of national intellectual property policy making and judicial enforcement. TRIPS requires nations to report to the TRIPS Council on developments in their intellectual property laws and policies.[39] The purpose of these reports is to enable the TRIPS Council to have advance knowledge of such developments, presumably so that it can consult with governments about these policies, practices, and developments. Should the TRIPS Council regard a particular policy or practice as undermining TRIPS norms, it may discourage adoption of this policy at the national level. TRIPS Council oversight may also serve a prophylactic function, obviating the need for disputes over intellectual property rights to be brought to the WTO. The TRIPS Council also has responsibility for determining whether new norms ought to be folded into TRIPS.[40] If an international consensus exists in support of modified or additional norms, the TRIPS Council can recommend to the WTO Ministerial Conference that the conference amend TRIPS to incorporate these new norms.

38. See, for example, Eric Smith, "Worldwide Copyright Protection under the TRIPS Agreement," *Vanderbilt Journal of Transnational Law* 29 (1996): 559.

39. TRIPS agreement, Art. 63.

40. Ibid., Art. 71.

The Complex Relationship of TRIPS and
WIPO-Administered Treaties

TRIPS has a complex interrelationship with WIPO-administered treaties. The complexity arises both as to long-standing treaties, such as the Berne Convention, whose norms TRIPS incorporates by reference, and as to later concluded treaties, such as the WIPO Copyright Treaty adopted in Geneva in December 1996.[41] This section explores some of these interrelationship issues. Although it focuses principally on the interrelationship of TRIPS and the Berne Convention, the same interrelationship issues arise in relation to other WIPO-administered treaties as well.

Professor Neal Netanel was among the first to explore in detail how Berne qua Berne (that is, the treaty in and of itself) might differ from Berne in TRIPS (that is, Berne treaty norms incorporated by reference into TRIPS).[42] The most obvious difference lies in the exclusion from TRIPS of the moral rights provision of the Berne Convention.[43] But Netanel points out that more subtle differences may manifest themselves as provisions incorporated by reference into TRIPS. Berne in TRIPS may, for example, have a somewhat different meaning from Berne qua Berne owing to differences in the purposes of each agreement. The main purpose of TRIPS, after all, is "to reduce distortions and impediments to international trade,"[44] whereas the main purpose of the Berne Convention is "to protect, in as effective and uniform manner as pos-

---

41. See WIPO Copyright Treaty.

42. Neil Netanel, "The Next Round: The Impact of the WIPO Copyright Treaty on TRIPS Dispute Settlement," *Virginia Journal of International Law* 37 (1997): 441. See also Paul Edward Geller, "Can the GATT Incorporate Berne Whole?" *European Intellectual Property Review* 12 (1990): 423.

43. TRIPS agreement, Art. 9(1).

44. Ibid., preamble.

sible, the rights of authors in their literary and artistic works."[45] Because TRIPS is largely indifferent to the rights of authors and the Berne Convention is largely indifferent to trade principles, some variance in meanings could arise. As Professors Dreyfuss and Lowenfeld have pointed out, the vocabularies of free trade and of intellectual property, as well as the core values of each field, are substantially different.[46] This too may contribute to variances in shades of meaning when interpreting the same norm in different contexts.

As yet unclear is the relative tolerance of the TRIPS council and WTO dispute panels, on the one hand, and the Berne Union, on the other, concerning national interpretations of Berne norms. As noted above, the Berne tradition has deferred heavily to established state practice, permitted some minor (and some not-so-minor) reservations to Berne norms, and left much to the discretion of national legislatures. Berne has concentrated on establishing norms, rather than enforcing them. Will the TRIPS Council and WTO panels be as accepting of national deviations as Berne has been? If not, this would widen the gap between Berne qua Berne and Berne in TRIPS.

One area in which the question of the relative toughness of TRIPS and Berne may play itself out concerns the permissible scope of exceptions and limitations to copyright.[47] Article 9(2) of the Berne Convention has permitted nations to adopt exceptions and limitations to authorial reproduction rights "in certain special cases provided that [the excepted] reproduction does not conflict with a normal exploitation of the work and does not unreasonably prejudice the legitimate interest of the author." WIPO and the

45. Berne Convention, preamble.

46. Dreyfuss and Lowenfeld, "Two Achievements of the Uruguay Round."

47. See, for example, Smith, "Worldwide Copyright Protection," p. 577; Netanel, "The Next Round," anticipating such challenges.

Berne Union have long tolerated a wide range of national exceptions and limitations within this framework. The U.S. accession to the Berne Convention, for example, was premised on the acceptability of the U.S. fair use doctrine and Article 9(2).[48] Article 13 of TRIPS broadens the principle of Article 9(2) by extending it to all exclusive rights.[49] (The wording of the two provisions is otherwise substantially the same.) In theory, this should mean that Article 9(2) and TRIPS Article 13 have the same meaning insofar as limitations on or exceptions to the reproduction right are concerned. But do they? If the U.S. fair use defense has been accepted as consistent with Article 9(2) of Berne, does that mean it is automatically acceptable under TRIPS? Some representatives of copyright industries may say no, seeing TRIPS as adopting a tougher standard. Fair use, they may argue, is not limited to "certain special cases" and often deprives publishers of revenues they regard as interfering with normal exploitations of protected works.[50]

It remains to be seen how this issue will be resolved in WTO disputes. However, WIPO's guide to the TRIPS agreement suggests that existing limitations and exceptions to author rights have essentially been grandfathered into TRIPS, for the guide assures readers that limitations and exceptions permitted by the Berne Convention should not violate Article 13 as long as they are correctly applied.[51] Astute nations concerned about fending off challenges to their exceptions or limitations may, however, find it worthwhile to ground their arguments for compliance with TRIPS on more than WIPO's assurances and to examine Articles 7 and 8

48. See, for example, U.S. Ad Hoc Report.

49. Cf. TRIPS agreement, Art. 13; Berne Convention, Art. 9(2).

50. See, for example, Samuelson, "U.S. Digital Agenda," discussing concerns of this sort.

51. World Intellectual Property Organization, "Standards Concerning Intellectual Property Rights at 22" (1996).

of TRIPS to find new possible groundings for exceptions and limitations that achieve legitimate national goals.[52]

Subsequent Agreements and TRIPS

TRIPS establishes most of its substantive norms by incorporating reference-specific provisions of existing intellectual property treaties.[53] Interesting questions arise about the obligations of WTO members when treaty provisions incorporated into TRIPS are subsequently amended or revised, when an incorporated-by-reference treaty is more generally amended or supplemented by a later treaty, and when wholly new international treaties on intellectual property matters are concluded. TRIPS contains some provisions establishing a formal process to extend its normative structure when an international consensus emerges on intellectual property norms.[54] The first step involves persuading the TRIPS Council that there is a consensus among WTO members for new or modified norms. The second step involves the council's recommendation to the WTO Ministerial Conference that it approve an amendment to TRIPS to incorporate such norms. The third step is for the ministerial conference to accept the council's recommendation. Some commentators suggest that there will also be informal ways to extend the normative reach of TRIPS.[55]

Article 71's formal process for amending TRIPS will almost certainly be used when a subsequent treaty establishes entirely new

52. See TRIPS agreement, Arts. 7–8, stating objectives and principles of TRIPS.

53. See, for example, TRIPS agreement, Art. 9(1), incorporating substantive provisions of the Berne Convention.

54. TRIPS agreement, Art. 71.

55. See, for example, Frederick M. Abbott, "WTO Dispute Settlement and the Agreement on Trade Related Aspects of Intellectual Property Rights," in *International Trade Law and the GATT-WTO Dispute Settlement System*, ed. E. U. Petersmann (London, Eng.: Kluwer Law International, 1996), pp. 387–409.

norms or when it addresses issues, such as parallel importation, which TRIPS expressly declined to address.[56] Had the December 1996 WIPO diplomatic conference yielded a treaty establishing a new form of intellectual property protection for the contents of databases, for example, representatives of the European Union (EU) and the United States would almost surely have asked the TRIPS Council to recommend an amendment to TRIPS to bind WTO members to this new treaty norm after WIPO had received enough accessions to declare that the new treaty was in force.[57]

Somewhat less clear is what will occur when, outside the WTO sphere, an international treaty is adopted that supplements or amends a treaty that TRIPS incorporates by reference, such as the WIPO Copyright Treaty concluded at WIPO headquarters in December 1996. Some commentators seem to think that norms embodied in any agreement that, for example, amends or supplements Berne will automatically be incorporated into TRIPS.[58] But the incomplete overlap between Berne Union and WTO memberships makes it doubtful that even a unanimous subsequent amendment to Berne would, by itself, establish consensus support for the norm among WTO members. An amendment to Berne that, for example, added twenty years to its current minimum copyright duration (i.e., life of the author plus fifty years) would almost certainly not bind WTO members unless the Article 71 process had been followed because Article 12 of TRIPS expressly estab-

56. TRIPS agreement, Art. 6.

57. See "Basic Proposal for the Substantive Provisions of the Treaty on the Intellectual Property in Respect of Databases to be Considered by the Diplomatic Conference," WIPO Doc. CRNR/DC/6, August 30, 1996. See also J. H. Reichman and Pamela Samuelson, "Intellectual Property Rights in Data?" *Vanderbilt Law Review* 50 (1997): 51, discussing the U.S. and E.U. strategies in relation to this treaty.

58. See, for example, Marci Hamilton, "The TRIPS Agreement: Imperialistic, Outdated, and Overprotective," *Vanderbilt Journal of International Law* 29 (1966): 613.

lishes life of the author plus fifty years as a TRIPS copyright norm.[59] However, I would argue that the same principle should apply even when TRIPS has merely incorporated a treaty norm by reference. The fact that such a provision might subsequently be amended outside the sphere of WTO (i.e., at WIPO) should not, in itself, increase the obligations of WTO members under TRIPS.

Nor should WTO members be bound by treaties that supplement treaty provisions incorporated by reference into TRIPS since supplementary agreements will, almost by their very nature, deal with matters on which consensus had not previously been achieved. Supplementary agreements to existing treaties do not even automatically bind signatories to the underlying treaty. Article 20 of the Berne Convention, for example, makes clear that agreements supplementing Berne will bind only those Berne Union nations that accede to them.[60] (The WIPO Copyright Treaty concluded in December 1996 describes itself as a special agreement under Article 20 of Berne.)[61] If this and other supplementary agreements to Berne do not automatically bind members of the Berne Union, it is difficult to believe that they could bind WTO members as TRIPS obligations unless the formal process contemplated by Article 71 had taken place.

In contemplation of a formal Article 71 amendatory process, organizers of any new diplomatic conference on intellectual property matters (e.g., WIPO) will likely seek to include as many WTO members as possible. This will help establish WTO member acceptance of any treaty norms that might emerge from the conference, easing and speeding along the Article 71 process. This may partly explain the decision of WIPO officials to open the

59. TRIPS agreement, Art. 12.
60. Berne Convention, Art. 20.
61. WIPO Copyright Treaty, Art. 1(1).

diplomatic conference that resulted in the WIPO Copyright Treaty to wider participation than Berne Union membership.

However, even if the overlap between negotiators at a diplomatic conference and WTO membership is complete, this should not automatically satisfy Article 71's requirement that WTO members accept the new norms. Many countries, the United States among them, have treaty ratification procedures that must be followed before the nation will consider itself bound to a treaty negotiated by its agents. If the U.S. Senate, for example, refused to ratify a treaty supplementing the Berne or Paris Conventions, the United States would surely defend its sovereignty if another nation complained about U.S. nonratification to WTO. Moreover, the drying of ink on a treaty does not, in itself, make the treaty effective. The WIPO Copyright Treaty, for example, provides that it will not be effective until ninety days after WIPO has received notice of thirty accessions or ratifications to the treaty.[62] However, gathering enough accessions to make the treaty effective may not establish WTO consensus on new treaty norms. It may be wise for the TRIPS Council to wait until there is wider accession by WTO member states to such a treaty. A formal denunciation of a new treaty by a WTO member may suffice to show a lack of consensus among WTO members on the treaty's norms.[63]

The international intellectual property policy-making community may be content, at least for now, to continue to utilize WIPO as a forum for conducting negotiations about possible supplements or amendments to existing treaties or possible new treaties. It remains to be seen whether a WIPO-proposes-and-TRIPS-disposes model will work in the long run. The search for a more efficient way to add new norms to TRIPS than the laborious WIPO deliberative process is likely to continue. Impatience with the full

62. Ibid., Art. 20.
63. See ibid., Art. 23, contemplating denunciations.

WIPO deliberative process probably contributed to U.S. and EU efforts to piggyback their proposals for a new treaty to protect the contents of databases onto ongoing WIPO negotiations on digital copyright issues.[64] They undoubtedly hoped that this would allow for far faster consideration of a database treaty than had occurred in respect to their digital copyright proposals (i.e., nine months for the database treaty and nearly eight years for the digital copyright proposals). But piggybacking onto ongoing WIPO processes will not always be feasible, and the WIPO consultative process is, by nature, drawn out. The failure of the proposed database treaty at the WIPO diplomatic conference in December 1996 may have partly resulted from resentment about efforts to short-circuit the full WIPO process.

If dissatisfaction with WIPO processes persists in the post-TRIPS environment, the TRIPS Council may be asked to take on responsibility of formulating proposals for new intellectual property norms. Although the TRIPS Council does not have such responsibility now, TRIPS contemplates the council will take on whatever additional responsibilities WTO members assign to it.[65] Some will likely argue the TRIPS Council is better situated to articulate emerging norms than WIPO by virtue of its oversight of national intellectual property developments. The TRIPS Council will surely be able to act faster than WIPO if unexpected developments (e.g., unforeseen technologies emerge that do not fall within existing treaties yet are vulnerable to market-destructive appropriations) arise that threaten to bring about the kind of trade distortion that TRIPS was meant to avert. Some may also argue that the TRIPS Council will be less political than WIPO (although it may, in reality, simply be political in a different way). Propo-

64. See, for example, Reichman and Samuelson, "Intellectual Property Rights in Data?"

65. TRIPS agreement, Art. 68.

nents of passing such responsibility to the TRIPS Council may hope that norms emanating from the council will be more protectionist than those that have typically emerged from WIPO compromise and consensus-building processes in the past. (For some WTO members, this will be a reason to resist giving the TRIPS Council this new responsibility.) There would certainly be some efficiency in having the TRIPS Council undertake not only the task of recommending new norms to the WTO Ministerial Conference under Article 71 but also formulating those norms.

Regardless of whether formal responsibility for new norms remains in WIPO or passes to the TRIPS Council, a separate set of issues arises about the extent to which new norms can or should be folded into TRIPS without invoking the formal process contemplated by Article 71. Some internationalists think that many norms will be incorporated into TRIPS as WTO dispute settlement panels decide that the norms at issue in a particular case have become customary rules of international law that WTO members must respect.[66] This amendment-by-interpretation mode of enhancing TRIPS obligations is certain to be controversial, although it is fair to say that TRIPS is a relatively skeletal agreement and that some means must be found to flesh out the obligations it imposes,[67] perhaps by taking account of how various WTO member states have construed their laws in relation to a question presented in a WTO dispute settlement process.

Consider, for example, a potential dispute between WTO members over whether TRIPS requires member states to extend copyright protection to user interfaces of computer programs. Article 10(1) of TRIPS requires WTO members to protect computer programs as literary works under the Berne Convention but says

66. See, for example, Abbott, "WTO Dispute Settlement."
67. See, for example, Geller, "TRIPS Dispute Settlement," p. 108, discussing minimalist and maximalist perspectives.

nothing about user interfaces. At least two factors caution against invoking a "customary rule of international law" approach to resolving this sort of controversy. One is that few nations have clear rulings on this subject: those that exist may not be entirely consistent (at least if U.S. case law is any guide).[68] Another is that, in acceding to TRIPS, WTO members did not intend to confer on WTO panels the power to ratchet up TRIPS obligations to ever-higher levels of protection in the course of dispute settlements. The Dispute Settlement Understanding states that WTO panels "cannot add to or diminish the rights and obligations provided in the covered agreements," which includes TRIPS.[69] WTO members will regard the formal amendatory process of Article 71 as the appropriate means for increasing the level of their obligations under TRIPS.

However, the practical fact is that proponents of the amendment-by-interpretation approach to extending the reach of TRIPS may be among those appointed to WTO dispute panels, giving them the chance to implement that approach without regard to what WTO members did or did not intend. They may feel justified in doing so on the ground that, if WTO panels eschew all attempts to engage in interpretative activities, it may be difficult for the larger objectives of TRIPS—to stabilize the world trading system—to be fulfilled.[70]

The customary rule of international law (or amendment-by-interpretation) approach may be more acceptable when the issue

---

68. Compare *Digital Communications Associates v. Softklone Distributing Corp.*, 659 F. Supp. 449 (N.D.Ga. 1987) (infringement based on command structure similarities) and *Lotus Development Corp. v. Borland Int'l, Inc.*, 49 F.3d 807 (1st Cir. 1995) (no infringement arising from command structure similarities).

69. "Understanding on Rules and Procedures Governing the Settlement of Disputes," December 15, 1993, GATT Doc. MTN/FA II-A2, reprinted in 33 I.L.M. 112, 115 (1994) (hereinafter DSU).

70. Geller, "TRIPS Dispute Settlement," p. 108.

presented in a dispute settlement matter has been well settled in virtually all WTO jurisdictions. It should be employed less often in relation to post-TRIPS issues and issues that were controversial at the time TRIPS was negotiated (e.g., whether decompiling a computer program is lawful under copyright law), even if a later consensus emerges on an issue (e.g., broad acceptance of a pro-decompilation privilege).[71] The Article 71 amendatory process should not be undermined by freewheeling WTO dispute resolution panels.

Apart from this, the customary rule of international law approach to amending TRIPS may contribute to manipulative gamesmanship by some nations. Certain high protectionist nations may find it useful to play on ambiguities about what is and is not a binding norm under TRIPS. Ambiguity may allow them to have it both ways: asserting both that something probably is a customary rule of international law (e.g., user interface protection by copyright) but that lingering doubts allow the complaining nation to take unilateral action against the offending nation insofar as the matter is outside TRIPS. (Unilateral action violates TRIPS if the norm is an express part of TRIPS.)[72]

How readily TRIPS obligations can be extended in the WTO dispute resolution process also depends on the TRIPS Council's decision on the scope and modality of "nonviolation complaints" (i.e., complaints that a particular state's practices are counter to the objectives of TRIPS even if the practices are not themselves, strictly speaking, in violation of TRIPS) that can be made to WTO.[73] In the first five years of its existence, the TRIPS Council

71. But see, for example, Charles R. McManis, "Taking TRIPS on the Information Superhighway: International Intellectual Property Protection and Emerging Computer Technology," *Villanova Law Review* 41 (1996): 207.

72. Ibid., pp. 229–30; DSU, Art. 23.

73. See, for example, Dreyfuss and Lowenfeld, "Two Achievements of the Uruguay Round," discussing nonviolation complaints.

is expected to develop a policy on nonviolation complaints.[74] If the TRIPS council adopts a policy allowing for an expansive scope for nonviolation complaints, this may be yet another way for new norms to be incorporated into TRIPS.

A Robust Model for Global Respect of Intellectual Property Rights

TRIPS is still a young agreement, and WTO is still ramping up its operations. There have been as yet few intellectual property disputes resolved by the WTO dispute resolution process, although a number of matters are in a precomplaint stage of mediation before the TRIPS Council.[75] The council is in the process of working out an accommodation with WIPO on the roles each institution will play in intellectual property matters.[76] WIPO itself is very much in transition, both as a result of having a new director general and as a result of taking on some new functions, such as providing arbitration services for resolving private disputes over intellectual property rights. WIPO's recent success in hosting a diplomatic conference that yielded two new international treaties addressing the challenges of digital technologies has buoyed its prospects for continuing as a significant player in the international intellectual property policy-making process.

The good news for U.S. industries is that there is now in place an international consensus in support of far-reaching minimum standards for protection of intellectual property rights, an international mechanism aimed at ensuring that nations effectively enforce these standards, and a system for building consensus to adopt

74. TRIPS agreement, Art. 64(2).

75. For a list of matters that have been informally resolved or are under consultation before the TRIPS Council, see *http://www.wto.org/ddf/daily/*.

76. TRIPS agreement, Art. 68.

new intellectual property norms as they are needed. WTO membership is sufficiently attractive to induce nations to conform their intellectual property laws and enforcement practices to TRIPS norms in order to be granted, or to retain, this status. China's desire to become a member of WTO may, for instance, be the strongest lever the United States could have to induce enforcement of intellectual property rights that will benefit U.S. industries. Even the prospect of U.S. complaints to WTO against countries that fail to protect intellectual property rights may have an enforcement-inducing effect beneficial to U.S. industries, without complaints needing to be made.

However, there may be more fragility built into the new global intellectual property rights framework than some would care to admit. The European Union set an unfortunate example recently, when it directed its member states to adopt a new form of intellectual property protection for the contents of databases on a material reciprocity basis. Thus EU member states have been ordered to protect the contents of EU databases but to deny protection to databases of foreign nationals unless the states from which the databases hail have adopted equivalent laws.[77] EU officials have frankly admitted that they intended for the material reciprocity clause to force other nations to adopt the EU model for such a law. Some U.S. scholars have asserted that this repudiation of national treatment principles violates TRIPS and other WIPO-administered treaties.[78] It is disturbing that the EU chose not to engage in international discussions on a proposed new international intellectual property norm until after it had ordered adoption of a reciprocity-

---

77. Directive 96/9/EC of the European Parliament and of the Council of 11 March 1996 on the legal protection of databases, 1996 O.J. (L77), Art. 11.

78. See, for example, McManis, "Taking TRIPS on the Information Superhighway," pp. 256–62.

based norm. This may trigger renegade reciprocity-based actions by other nations.[79] It would be ironic if intellectual property laws become more disparate in the aftermath of TRIPS rather than less so.

WIPO and the TRIPS Council face many institutional challenges as they struggle to guide nations toward enhanced respect for intellectual property norms and to form and enforce rules that will regulate the global information economy. The remainder of this chapter discusses four recommendations that WIPO and the TRIPS would do well do heed if they wish to fulfill their potential as respected regulators of the global information economy.

Pay Attention to Competition Policy

Owners of intellectual property rights and other intellectual property professionals often invoke economic analysis to justify intellectual property laws.[80] Without a grant of exclusive rights, they say, that permits creators (and their assignees) to recoup investments in intellectual work and the dissemination of it, levels of investment in such work would be low and society would be the worse for it. TRIPS is based in substantial part on this economic rationale and on the related notion that inadequacies in intellectual property protection can distort trade in a competitively unhealthy way.[81]

As willing as rightsholders and intellectual property profession-

79. See, for example, J. H. Reichman, "From Free Riders to Fair Followers: Global Competition under the TRIPS Agreement," *New York University Journal of International Law and Policy* (1997).

80. See, for example, Report of Working Group on Intellectual Property Rights of Information Infrastructure Task Force, Intellectual Property Rights and the National Information Infrastructure, Appendix (Sept. 1995).

81. See, for example, Leaffer, "Protecting United States Intellectual Property Abroad," p. 277.

als may be to invoke economic theory when it cuts in favor of initially granting or later strengthening intellectual property rights, they are less keen about invoking it when it raises doubts about proposals to extend or interpret intellectual property rights in an expansive way. Rightholder resistance to economic learning has been especially evident in discourse about proposals to lengthen the term of existing copyrights for twenty years and in national and international debates over the legitimacy of decompiling or disassembling executable forms of computer programs undertaken to get access to information with which to develop a program that will interoperate with another program.[82]

The principal (if not the only) reason that the European Union's 1991 directive on the legal protection of computer programs contains a provision permitting decompilation for interoperability purposes is that the Competition Directorate of the European Commission (EC) insisted that such a provision was critical to European competitiveness in the world market for software.[83] Left to its own devices, the commission's Intellectual Property Directorate would almost certainly have decided that interfaces of computer programs should be protected by copyright law (as long as they exhibited a minimal level of intellectual creation) and that decompilation or disassembly of program code should be unlawful as an unauthorized reproduction of the work.

U.S. trade officials and representatives of certain leading U.S. computer companies, including IBM, fought long and hard in sup-

---

82. See, for example, Peter A. Jaszi, "Goodbye to All That: A Reluctant (and Perhaps Premature) Adieu to a Constitutionally Grounded Discourse of Public Interest in Copyright Law," *Vanderbilt Journal of International Law* 29 (1966): 595; McManis, "Taking TRIPS on the Information Superhighway," pp. 233–52, discussing interoperability issues.

83. See, for example, Pamela Samuelson, "Comparing U.S. and E.C. Copyright Protection for Computer Programs: Are They More Different Than They Seem?" *Journal of Law and Commerce* 13 (1994): 279.

port of the stricter rule, even though other U.S. companies, including Sun Microsystems, favored decompilation for interoperability and other legitimate purposes.[84] U.S. officials and high protectionist computer companies regarded the EC Competition Directorate's proposal for an interoperability privilege as an unwarranted seizure of U.S. intellectual property. Even after losing the interoperability battle in Europe,[85] U.S. officials and representatives of those same companies have vigorously opposed interoperability-related initiatives in the United States and other countries. They continue to do so to this day.[86]

Copyright protection for program interfaces and outlawing decompilation would insulate certain leading software and hardware companies, such as Microsoft and IBM, from certain kinds of competition. There is, however, a fairly strong consensus among economists who have studied intellectual property rights issues in the software industry that a high protectionist rule would harm competition and follow-on innovation in the software industry out of proportion to any ensuing social benefit.[87] Courts in the United States have accepted these economic arguments, ruling that copyright protection for computer programs does not extend to interface specifications and that decompilation for a legitimate purpose such as promoting interoperability is lawful.[88] Five years after the

84. See, for example, Thomas C. Vinje, "The Legislative History of the EC Software Directive," in *A Handbook of European Software Law*, vol. 39, ed. Michael Lehmann and Colin Tapper (Oxford, Eng.: Clarendon Press, 1991).

85. See Council Directive 91/250 on the Legal Protection of Computer Programs, 1991 O.J. (L122) 42.

86. See, for example, McManis, "Taking TRIPS on the Information Superhighway," pp. 232–52.

87. See, for example, Frederick Warren-Bolton, Kenneth C. Baseman, and Glenn A. Woroch, "POINT: Copyright Protection of Software Can Make Economic Sense," *Computer Law* 12, no. 2 (February 1995): 20–21.

88. See, for example, *Sega Enterprises Ltd. v. Accolade, Inc.*, 977 F.2d 1510 (9th Cir. 1992).

first appellate court decisions promulgating prointeroperability rules, competition in the development of computer software is healthy. Many believe this is due to an acceptance in the United States and elsewhere of copyright rules that allow companies to develop programs that interoperate with existing programs.[89]

Despite the seeming success of interoperability, U.S. officials and protectionist U.S. software and hardware companies opposed including prointeroperability and prodecompilation rules in the digital copyright treaty to supplement the Berne Convention eventually concluded in December 1996. WIPO officials were apparently content to let the idea drop. WIPO has no competition bureau and no economists in influential positions who might have suggested that competition policy should limit the extent of legal protection available to computer programs, among other works, in the course of international intellectual property policy making. WIPO's inattention to economic analysis and to competition policy may partly be attributable to the Berne Convention's focus on protecting the rights of authors.[90] Having author protectionism as one's goal may incline one to favor ever-stronger protection measures and to ignore deleterious competition effects of stronger rights. WIPO officials evidenced their adherence to author protectionism in their support for the maximalist digital agenda that U.S. officials were pursuing in Geneva in December 1996.[91] They were unsympathetic to the competition concerns of computer hardware and software companies.

89. See, for example, McManis, "Taking TRIPS on the Information Superhighway"; Pamela Samuelson, Randall Davis, Mitchell D. Kapor, and J. H. Reichman, *Columbia Law Review* 94 (1994): 2318, 2401–04.

90. Berne Convention, preamble.

91. See, for example, Mihaly Ficsor, "Toward a Global Solution: The Digital Agenda of the Berne Protocol and the New Instrument," in *The Future of Copyright in a Digital Environment*, ed. P. Bernt Hugenholtz (Amsterdam: Kluwer, 1996), pp. 118–35, discussing WIPO's digital agenda for these treaties; Samuelson, "U.S. Digital Agenda."

Also contributing to WIPO officials' inattention to competition policy matters is their deference to senior executives of major copyright industries and copyright collecting societies. No longer do we hear complaints that WIPO is too sympathetic to the concerns of developing countries. WIPO officials may, however, have swung from one extreme (too much tolerance of developing nations' concerns) to the other (too much sympathy with the concerns of rightsholders from developed nations) without exploring the middle ground in between.

WIPO officials do not seem to have noticed that copyright industries have lately been posturing themselves in the international intellectual property policy arena as though their interests and the interests of authors coincide when, in fact, they diverge in some significant respects. Subsequent authors may, for example, need to borrow from preexisting works to create new works. Fair use law promotes authorship; it is generally publishers who object to fair use. In failing to recognize the differences between author and exploiter interests, WIPO officials may inadvertently be impeding Berne's purpose of promoting authors' interests.

It is not too late for WIPO, and certainly not too late for the TRIPS Council, to take competition and economic analysis into account in forming judgments about the proper contours of intellectual property rights for the information age. Consideration of economic factors will sometimes lead to recommendations of stronger intellectual property rights and sometimes to recommendations of lesser levels of protection. WIPO and the TRIPS Council should be guided by this learning in both situations, even if it may not always yield definitive results given that economists and competition policy analysts do not agree on all issues. Indeed, they must do so if they are to avoid becoming mere tools of global information monopolists.

There is reason to be hopeful that the TRIPS Council will be more attentive to competition policy issues arising in intellectual property matters than WIPO has historically been. TRIPS, after all, is a trade-related agreement; its very purpose is to promote adequate and effective intellectual property protection to "reduce distortions and impediments to international trade."[92] This includes a concern "to ensure that measures and procedures to enforce intellectual property rights do not themselves become barriers to legitimate trade."[93] TRIPS recognizes that abuses of intellectual property rights may occur and that states have a legitimate interest in taking action to curb that abuse.[94] The TRIPS Council should perceive its job as including consideration of competition policy and economic learning.

Because competition and trade policy are such fundamental components of TRIPS and the WTO framework, there might seem to be nothing to worry about. Surely the TRIPS Council will carry out the treaty's purpose. Two factors make the prospects for this somewhat less sanguine than they might appear. First, the TRIPS Council will almost certainly rely on WIPO for substantive expertise on many TRIPS-related matters (e.g., state practices under WIPO-administered treaties).[95] It will also look to WIPO for experts to serve on WTO dispute resolution panels when nations allege that other WTO members have violated the TRIPS agreement. In giving advice on treaty interpretation and in recommending intellectual property professionals to serve on WTO panels, it would be consistent with past conduct for WIPO officials to ignore competition policy issues and economic learning. This may carry over to inform the TRIPS Council's understanding of WIPO-ad-

92. TRIPS agreement, preamble. See also Dreyfuss and Lowenfeld, "Two Achievements of the Uruguay Round."

93. TRIPS agreement, preamble.

94. Ibid., Art. 8(2).

95. See, for example, Abbott, "WTO Dispute Settlement," pp. 398–99.

ministered treaties and the results of WTO dispute resolution panel decisions.

In addition, the TRIPS Council and the staff that serves it will tend to be drawn from the ranks of intellectual property professionals who have worked for WIPO or for rightsholders' organizations that tend to favor protectionist positions. High protectionist Hugh Hanson surely thought he was speaking for the overwhelming majority of intellectual property professionals when he wrote that the conversion of the masses to high protectionist norms in the aftermath of TRIPS would be made "by the sword" if this became necessary.[96]

One hopes that the TRIPS Council will not fall victim to the high protectionist ideology that besets so many WIPO officials these days. One way for the TRIPS Council to demonstrate that its attention to competition policy and economic analysis in the process of overseeing TRIPS compliance would be to establish a competition bureau; WIPO would do well to follow the same example. Failure to focus on these concerns is not in the interest of the global information economy, which will only flourish in a competitive environment—failure to do so will jeopardize the chances that WIPO and the TRIPS Council will be viable institutions in the long run.

Acquire Expertise about Advanced Information Technologies

The past few decades have witnessed a proliferation of advanced information technologies, such as computer programs,

---

96. Hugh C. Hansen, "International Copyright: An Unorthodox Analysis," *Vanderbilt Journal of Transnational Law* 29 (1996): 579, 592. See also Rebecca Mead, "A New Plan to Take Out Saddam Hussein, Courtesy of Hollywood," *New Yorker* (March 16, 1996), pp. 26–27, wryly suggesting a surgical strike as a U.S. response to an unauthorized Iraqi television broadcast of *Wag the Dog* to demonstrate that U.S. presidents start wars to deflect attention from sex scandals.

computer databases, and semiconductor chip designs, which have presented vexing intellectual property policy issues.[97] Partly owing to the technical complexity of these works, it has been difficult for legal decision makers to craft appropriate forms and levels of intellectual property protection. Although some advanced technology products (e.g., computer programs) have been folded into existing legal frameworks, others (e.g., semiconductor chip designs) have been the subject of sui generis legislation.[98] (Advanced high-technology challenges are not limited to computing and networking technologies; biotechnology has also presented some difficult challenges for intellectual property systems.)[99]

Deciding on a basic legal framework for protecting emerging high-technology products does not, of itself, end intellectual property controversies or the difficulties of adapting the law to those technologies. Just because a nation has decided to protect computer programs by copyright law does not mean that it has thought through whether, for example, this law should protect the "look and feel" of computer programs.[100] Scope of protection decisions often raise difficult policy issues that require technical, as well as economic, expertise to resolve in a sound manner. Copyright case-law, which largely concerns such fanciful subject matter as fabric designs and dramatic plays, provides scant guidance on matters raised in computer program cases.[101] In addition, judges must acquire considerable expertise if they are to make technically as well as legally sound decisions on computer program protection issues (and not all have done so). Even laws specially tailored to address

97. J. H. Reichman, Legal Hybrids between the Patent and Copyright Paradigm, *Columbia Law Review* 94 (1994): 2432.

98. Ibid., pp. 2478–88.

99. Ibid., pp. 2465–72.

100. See, for example, Samuelson, et al., "Manifesto," pp. 2395–99, discussing "look and feel" lawsuits.

101. Ibid, pp. 2342–56.

the needs of an advanced high technology, such as the sui generis legislation adopted to protect semiconductor chip designs, have sometimes proven troublesome because they have been too technology specific, leading to premature obsolescence.[102] The U.S. semiconductor design law, for example, focused on protecting "masks" that are no longer used in the process of manufacturing semiconductor chips.[103]

There is every reason to expect that new information technologies will continue to proliferate and present challenges for intellectual property systems. This will almost certainly lead to new proposals either to fold an unforeseen advanced high-technology product into an old legal category or to formulate new intellectual property rights for it. To make well-informed decisions on such proposals, intellectual property policy makers, both at national and international levels, need disinterested expertise and advice from the appropriate technology communities.

Unfortunately, WIPO has thus far shown no inclination to seek such disinterested technical expertise. Indeed, some WIPO officials appear to be actively hostile to the idea of consulting technical experts in the course of making intellectual property policy decisions on new technology issues. In the near term, the TRIPS Council, as long as it looks to WIPO processes for international policy formation, is unlikely to perceive the need for having its own source of advanced technology expertise or to convene meetings on advanced high-technology protection issues. Yet both WIPO and the TRIPS Council risk their reputations as respected guides on important intellectual property policy matters unless they become more technically sophisticated internally or find ways to seek disinterested advice on advanced technology issues. Sound intellec-

---

102. See, for example, Goldberg, "Semiconductor Chip Protection," pp. 331–34, discussing limitations of semiconductor design laws.

103. See 17 U.S.C. sec. 901 et seq.

tual property policy cannot be made without an appreciation of the advanced technology environment.

WIPO's willingness to move forward with major policy initiatives on wide-ranging high-technology intellectual property matters without the aid of disinterested technical expertise was especially evident in meetings and negotiations leading up to adoption of the WIPO Copyright Treaty. In anticipation of an eventual treaty on "digital agenda" issues, WIPO hosted a number of symposia about the challenges of digital technology for intellectual property law at major academic institutions, including the Harvard Law School.[104] WIPO chose not to include on the program well-known technologists or skeptics who might raise questions about how well suited copyright law was to the regulation of digital networked environments. Rather, WIPO salted the speaker list with representatives of major copyright industry groups and other well-known high protectionists who could be counted on to answer questions posed by the conference organizers as to whether copyright law could meet the challenges posed by digital technology with a resounding yes. The Harvard symposium, which was sponsored by WIPO and which this author attended, was an orchestrated event designed to produce the verdict that the organizers wanted to hear.

The principal reason that the December 1996 WIPO-sponsored diplomatic conference on "digital agenda" issues did not adopt the imbalanced and technologically ignorant treaty initially supported by WIPO officials was that representatives of high-technology companies from around the world attended the conference as nongovernmental observers. They educated national delegations about the adverse consequences that would flow from adopting the

104. See, for example, *Proceedings of the WIPO Worldwide Symposium on the Impact of Digital Technology on Copyright and Neighboring Rights*, March 31–April 2, 1993 (Cambridge, Mass.: Harvard University Press, 1993).

overbroad regulation of temporary copies and of technologies capable of infringement-enabling technologies in the draft treaty.[105] It remains to be seen whether WIPO officials will succeed in their current efforts to insist that nations accept that the WIPO Copyright Treaty requires adoption of the very provisions on temporary copying and on infringement-enabling technologies that were rejected at the diplomatic conference. This effort may instead undermine the credibility and prestige of those officials.

Sadly, WIPO officials do not seem to realize the disadvantage at which their technical ignorance puts them. Even though representatives of some technology firms may recommend a particular kind or level of legal protection for their industry, such recommendations will inevitably reflect the stake those firms have in the matter. If WIPO officials have no independent basis for assessing those recommendations, they will inevitably find themselves attempting to exercise leadership on high-technology matters without a firm grasp of the issues or the larger implications of their decisions, which could lead to adoption of policies that favor the major players on whose self-interested advice WIPO officials might rely. Both WIPO and the TRIPS Council must find a way to gain disinterested expertise on advanced technology issues if they are to provide sound guidance in formulating intellectual property policy for the global information economy.

Be Open to New Intellectual Property Paradigms

The norms enshrined in the Paris and Berne Conventions and incorporated by reference in TRIPS developed largely in response to the needs of manufacturing-based economies of the nineteenth and twentieth centuries, but the global information economy may require new paradigms for intellectual property protection. Some

---

105. See, for example, Samuelson, "U.S. Digital Agenda at WIPO."

sui generis legal regimes have already been adopted for new information technologies that do not fit comfortably within the patent and copyright paradigms, such as those adopted to protect semiconductor chip designs and computer databases. Some say those regimes are harbingers of a broader need for new intellectual property paradigms.[106] Perhaps the needs of advanced information technology-based economies will be significantly different from the needs of traditional manufacturing-based economies. WIPO and the TRIPS Council need to have an open mind about the possible emergence of new intellectual property paradigms for the information age and to embrace them as the need for them becomes more evident.

There is as yet no consensus among intellectual property professionals either as to the appropriateness of new paradigms or as to the contours of any such paradigms. However, a number of intellectual property scholars have proposed new norms to outlaw malcompetitive copying of unpatentable and uncopyrightable information-rich products.[107] Among the scholars exploring those issues is Professor Jerome Reichman, who believes that the recent proliferation of sui generis laws are attributable to

> the advent of new, information-based technologies, including computer science and biogenetic engineering, whose industrial applications [are] costly to develop but vulnerable to rapid duplication . . . Incremental advances in technical know-how emanating from these nontraditional forms of innovation fit imperfectly in the patent and copyright paradigms. Yet, because they become embodied in products distributed in the open market, the domestic trade secret laws often fail to impede

106. See, for example, Reichman, "Legal Hybrids"; McManis, "Taking TRIPS on the Information Superhighway," pp. 222–26.

107. See, for example, Wendy J. Gordon, "On Owning Information: Intellectual Property and the Restitutionary Impulse," *Virginia Law Review* 78 (1992): 149, 222–58; Samuelson et al., "Manifesto."

second comers from appropriating these same advances without incurring the time and costs of reverse engineering.[108]

Reichman proposes a new intellectual property paradigm based on principles drawn largely from trade secrecy law that would provide artificial lead time to "incremental innovation bearing know-how on its face," which he believes characterizes many of today's most commercially valuable information-based products.[109]

Other scholars have expressed concern that TRIPS, despite its broad sweep and lofty aspirations, may already be outdated because it is wholly silent about intellectual property matters that arise in global, digital networked environments.[110] Professor Marci Hamilton observes that

> The TRIPS Agreement appears in the midst of the on-line era, but is oblivious to this era's fundamental change in intellectual product transmission and generation. The on-line era, with its worldwide communication bridge, massive access capacity, and private home receipt of mountains of information, questions the existing fences and gates of intellectual property ownership and invites a reassessment of their proper placement in virtual space. Determining the optimal balance between ensuring a steady and ample supply of information to recipients and remunerating the authors of original contributions to the cultural store is a vexing problem . . . There is no easy, automatic answer.[111]

Although Hamilton's views may not be widely shared, history is replete with examples of institutions that failed to notice or adapt to significantly changed circumstances, including new technology, and thereafter failed as institutions.

108. Reichman, "Legal Hybrids," p. 2443.
109. Ibid., pp. 2444, 2511–21.
110. Hamilton, "The TRIPS Agreement," pp. 614–15.
111. Ibid., p. 620.

WIPO and the TRIPS Council should maintain an open mind toward new ideas on intellectual property issues. They should take a self-critical look at their institutional structure and at the treaties and legal regimes they are charged with administering to ensure that these agreements are truly responsive to the needs of the emerging information economy. Such a self-critical perspective will also enhance the long-term prospects of those institutions.

Promote Intellectual Capital

As many chapters in this book reveal, intellectual property is a component of intellectual capital. It is, however, far from the only component of such capital. Intellectual property may not even be the most important component of intellectual capital. If the health of an information economy depends on its cultivation of intellectual capital, then it makes sense to keep intellectual capital in mind in the process of forming intellectual property policy. This will help ensure that intellectual property is promoting intellectual capital. Neither WIPO nor the TRIPS Council has such an orientation today, but broadening their perspective to include such considerations may facilitate the long-term adaptability of these institutions and promote the long-term health of the global information economy.

Most of the writing on intellectual capital thus far has focused on recognizing its value to individual companies.[112] However, just as "the true value of a company's performance lies in its ability to create sustainable value by pursuing a business vision and its resulting strategy,"[113] the true value of a nation's performance may lie in pursuing its information economy vision and devising strategies to

112. See, for example, Leif Edvinsson and Michael S. Malone, *Intellectual Capital* (New York: Harper Collins, 1997).
113. Ibid., p. 17.

accomplish it. Human capital, "the combined knowledge, skill, innovativeness, and ability of . . . skilled employees to meet the task at hand.[114] Many national policies aim to promote human capital, including educational and training-related policies, labor and employment policies, and entrepreneurship policies.

Nations, like companies, also have structural capital that contributes to intellectual capital. Structural capital, according to one source, consists of (1) organizational capital (systems and tools), (2) process capital (work processes and techniques), and (3) innovation capital (intellectual properties),[115] the effective interaction of which is essential to the success of companies. This is also true for national economies. Among the other policies besides intellectual property law that promote the growth and value of intellectual property assets is tax policy. Consider, for example, Ireland's decision not to tax the royalty income of authors if they emigrate to and live in Ireland. This has led to a blossoming of intellectual property and intellectual capital in Ireland. Recognizing the relationship between intellectual property and intellectual capital might enable WIPO or the TRIPS Council to address, in the context of nonviolation complaints, ways in which state practices on taxation or accounting policies may interfere with intellectual property rights and impede the free movement of information goods and services in the global economy.

It would be unfortunate if WIPO or the TRIPS Council, in considering intellectual capital in intellectual property policy formation, were to conclude that it was critical to strengthen the rights of employers as regards their employees on an international scale. If a firm's intellectual capital depends in part on the combined knowledge and skill of its employees, companies might initially seem to need stronger ownership rights in their employees'

114. Ibid., p. 11.
115. Ibid.

skills and knowledge as a way of maintaining this component of their intellectual capital. TRIPS moves somewhat in this direction by being the first international intellectual property treaty to address trade secrecy issues that affect, among others, employer-employee relationships.[116] Stronger regulation of human capital assets of companies might lead to policies that would restrict employee mobility. However, those who have studied intellectual capital realize that human capital is something that companies and nations possess—and the more the better—without owning it.[117] Employee mobility, both within national boundaries and beyond, will promote the free trade goals of TRIPS and other WTO agreements. The global information economy does not need to close off worker mobility as the Venetian doges once closed off opportunities to glassblowers from the islands of Murano (who were killed if caught fleeing the site of their employment). Considering intellectual capital in the formation of intellectual property policy would also, it is hoped, promote a healthy respect for other factors besides intellectual property that contribute to the health of the global information economy and to provide principles with which, on occasion, to limit the reach of intellectual property policy insofar as it would impede, instead of promote, intellectual capital.

There is a parallel between promoting intellectual capital and the policy underlying the clause in the U.S. Constitution that empowers Congress to enact intellectual property laws to "promote the progress of science and useful arts."[118] The constitutional concern is to promote knowledge, creativity, and innovation, not to promote the interests of intellectual property rightsholders as such. The founders recognized that protecting intellectual property rights was a useful means to accomplishing the larger public inter-

116. TRIPS agreement, Art. 39.
117. Edvinsson and Malone, *Intellectual Capital*, p. 11.
118. U.S. Constitution, Art. I, sec. 8, cl. 8.

est goal but should not be an end in itself.[119] This tradition calls on legal decision makers to take a longer-term perspective when promoting public interest in sustainable innovation than today's best lobbyists might prefer. Concerns with sustainable value and innovation also underlie the concept of intellectual capital.

Sustainable innovation is also a concern of TRIPS. The reason this treaty regulates intellectual property rights is to avert distortions and impediments so that international trade will flow more freely and promote further innovation and trade among those who engage in it. Article 7 of TRIPS reflects this fundamental policy: "The protection and enforcement of intellectual property rights should contribute to the promotion of technological innovation and to the transfer and dissemination of technology, to the mutual advantage of producers and users of technological knowledge and in a manner conducive to social and economic welfare, and to a balance of rights and obligations."[120] This clause resonates with the U.S. constitutional tradition. Moreover, Article 8 indicates that member states may tailor their intellectual property laws and regulations "to promote the public interest in sectors of vital importance to their socioeconomic and technological development, provided that such measures are consistent with the provisions of this Agreement."[121] This suggests that WIPO and the TRIPS Council should accord nations considerable discretion in configuring intellectual property policies to achieve national social goals that might include, for example, promoting intellectual capital.

The true mission of TRIPS is not to raise levels of intellectual property protection to ever higher and higher planes, as some rightsholders might wish, but to encourage countries to adopt in-

119. See, for example, *Sony Corporation of America v. Universal City Studios, Inc.*, 464 U.S. 417 (1984).
120. TRIPS agreement, Art. 7.
121. Ibid., Art. 8.

tellectual property policies that promote their national interests in a way that will promote free trade and sustainable innovation on an international scale. WIPO and the TRIPS Council would do well to keep this larger goal in mind when crafting policies in the coming decades to regulate the global information economy. Doing so can help WIPO and the TRIPS Council achieve respect as sound regulators of a prosperous global economy.

Epilogue

As made evident in the preceding chapters, commerce is now intermingled with knowledge and information in ways that were unheard of a generation ago. Increasingly, speaking about commercial enterprises means speaking about the creation, the management, the protection, and the application of intellectual capital. This is true whether the subject is approached from the traditional perspective of intellectual property law or from the more expansive perspectives that attempt to value relationships and skill sets.

Meanwhile, however, commerce itself is a grander activity than what we might sometimes think. Alexis de Tocqueville once remarked that, "in democracies, nothing is greater or more brilliant than commerce. It attracts the attention of the public and fills the imagination of the multitude." If this observation resonates for an emerging global economy as well as it did for a young American nation (and I think it does), then intellectual capital has a broader role in the next century than just a resource for business success.

The challenge is evident wherever we look. The need for school reform, the threat of technomonopolies, the ethics of biotechnology, the search for harmonious trade relations, and the dilemmas of employer-employee relationships reflect in different ways concerns about intellectual capital—how we can get it, how we can use it, and how we should share the rewards. These are not just economic or ethical problems of one constituency, firm, or industry but issues that shape a culture where the significance of intellectual assets is obvious.

In effect, progress toward a global environment of vibrant democracies and free markets depends in great measure on our ability to accommodate the promise and the challenge of intellectual capital. The expansion of material well-being is only one aspect. If we do our task well, the experience will be a narrative of the increasing awareness of the bond among economic success, social good, and individual liberty.

Appendix

Conference Agenda
and Participants

HOOVER INSTITUTION CONFERENCE
Intellectual Capital

Stauffer Auditorium
Herbert Hoover Memorial Building
Stanford University
June 19–20, 1997

Thursday, June 19

8:30 A.M. *Welcome and Introduction*
John Raisian and Nicholas Imparato

8:45 A.M. Michael S. Malone, "Intellectual Capital"

9:30 A.M. *Intellectual Capital, Economic Growth, and Public Policy*
Paul Romer, "Knowledge and Economic Growth"
John Barton, "Intellectual Property Rights and Innovation"
Robert Barro, "Intellectual Capital: Policy Issues"

10:45 A.M. *Intellectual Capital: Practical Applications*
Joseph Costello, "Intellectual Capital and Global
Competitiveness"
Crawford Beveridge, "Government Leadership and
Cooperative Efforts"
Åke Freij, "Skandia: Three Generations of Intellectual
Capital"

1:00 P.M. *Issues in Law, Regulation, and Property Rights*
Clarisa Long, "Patents and Copyright Law in
Biotechnology"
Mark Radcliffe, "Patents and Copyright Law"
George Johnston, "Exclusivity: The Life Blood for
Continued Pharmaceutical Industry Innovation"
Margaret Jane Radin and Erin Sawyer, "Nonproprietary
Technologies: A Challenge to the Standard Economics of
Intellectual Property"
Philip White, "Employer-Employee Relations"
Edward Lazear, discussant

2:45 P.M. *Issues in Law, Regulation, and Property Rights*
David Dolkas, "Consumer Perspectives in Big Ticket
Litigation"
Jay Folberg, "Alternative Dispute Resolution"
Robert Hall, "Resolution of Disputes about Intellectual
Property"
Abraham D. Sofaer, discussant

4:00 P.M. *Societal and Ethical Issues*
Peter Keen, "The Trust Economy vis-à-vis the Contract
Economy"

4:45 P.M. David Henderson, "Ruminations on Day One"

Friday, June 20

8:30 A.M. Steven M. H. Wallman, "Importance of Measuring
Intangible Assets"

9:15 A.M. *Measuring the Value of Intellectual Capital*
Patrick Sullivan, "Extracting Value from Intellectual
Capital: Policy and Practice"
Tim Draper, "Assessing Intellectual Capital for Startups"
David Teece, "Licensing"
Gordon Petrash, "Balance Sheet Accounting"
Kenneth Judd, discussant

10:45 A.M. *Learning from Industry*
Barbara Simons, "Computer Industry"
Thomas White, "Genomics"
Sean Johnston, "The Costs of Uncertainty in Mapping the
Legal Terrain"
Douglas Fairbairn, "The Virtual Socket Interface Alliance:
The Drive for Legally Safe Standards"
John Barton, discussant

1:00 P.M. Michael Brown, "Intellectual Capital and the
Internationalization of Equity Markets"

1:45 P.M. *International Issues: Global Complexities*
Marc Pearl and Glee Cady, "Lowering Protection Standards
to Common Levels"
Pamela Samuelson, "World Intellectual Property
Organization"

Peter Richardson, "International Standards for Patent
Protection"

Bruce Bueno de Mesquita, "Protectionism in International
Equity Markets"

Glee Cady, discussant

3:15 P.M.   *International Issues: Regional Perspectives*
Clarisa Long: Latin America
Donald Weadon: Asia
G. William LaRosa: Europe
Dennis Bark, discussant

4:15 P.M.   Nicholas Imparato, "Going Forward: Next Steps"

4:45 P.M.   Rich Karlgaard, "Ruminations on Intellectual Capital"

Participants

Dennis Bark—Senior Fellow, Hoover Institution

Robert Barro—Senior Fellow, Hoover Institution; Robert C.
Waggoner Professor of Economics, Harvard University

John Barton—George E. Osborne Professor of Law, Stanford Law
School, Stanford University

Crawford Beveridge—Chief Executive Officer, Scottish Enterprise,
Glasgow, Scotland, United Kingdom

Michael Brown—Chief Financial Officer, Microsoft Corporation

Bruce Bueno de Mesquita—Senior Fellow, Hoover Institution;
Professor (by courtesy), Department of Political Science, Stanford
University

Glee Cady—Manager, Public Policy, NETCOM On-Line
Communication Services

Joseph Costello—Chief Executive Officer, Cadence Design Systems

David Henry Dolkas—Attorney at Law, Gray, Cary, Ware and
Freidenrich

Tim Draper—Managing Director, Draper Fisher Associates

Richard A. Epstein—James Parker Hall Distinguished Service Professor
of Law, University of Chicago

Douglas Fairbairn—President, Virtual Socket Interface Alliance; Vice
President, Strategic Programs, Cadence Design Systems

Jay Folberg—Dean and Professor, School of Law, University of San
Francisco

Åke Freij—Chief Operating Officer, Skandia Process Development
Center, Berlin, Germany

Robert Hall—Senior Fellow, Hoover Institution; Professor,
Department of Economics, Stanford University

David Henderson—Research Fellow, Hoover Institution; Professor,
Department of Economics, Naval Postgraduate School

Nicholas Imparato—Research Fellow, Hoover Institution; Professor,
University of San Francisco

George W. Johnston—Vice President/Licensing and Chief Patent
Officer, Hoffmann-LaRoche

Sean Johnston—Senior Patent Counsel, Genentech

Kenneth Judd—Senior Fellow, Hoover Institution, Stanford University

Rich Karlgaard—Editor, *Forbes ASAP*

Peter G. W. Keen—Founder and Chairman, International Center for
Information Technology

G. William LaRosa—Vice President, Europe, Middle East, Africa
Marketing and Sales, IBM Microelectronics

Edward Lazear—Senior Fellow, Hoover Institution; Jack Steele Parker
Professor, Graduate School of Business, Stanford University

Clarisa Long—Abramson Fellow, American Enterprise Institute

Michael S. Malone—Contributing Editor, *Forbes ASAP*, *Wired*, and
Upside magazines

Marc Pearl—General Counsel and Vice President of Government
Affairs, Information Technology Association of America

Gordon Petrash—Global Director, International Asset and Capital Management, Dow Chemical Company

Mark F. Radcliffe—Attorney at Law, Gray, Cary, Ware and Freidenrich

Margaret Jane Radin—Professor, Stanford Law School, Stanford University

John Raisian—Director and Senior Fellow, Hoover Institution, Stanford University

Peter C. Richardson—Senior Assistant General Counsel and Assistant Secretary, Pfizer, Inc

Paul Romer—Senior Research Fellow, Hoover Institution; Professor, Graduate School of Business, Stanford University

Pamela Samuelson—Professor, School of Information Management and Systems and Professor, School of Law, University of California, Berkeley

Erin Sawyer—J.D. Candidate (1998), Stanford Law School, Stanford University

Barbara Simons—Chair, U.S. Public Policy Committee, Association for Computing Machinery

Abraham D. Sofaer—George P. Shultz Senior Fellow in Foreign Policy and National Security, Hoover Institution; Professor (by courtesy), Stanford Law School, Stanford University

Patrick H. Sullivan—Principal, ICM Group LLC

David Teece—Director, Institute of Management, Innovation and Organization, Haas School of Business, University of California, Berkeley

Steven M. H. Wallman—Commissioner, U.S. Securities and Exchange Commission

Donald Alford Weadon Jr.—Adjunct Professor, International Institute, Institute of Public Policy, George Mason University; Principal, Weadon & Associates

Phillip E. White—President, Chief Executive Officer, and Chairman, Informix Software

Thomas White—Vice President, Research and Development, Roche Molecular Systems

The Hoover Institution gratefully acknowledges generous support from the Founders of the Program on American Institutions and Economic Performance: Tad Taube, the Taube Family Foundation, and the Koret Foundation; and Cornerstone Gifts from Joanne and Johan Blokker and the Sarah Scaife Foundation.

This Hoover Institution conference was made possible by funding from Cadence Design Systems, Informix Software, Pfizer Inc, and Roche Holding Ltd.

Contributors

ROBERT J. BARRO is a senior fellow at the Hoover Institution and the Robert C. Waggoner Professor of Economics at Harvard University. He is also a viewpoint columnist for *BusinessWeek* and a contributing editor of the *Wall Street Journal*. His recent books include *Getting It Right: Markets and Choices in a Free Society*, *Macroeconomics*, and *Money, Expectations, and Business Cycles*. He is a fellow of the American Academy of Arts and Sciences and vice president of the American Economic Association.

JOHN H. BARTON is a specialist in international technological law issues, the George E. Osborne Professor of Law at the Stanford University Law School, and codirector of the Stanford Law and Technology Policy Center. He works particularly on issues of international patent and antitrust policy, and on issues of development and transfer of biotechnology for application in developing nations. Barton is the author of *The Politics of Peace* and coauthor of *Law in Radically Different Cultures*. He has consulted with the World Bank, the Organization for Economic Cooperation, the Food and Agriculture Organization and a variety of international research institutions. He is also on the roster of NAFTA dispute resolution panelists.

CRAWFORD BEVERIDGE is the chief executive of Scottish Enterprise, a government-sponsored agency that is responsible for developing the economy, enhancing the skill base, and improving the business environment of Scotland. Beveridge was the vice president of Corporate Resources at Sun Microsystems from 1985 to 1991, a period when sales grew from $100 million to $3 billion and staff grew from 800 to 12,000. He is a nonexecutive board member of the U.S. Smaller Companies Trust and Autodesk, a U.S. software supplier. Since 1994, he has been a visiting professor at the University of Paisley.

JOSEPH COSTELLO is managing director and chairman of Cad Lab, Inc. Until 1997 he served as the founding president and CEO of Cadence Design Systems, the world's leading supplier of electronic design software and services. In 1997 he was named the top performing CEO of all publicly traded companies in North America by *Chief Executive Magazine*. Costello has demonstrated an active interest in intellectual property issues and played a key role in the formation of the Virtual Socket Interface Alliance in 1996, a 150-member consortium dedicated to the development of standards for the development and exchange of IP among high-technology firms. He has also been a vocal supporter of legal, educational, and business reform related to intellectual property issues.

DAVID HENRY DOLKAS is a partner in the law firm of Gray Cary Ware & Freidenrich, a California-based law firm with offices in various cities, including San Diego, Palo Alto, San Francisco, and Austin, Texas. He has arbitrated well over 100 matters before court-appointed and private arbitrators, including Judicial Arbitration and Mediation Services, the American Arbitration Association, and the New York Stock Exchange. Dolkas frequently lectures and writes about various matters pertaining to intellectual property litigation, including liability issues on the Internet. His articles related to intellectual property issues have appeared in the *California Business Journal*, the *Journal of Intellectual Property Section of the State Bar of California*, and the *National Law Journal*.

TIM DRAPER is the founder and managing director of Draper Fisher Jurvetson (formerly Draper Associates), a leading early-stage venture capital firm with over $300 million under management. He has funded more than 120 start-up companies, 40 in which he was the founding seed investor. Draper was a seed investor in Parametric Technology, a public company now worth more than $7 billion, and other successes such as Hotmail (acquired by Microsoft), Four 11 (acquired by Yahoo!), Digidesign (acquired by Avid), Combinet (acquired by Cisco), Redgate (acquired by AOL), Preview Travel, CellNet Data Systems, and Jet Fax. He currently serves on the boards of Upside Media, PLX Technology, iTV, Chroma, aVEO, Troika Networks, Photonic Power, and I-Cube. He serves as partner/adviser to three regional venture capital firms (Wasatch Ventures in Utah, Timberline in Oregon, and Polaris in Alaska). In 1997 he founded Action in California Education (ACE), a nonprofit organization dedicated to improving education. ACE's first project is BizWorld, a course dedicated to teaching elementary schoolchildren entrepreneurship and business concepts.

LEIF EDVINSSON is vice president and corporate director of Intellectual Capital at Skandia AFS of Stockholm, Sweden. During 1996 he was honored by both the American Productivity and Quality Center (United States) and Business Intelligence (United Kingdom) for his pioneering work in intellectual capital. Edvinsson recently coauthored *Intellectual Capital* (with Michael Malone). He has been a special adviser on service trade to the Swedish Ministry of Foreign Affairs, a special adviser to the United Nations International Trade Center and is cofounder of the Swedish Coalition of Service Industries.

RICHARD A. EPSTEIN is the James Parker Hall Distinguished Service Professor of Law at the University of Chicago. He is a member of the American Academy of Arts and Sciences and a senior fellow of the Center for Clinical Medical Ethics at the University of Chicago Medical School. He is the editor of the *Journal of Law and Economics*, and previously served as editor of the *Journal of Legal Studies*. His books include *Mortal Peril: Our Inalienable Rights to Health Care?*, *Simple Rules for a Complex World*, and *Forbidden Grounds: The Case against Employment Discrimination Laws*.

ÅKE FREIJ is the vice president, Business Reporting Development, of the Skandia Process Development Centre in Berlin, Germany. Since 1997 he has also been project manager for Skandia's Transparency Project, focusing on reengineering reporting workflows and packaging value-adding business information. He has spoken frequently on topics related to intellectual capital, information technology, and knowledge management throughout Europe for organizations as diverse as the Swedish IT Commission and the Institute for International Research in Vienna.

NICHOLAS IMPARATO is a research fellow at the Hoover Institution and professor of management and marketing at the University of San Francisco. He is coauthor of *Jumping the Curve*, serves on the Board of Editors for the *Business Encyclopedia* (Time Warner/ Knowledge Exchange), and is a columnist for and contributing editor to *Intelligent Enterprise* magazine. Primary research interests are in the intersection of business strategy and public policy. Imparato has served in senior corporate positions, including chief operating officer and board member, of both public and closely held companies. He consults and speaks frequently regarding intellectual capital, change, and sustainable innovation with private-sector firms and government agencies in the United States, the Middle East, Asia, and Europe.

PETER G. W. KEEN is the founder and chairman of Keen Innovations (formerly known as the International Center for Information Technologies). He has served on the faculties of Harvard, MIT, and Stanford, with visiting positions at Wharton, Oxford, and the London Business School, among others. He is currently a visiting professor at Duke University. His books include *The Process Edge*, *On-Line Profits: Every Manager's Guide to Business Multimedia*, and *Shaping the Future: Business Design through Information Technology*. He has worked as a consultant and long-term adviser to top managers in firms in Europe and North America, helping them fuse business choices and technology decisions.

EDWARD P. LAZEAR is a senior fellow at the Hoover Institution and the Jack Steele Parker Professor of Human Resources, Management, and Economics at Stanford University's Graduate School of Business. He is the current and founding editor of the *Journal of Labor Economics* and president of the Society of Labor Economists. His recent books include *Personnel Economics* (MIT Press, 1995) and *Personnel Economics for Managers* (Wiley, 1998). Lazear has been an adviser to the governments of the former Czechoslovakia, Romania, Ukraine, and Russia.

CLARISA LONG is the Abramson Fellow at the American Enterprise Institute for Public Policy Research. She also holds a dual appointment at Harvard University as research fellow at the Kennedy School of Government and as a research fellow at the Center for Business and Government. Her interests include the legal, economic, and policy issues surrounding intellectual property rights, genetic research, and the biotechnology industry. Additionally, she works with Harvard's Information Infrastructure Project on intellectual property issues. Long is the coauthor of *U.S. Foreign Policy and Intellectual Property Protection in Latin America* and is a regular contributor to *Intellectual Property News*.

MICHAEL S. MALONE is a contributing editor to *Forbes (ASAP)*, *Fast Company*, and *Upside* magazines. Raised in Silicon Valley, he joined the *San Jose Mercury-News* as the nation's first daily high-tech reporter. As an investigative reporter with the paper, he helped break the first stories on toxics, drugs, sweatshops, and espionage in Silicon Valley. His editorials have appeared in the *Wall Street Journal* and the *Los Angeles Times*. He also spent two years as a columnist for the *New York Times*. Malone coauthored *The Virtual Corporation* and *Intellectual Capital*. Other books include *The Big Score* and *The Microprocessor: A Biography*. His nationally syndicated television program, *Malone*, is in its ninth season.

GORDON P. PETRASH is partner for PricewaterhouseCoopers. Until 1998 he was the global director of Intellectual Asset and Capital Management for the Dow Chemical Company. He has been a speaker at numerous conferences regarding intellectual assets hosted by the Institute for International Research, MIT, the Securities and Exchange Commission, and other prominent organizations. Petrash has authored numerous articles and reports regarding intellectual capital for a wide spectrum of publications and organizations, including the *European Management Journal* and the Conference Board. He has served frequently as conference chairman for international conclaves on knowledge management and has been honored for his contributions to the area.

MARGARET JANE RADIN is the William Benjamin Scott and Luna M. Scott Professor of Law at Stanford University, where she teaches in the fields of intellectual property, cyberspace law, and legal theory. As a property theorist, Professor Radin is well known for extensive treatment of "commodification" (exploring the limits of markets and market rhetoric), as well as other aspects of property as a right and as an institution. These themes are developed in her two books, *Contested Commodities* and *Reinterpreting Property*. Radin's most recent work deals with nonproprietary technologies, electronic commerce, and Internet governance. She is cofounder and codirector of the Cyberspace Law Institute.

PAMELA SAMUELSON is a professor at the University of California, Berkeley, with a joint appointment in the School of Information Management & Systems and in the School of Law, where she is codirector of the Berkeley Center for Law and Technology. She has written and spoken extensively about the challenges that new information technologies pose for traditional legal regimes, especially for intellectual property law. In 1997 Samuelson was named a fellow of the John D. and Catherine T. MacArthur Foundation. She is also a fellow of the Electronic Frontier Foundation. As a contributing editor of *Communications of the ACM* (Association of Computing Machinery), she writes a regular column, "Legally Speaking." She also serves on the Lexis-Nexis Electronic Advisory Board and on the editorial boards of the *Electronic Information Law and Policy Report* and the *Journal of Internet Law*.

ERIN SAWYER is a third-year law student at Stanford Law School and received her J.D. in June 1998. Before law school she worked in the corporate public relations department at Sun Microsystems and researched issues relating to encryption and export control legislation. She was the recipient of a 1997 Summer Research Fellowship from the John M. Olin Program in Law and Economics. In addition, Sawyer was the features editor for the *Stanford Law and Policy Review* and is an active member of the Stanford Law and Technology Association.

BARBARA SIMONS is chair of the U.S. Public Policy Committee of the Association of Computing Machinery (ACM), the leading organization of computing professionals, and spent most of her professional career as a computer science researcher at IBM Research. She is a fellow of both the American Association for the Advancement of Science and the ACM and was cofounder of the University of California, Berkeley, Computer Science Department Reentry Program for Women and Minorities in 1984. Simons has won numerous honors, including the Norbert Wiener Award for Professional and Social Responsibility in Computing and the Pioneer Award of the Electronic Frontier Foundation. She has authored numerous papers and patents and has testified at technology policy hearings on cryptography, medical privacy, authentication for access to on-line records, and intellectual property on the Internet.

JOHN J. SNINSKY is the senior director of discovery research at Roche Molecular Systems, where he oversees efforts in the Departments of Infectious Diseases and Human Genetics as well as the program in core research. Sninsky has been recognized for his accomplishments in advancing the technology in the application of polymerase chain reaction to virology through such awards as the Charles C. Shepard Science Award from the Centers for Disease Control and the 1997 Hoffman–LaRoche 1997 R&D Prize Award. He has served on advisory and review panels and as a consultant for the National Institutes of Health, Department of Energy, and Department of Defense.

ABRAHAM D. SOFAER is the George P. Shultz Senior Fellow in Foreign Policy and Diplomacy at the Hoover Institution and professor of law (by courtesy) at the Stanford Law School. His *War, Foreign Affairs and Constitutional Power* is among various works that contribute to his status as a scholar of international prominence. He has served as United States district judge in the Southern District of New York and as the legal adviser to the U.S. Department of State under Presidents Reagan and Bush. He received the Distinguished Service Award in 1989, the highest State Department award given to someone who is not a civil servant. He is a member of numerous bar and civic associations, serves as a director on several corporate boards, and writes for many journals and other publications.

PATRICK H. SULLIVAN is a founding partner of the ICM Group, a consulting company focused on the extraction of value from intellectual capital. He advises companies on how to maximize their profits from intellectual assets. He is the author of *Profiting from Intellectual Capital* and coeditor of *Technology Licensing—Corporate Strategies for Maximizing Value*. He is a frequent speaker on topics concerning the management of intellectual capital and is a member of the Licensing Executive Society, where he was founding chairman of the Intellectual Capital Committee. He is also a member of the American Bar Association Intellectual Property Licensing Section and the World Intellectual Property Trade Forum.

STEVEN M. H. WALLMAN is a senior fellow (nonresident) at the Brookings Institution. Before taking his position at Brookings, Wallman was a member of the United States Securities and Exchange Commission, from July 1994 through October 1997. As a commissioner, he led the commission's agenda concerning the impact of technology on market structure, securities offerings, and trading. In addition, Wallman chaired the Commission's Advisory Committee on Capital Formation, which recommended major changes to the current securities issuance process to reduce costs of raising capital while enhancing investor protection. He is the author of numerous articles that have appeared in a variety of academic, professional, and popular journals.

THOMAS J. WHITE is vice president of research and development at Roche Molecular Systems and visiting scholar in the Department of Plant and Microbial Biology at the University of California, Berkeley. He is responsible for Hoffman–La Roche's research and development of polymerase chain reaction (PCR)–based clinical diagnostic tests and instruments for infectious disease, genetic disease, and cancer. He has published more than sixty articles in the scientific literature and has coauthored three books: *PCR Protocols*, *Diagnostic Molecular Microbiology*, and *Molecular Evolution*. He has served on advisory and review panels and as a consultant for a diverse group of organizations including the Department of Health and Human Services, National Institutes of Health, and the Pacific Center for Health Policy and Ethics.

Index